Greece by Rail
With Major Ferry Routes

Zane Katsikis

Bradt Publications, UK
The Globe Pequot Press Inc, USA

First published in 1997 by Bradt Publications,
41 Nortoft Road, Chalfont St Peter, Bucks SL9 0LA, England.
Published in the USA by The Globe Pequot Press Inc, 6 Business Park Road,
PO Box 833, Old Saybrook, Connecticut 06475-0833.

British Library Cataloguing in Publication Data
A catalogue record for this book is available from the British Library
ISBN 1 898323 44 5

Library of Congress Cataloging-in-Publication Data
Katsikis, Zane
    Greece by Rail/Zane Katsikis.
        p. cm. — (Bradt guides)
    Includes index.
    ISBN 1-898323-44-5 (Globe Pequot Press)
    1. Greece–Guidebooks. 2.Railroad travel–Greece–Guidebooks.
I. Title. II. Series.
DF718.K37   1997
914.9504′7—dc21   96-47292
                                                    CIP

Cover photographs Zane Katsikis
Front: Koroni
Back: Recently restored Diakofto–Kalavrita rack and pinion
steam locomotive built in 1896
Colour photographs Artemis Klonos (AK); Zane Katsikis
Maps *Inside covers*: Steve Munns
Athens and Gradient charts: Quail Maps
Others: Patti Taylor from the author's originals

Typeset from the author's disc by Patti Taylor, London NW10 1JR
Printed and bound in Spain by Grafo SA

CONTENTS

Introduction

WHY TRAVEL THROUGH GREECE BY RAIL?

The purpose of this book is to explain the Greek railway system in a clear, concise manner, then offer suggestions and possibilities (routes, stations, access to major attractions) both out of train windows and at stops throughout Greece – one of the world's most exotic travel destinations.

Most tourists, travellers and even locals do not consider train travel in Greece. Athenians ask if, other than their own single-line suburban system, trains exist in the land where travel has always been synonymous with the sea. Pensioners, young men doing obligatory national service and some spendthrift students taking advantage of reduced fares use the train, but most Greeks just smile politely when the rail travel option is mentioned. Young foreigners, using one of the plethora of European rail passes currently available, can be seen aboard the trains of the Hellenic Railways Organisation (OSE), but others are scared off by meagre or non-existent guidebooks and mention of dilapidated, slow trains that go nowhere, and simply don't bother to travel by train.

But it is possible to base an entire visit to the land considered the birthplace of Western civilisation by train – travelling to the far corners of Thrace or the Peloponnese. It is also possible to use the trains for short, scenic hops between major points such as Patras and Corinth, long hauls between Athens and Thessaloniki or even within the Athens–Piraeus metropolitan area. Those who want to wander the ancient paths of the mountains of Greece are advised to take a train to the trailhead. The ornate Volos railway station provides an excellent introduction to both the mysterious Pelion Peninsula of Centaur fame and the Sporadic Islands of Skiathos and Skopelos.

Despite the lack of rail services in mountainous Epirus or western Greece, OSE trains serve a surprisingly large area of the country, and fares are usually lower than the bus. The railways came late to Greece – almost 40 years after Stevenson's pioneer train first chugged down unsteady tracks in 1830 – and paved roads came even later. No road is to be seen the entire 22km length of the tiny 75cm gauge Swiss ABT type cog railway line which runs between Diakofto and Kalavrita on the dramatic Peloponnesian Achaian alpine-type coast (hikers take note of the terrific possibilities here). And canoeists should know that the swift running Nestos River west of appropriately named Drama in Thrace runs through a canyon reserved exclusively for the tracks of OSE trains.

Obviously, there is no rail service to or on the many islands (although a rusting steam locomotive is prominently displayed near the docks in Iraklion, Crete). But virtually all mainland ports – major and minor – are served by frequent rail services. Greece's renown amongst travellers is due mainly to its plethora of exotic islands, and ferries of all types and sizes sail from most seaside towns and villages. Often these ports are linked to inland areas by railways.

Rail fans should find a great deal of pleasure in experiencing a variety of new and old rail rolling stock, track gauges and operating procedures fast disappearing everywhere else in Europe.

Why travel by train? To relax, to meet the voluble outgoing local people and certainly to discover a Greece rarely visited by most travellers.

Zane Katsikis
email: ZaneKat@aol.com

ACKNOWLEDGEMENTS

So many people helped in the creation of this book that it seems almost futile to try to list all of them, but I must try: Spyros Fassoulas, Artemis Klonos, George Nathenas and Dimitris Papadimitriou among the other dedicated members of the Hellenic Association of Railway Friends (these gentle people can be reached at their attractive meeting room and rooftop terrace overlooking the northern approach tracks to the Athens rail stations. They are located on the second floor of the Hellenic Railway Museum, Siotou St 4, 104 43 Athens); Zisis Protopappas of the Panhellenic Federation of Railwaymen; Mrs Stella Karacosta from the Hellenic Railways Organisation Public Affairs Office; and all the railway workers of Greece.

I'd also like to thank Eric, Fotis, and Nicos of Digital Motion Computer Technologies (Dervenion 22 – Exarchia, Athens; 01 33 03 410) for their help with the graphics and assistance with my errant computer.

John Younge and his Quail Map Company (2 Lincoln Road, Exeter EX4 2DZ, England, tel: 01392 430277) also deserve a mention for their assistance with railway maps in Greece.

Part One

INTRODUCTION

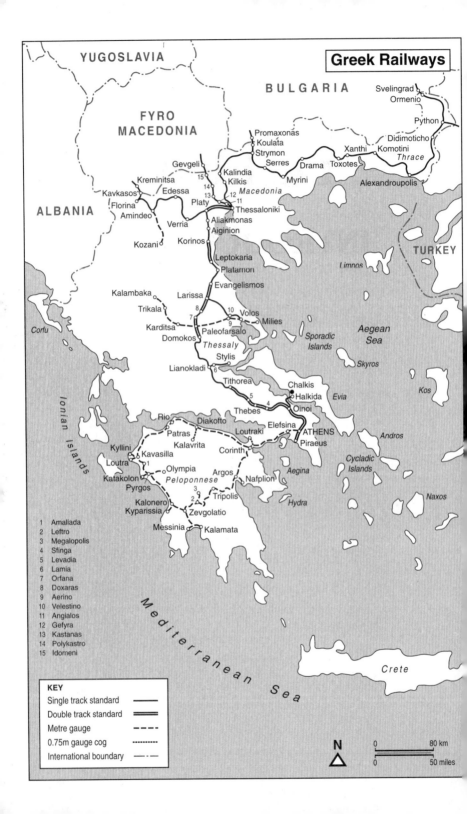

Chapter One

Practical Information

GETTING TO GREECE
By air
This is straightforward, as Athens, and increasingly Thessaloniki, are well served with regular and charter flights by most major international carriers. Discount and charter operators flourish, and inexpensive flights are more and more the rule. Remember, though, that round-trip tickets usually require that the traveller returns from the same airport as on arrival in Greece, unless prior arrangements are made or at hefty additional cost. Charter flights seem to be available to even the most out-of-the-way airports but, once again, return travel is from the airport you arrive at and only on the return flight specified. Domestic flights to smaller airports usually operate with Athens or Thessaloniki as hubs, are often not daily, and are not scheduled to co-ordinate with international charter flights. This should be kept in mind by those coming to Greece by charter for two weeks, but who stray far from their arrival airport. Improvising won't help much if a charter flight is on a Tuesday from Prevesa in western Greece and you find yourself, having wandered by bus and rail, on Monday evening in Alexandroupolis, Thrace, over 800 miles away.

By international bus
These do still exist, but are usually as expensive as flying – though travel by bus does permit more spontaneity. Eurolines has an extensive European network and can be contacted at:
UK National Express, 52 Grosvenor Gardens, Victoria, London SW1, tel: 0171 730 0202
France 55 rue St Jacques, 75005 Paris, tel: 01 43 54 11 99
Germany Deutsch Touring, Am Romerhof 17, 6000 Frankfurt 90, tel: 069 7 90 30
   Deutsch Touring, Arnulfstrasse 3, Munich, tel: 089 59 18 24
Holland Eurolines/Budget Bus, Rokin 10, Amsterdam, tel: 020 627 5151
Italy Lazzi Express, Via Tagliamento 27, Rome, tel: 06 841 74 58

By rail

Greece can be reached through Yugoslavia, Bulgaria, Turkey and Italy (by ferry). A variety of Rail Passes and special discount fare plans are available:

Interrail Passes for persons under 26 years old

Interrail 26+ for those over 26
These passes are available to residents of Europe and to selected other persons but are not available in all countries – check with local railways for specific details.

Eurail Passes of many types are available to non-residents of Europe and can be purchased before arriving in Europe or from selected major European railway ticket offices. Prices are slightly higher when purchased in Europe and some passes are not available in all countries.

Specific tickets – one way and round-trip – are available through the Wasteels Agencies. Rail routes are predetermined, but stopovers are permitted.

From Europe

Rail travel to Greece from Europe will necessitate a ferry crossing from Italy as the situation in the former Yugoslavia is not yet settled enough to ensure safe and on-time travel. Through trains are scheduled between Munich, Vienna and Thessaloniki (connecting there for Athens) but are not recommended because of frequent delays. Some travellers may need additional visas for travel through Bulgaria, Hungary and Serbia. These countries are constantly changing their entry procedures for travellers in transit. Those travellers planning on crossing through these countries are advised to check with their embassies for current requirements.

Five Italian ports offer regular all-year ferry services to Greece: Trieste, Venice, Ancona, Bari and Brindisi. Otranto further down the Italian boot from Brindisi offers a regular high summer season service to Corfu and Igoumenitsa. By far the most frequent and convenient service with the newest ships is through the Port of Ancona. Rail pass holders will have to use the well-known and often dreaded southern Italian port of Brindisi for the overnight passage on older, slower, often crowded and dirty Adriatica or Hellenic Mediterranean Lines ferries. Consult the monthly *Thomas Cook Continental Timetable* for full details of schedules.

From Asia

It is possible to travel from many Asian points (Hong Kong, Singapore, Saigon, Beijing, Vladivostok) to Athens. Though the days of extended overland rambles by hardy Australians, New Zealanders and others coming from the Antipodes are long past, rail travel options have multiplied in the last few years and today a variety of routes exist including the classic Trans-

Siberian route from Vladivostok or Beijing.

Intrepid rail travellers can now travel through western China (via Urunqui to Alma Ata, Kazakhstan) then either rejoin the classic Trans-Siberian route or use another more exotic route further south through Tashkent. With the opening of Vietnam, it is once again possible to go by rail from Saigon through Hanoi to Kunming (or Beijing), China, then up to Urunqui and west. *Thomas Cook's Overseas Timetable*, updated every other month, will provide current information on all these and other possibilities.

In most cases it will be necessary to travel through Moscow. From there the Pushkin Express departs at least twice weekly from the Kievskaya station for Thessaloniki.

Alternatively, a daily service from the same Moscow station provides a connection at Sofia, Bulgaria, with the Trans-Balkan Express for Thessaloniki. For full details on routes and schedules west of Moscow, it is advisable to consult the monthly *Thomas Cook Continental Timetable*. Note that international trains to Greece all terminate in Thessaloniki. None continues on to Athens.

Finally, there are two routes through Western Turkey for Greece; these will be discussed in the chapter on Eastern Thrace.

PREPARATIONS
Passports and visas
European Union (EU) nationals need only a valid passport or ID card – no stamp is issued on arrival or departure. Most non-EU Europeans, US, Canadian, Australian and New Zealand citizens must show a valid passport and will receive 90-day visas on arrival.

Longer visits require permission from a Greek Embassy or consulate before arrival in Greece or, if already in Greece, extension requests must be made at least one month in advance of valid visa expiration date at the Aliens Bureau in major cities – Thessaloniki, Patras, Athens (Leoforos Alexandras 173, tel: 01 770 5711) – or at a local police station in outlying areas. Regulations constantly change as to photo requirements and costs for the extension, but protracted bureaucratic entanglement is a certainty. Patience is the key to success.

Greek embassies overseas
Australia 9 Turrana St, Yarralumba, Canberra ACT 2600; tel: 062 273 3011
Canada 76-80 Maclaren St, Ottawa, Ontario K2P 0K6; tel: 613 238 6271
Japan 16-30 Nishi Azabu 3-chomo Minato-Ku, Tokyo 106; tel: 03 403 0871/2
New Zealand 235-237 Willis St, PO Box 27157, Wellington; tel: 04 847 556
South Africa 995 Pretorius St, Pretoria 0083; tel: 012 437 352
USA 2221 Massachusetts Ave NW, Washington, DC 20008; tel: 202 667 3169.

Information and maps

These abound, but be wary. Since Greece's accession to full European Union membership in 1988, the country has evolved at an astounding rate. Athens is the most vivid example. Its centre is a veritable construction site with many major traffic arteries blocked for tunnelling work related to the two new metro lines that should, when they are put into service in late 1997 or early 1998, immensely improve the city's notorious transport problems. All streets in front of the main railway station – the Larissis station – are currently closed to traffic, creating havoc for travellers, taxi drivers and locals alike.

General information and simple maps on the country can be had from Greek National Tourist Offices (EOT) overseas – and from the plethora of guidebooks. Most, though, only offhandedly mention OSE rail routes and usually omit several rail lines.

EOT offices abroad

Australia 51 Pitt Street, Sydney, NSW 2000, tel: 02 241 1663
Canada 1300 Bay Street, Main Level, Toronto, Ontario M5R 3K8, tel: 416 968-2220
1223 rue de la Montagne, Montreal, Quebec QCH 3G, tel: 514 871 1535
Denmark Copenhagen Vester Farimagsgade 1, 2 DK 1606 Kobenhavn V, tel: 325 332
Netherlands Leidsestraat 13, Amsterdam NS 1017, tel: 20 254 212
Norway Ovre Stottsgate 15B, 0157 Oslo 1, tel: 2 426 501
Sweden Grev Turigatan 2, PO Box 5298, 10246 Stockholm, tel: 8 679 6480
UK 4 Conduit St, London W1R 0DT, tel: 0171 734 5997
USA 645 Fifth Avenue, NYC, NY 10022, tel: 212 421 5777
168 North Michigan Avenue, Chicago, Illinois, tel: 312 782 1084
611 West 6th St, Los Angeles, CA, tel: 213 626 6696

For other countries not listed, check with the Greek Embassy. At the time of writing there are no EOT offices in New Zealand. EOT offices are scattered throughout Greece but most do not carry a complete supply of brochures. In the off-season (Oct–May), they may not have any at all. The most helpful EOT office is inside the National Bank of Greece building on Sindagma Square in Central Athens. Recently, the most frequented tourist sights, like Delphi, have been employing their own tourist information personnel. If this is the case, they may or may not have information on sights other than local ones.

Maps

General maps of Greece are provided by several major publishers who, unfortunately, transliterate the Greek language as they see fit. As there is no standard transliteration, confusion abounds.

Maps can be obtained in:

UK Stanfords, 12-14 Long Acre, London WC2E 9LP or by mail or phone order, tel: 0171 836 1321
USA Rand McNally Company, tel: 1 800 333-0136 ext 2111 for location of nearest store or direct mail order outlet
Greece The Army Geographical Service (YIS) provides the standard map references, though their topographical maps are older and often neglect to mention strategically sensitive sites like railways. But, once again, patience (and Greek language skills) is the order of the day when dealing with the entrenched bureaucracy. YIS is at Evelpidon 4, north of the Arios Park in Athens (08.00 to 12.00 on Mon, Wed and Fri).

Railway timetable brochures (pocket size) containing current maps are updated once per year and are generally available at major OSE ticket offices and stations in Greece only (see *Railway Travel Information* page 23 for details).

IN GREECE

Population: 10,000,000
Land area: 131,944km²

Currency
The unit of currency is the drachma.
Coins: 5, 10, 20, 50, 100, 200.
Notes: 100, 200, 500, 1,000, 5,000, 10,000.

Study the denomination of the notes carefully as the 100 and 1,000 notes as well as the 500 and 5,000 resemble each other in size and colour.

Exchange rates have been steady for several years as Greece tries to stabilise its currency for eventual entry into the single European currency. Inflation currently runs near 8.5% annually. At the time of going to press (March 1997), exchange rates were as follows:

Australian dollar	208
Canadian dollar	192
French franc	47
German mark	161
Japanese yen	2.14
NZ dollar	185
Swiss franc	185
UK pound	454
US dollar	270

Prices in this book are quoted in drachmas.
    ATM and automatic currency exchange machines have proliferated over the last few years. Travellers cheques still abound, but given the legendary

slowness with which Greek clerks of all types proceed and the cost of international banking when receipts and tracers are necessary, it is best to use a piece of plastic.

Most museums and major archaeological sites have a three-tiered pricing system. In this book the first citation is for adults, the second refers to school children and the third to students. Who fits into what category depends on the guard's discretion and the visitor's ability to convince the guard.

Language

Modern Greek is an Indo-European language and though it is similar to ancient Greek (Socrates could order bread today, but it's doubtful if he could reserve rail passage), it has had over two thousand years to evolve. There is no standard transliteration. A handy pocket-sized phrase book (like the one published by Lonely Planet Publications) would be a good investment and give some insight into the language.

English-language publications proliferate. A lively daily newspaper *The Athens News*, the monthly *The Athenian* and the bi-monthly *Odyssey* are available at kiosks throughout Athens and most of Greece. Though they provide excellent coverage and in-depth insights into Greek events, they concentrate their entertainment listings on Athenian events, virtually ignoring the vibrant northern city of Thessaloniki not to mention the rest of the country. All British and European daily newspapers and magazines are available from central Athens kiosks the day they are published but usually at least a day late outside Athens.

OSE station and on-board staff that deal with the travelling public all know some English. In fact, most Greeks who deal regularly with the travelling public communicate well in English. This book assumes that all those who work in hotels, restaurants, museums and other travel related services have a working knowledge of English.

But remember, the latest slang might not have made it to the far end of Thrace yet. Use regular English and enunciate clearly. All railway stations are clearly signposted in Greek and in Roman letters, although spellings are sometimes in French rather than in English (Athènes rather than Athens, but it could be Athine).

Even in the tiniest, most out-of-the-way station, someone will be able and most willing to assist in breaking the language barrier.

Telecommunications

The Hellenic Telecommunications Organisation (OTE) has a well-deserved reputation of providing less than adequate telephone services. It used to be necessary to go to their offices to use a phone, then try to get through, or to use the antiquated dial phones at the plethora of busy kiosks throughout Greece. Now a new system of prepaid card phones has saturated the country.

Prepaid cards can be purchased in many locations and cost 1,300 drachma for 100 units, 6,000 for 500 and 11,000 for 1000. Remember that the quickest call to Australia or the US will easily use up a few dozen units. Conversely using a kiosk pay telephone to hook into an international satellite system like Sprint or AT&T could save money but will certainly not endear you to the kiosk keeper who usually won't understand how someone can chit-chat for twenty minutes without his metre turning at all. Mobile phones have recently become extremely popular in Greece.

The international calling code for Greece is 30. In this book telephone numbers will be listed as follows: city code/tel number. Remember when phoning to Greece to omit the first 0 in the city code. Within Greece the 0 should be included.

Domestic travel

Air travel is by the heavily subsidised Olympic Airlines (OA) which uses some of the older aircraft still plying the world's airways. Basic airports exist throughout the mainland and most of the islands. No train to the plane service exists in Greece although one is planned for the new Athens area airport at Spata by the Attica Metro now under construction. All airports are well served by local buses and taxis.

Intercity buses of the loosely amalgamated KTEL organisation serve virtually every nook and cranny of Greece with some of the most creative though unfathomable schedules possible. The large green KTEL road coaches are about 30% more expensive than regular trains and suffer from a lack of a central information source. It is necessary to check in advance with each local bus terminal or risk waiting for a next day connection. When possible, bus connections with rail services will be suggested.

Urban transit networks using diesel and electric **trolley buses** exist in Athens and Thessaloniki. These two major cities have an extremely wide ranging and dense system of public transit. Unfortunately both cities are in the midst of extensive reorganisation of their networks: Athens because of the Attica Metro tunnelling and construction and Thessaloniki because it is preparing to be the 1997 European Cultural Capital.

With Greece being so intimately associated with the sea, it is not surprising that sea transport – in the form of **ferry and shipping services** – is well developed. Unlike the anarchic though politically well connected KTEL bus organisation, shipping company schedules are known and publicised and available from most travel agencies. The handy annual *Thomas Cook Guide to Greek Island Hopping* is comprehensive and reliable. EOT publishes a weekly flyer (issued on Thursdays), available from the Athens Syntagma Square branch with schedules from Piraeus to the islands. Given the speed with which shipping companies adjust to changing markets – adding large ferries or swift hydrofoils as needed – it is best to consult the appropriate travel agencies in local areas for precise details.

OSE trains serve most major seaports throughout Greece. A list of such rail-sea junctions appears in the next chapter and each port is described in the appropriate section of this book.

No description of domestic Greek travel would be complete without a mention of the ubiquitous **taxi**. Many travellers are convinced that the pre-twentieth century tradition of armed banditry in the Greek countryside did not just fade away. Bandits simply laid down their cutlasses and muskets and replaced them with a yellow or grey diesel Mercedes taxi equipped more often than not with a "broken" meter. Taxis are available 24 hours a day – usually with the same individual behind the wheel for Herculean stretches of time, and they will go anywhere – for a price. The key is to negotiate the price before entering the car and to stick by it despite the driver's lamentations en route.

A favourite trick of unscrupulous taxi drivers is to confront foreigners arriving at rail stations and offer discounted long-distance rides for small groups. The main advantage is faster travel time. The disadvantages are legion. First, these drivers do not have proper authorisation to make these trips which means that they are not insured against accidents. Then, they often will not go directly to a traveller's destination. Travellers are left on their own, often at the edge of a town, requiring more time and expense to arrive where they wanted to go in the first place. Patras and Athens are the two preferred cities for this scam.

All major and minor **car rental agencies** can be found. Caution is the keyword when negotiating with the lesser known companies, especially during the high season when fast car turn-around time eliminates the possibility of preventive maintenance, and simple check-up on such essentials as brakes and clutch systems is ignored. Greece rivals only Portugal for having the worst drivers and highest accident rates in the EU. Police estimate that one in ten motorists take to the wheel with a blood alcohol count exceeding the legal limit.

Motorbikes and **push bikes** are available for rental, though push bikes are not advised in major cities, or during the extremely hot summer months in the countryside. Greek motorists, especially bus and truck drivers, are aggressive and not used to yielding the right of way for anything – man, beast or smaller vehicle. All OSE trains accept bikes of all kinds, but owners are advised to oversee the loading process. (See the *Hellenic Railways Organisation* chapter for details.) Proposed rental vehicles should be thoroughly checked as maintenance is often neglected.

Public holidays

One of the most impressive sights in peacetime Europe must be holiday departure time from Greek metropolitan rail, bus, boat and air ports. That's when what seems like the majority of urban populations try to leave, all at once, creating an exodus bordering on chaos and sheer anarchy that overloads capacity in all transit modes.

Savvy visitors know to work around these dates (fixed and moveable) by either not travelling or reserving space well in advance.

The most likely dates to cause travel difficulties include: January 1 and 6, March 25, the Orthodox Easter celebrations including the first Monday of Lent, Easter weekend, May 1, Whit Monday (usually in June), August 15, October 28, December 25 and 26. Irregularly scheduled national election days also wreak havoc as many people return to their towns and villages to vote.

Landscape and leisure

Most travellers to Greece realise that the sea is rarely out of sight. Fully one-third of the Mediterranean's 45,000km shore line is Greek and no point on the Greek mainland is more than 150km from the sea.

Those who stray from the many sun soaked beaches will quickly understand that Greece is an extremely mountainous land. It is said that almost 75% of the country is non-arable, uninhabited rugged mountain uplands. Anyone riding the train from Patras to Corinth will realise this. Rail lines, mostly built in the first part of this century and not rebuilt since, follow geographic contours usually along the highly scenic coastal plains. Tunnels are only now beginning to pierce the coastal mountain ranges of Central Greece.

With fully half the Greek population crowding the metropolitan Athens area, the rugged interior – responsible for the aura of fierce devotion to individual freedom displayed throughout centuries of foreign domination – is rapidly emptying. Hikers and trekkers are discovering a wonderland of wildflowers and fauna relatively easily accessible by foot along well developed high country paths built centuries ago.

Only recently have Greeks, mostly young upscale city dwellers, rediscovered the natural beauty of their country. Adventure travel is a recent phenomenon as well. The Hellenic Alpine Club (EOS) (in Athens: 01 72 12 773; Nafpaktos: 0634 29 563; or in local offices like Lamia and Karpenissia) can provide further information. The Association of Greek Climbers in Thessaloniki (031 224 710) and the Hellenic Mountaineering and Skiing Federation in Athens (01 32 34 555) are also valuable.

The oldest and best-established private outfit organising rafting, kayaking, canoeing and other adventure travel expeditions is Trekking Hellas. They have offices in Athens at Philellinon St 7, Syntagma 10557 (tel: 01 325 0317 0853 1958 and fax: 01 323 4548) and Thessaloniki at Aristotelos 11, Thessaloniki 54624. In the UK, contact Sunvil Holidays (Sunvil House, Upper Square, Old Isleworth, Middlesex TW7 7BJ; tel: 0181 568 4499, fax: 0181 568 8330). Their American agent is Hellenic Adventures (4150 Harriet Ave South, Minneapolis, Mn 55409; tel: 612 827 0937, fax: 612 827 2444).

The first environmental volunteer-led programme created to clean up many trash-filled ravines and river banks, co-ordinated by the Hellenic Society for the Protection of Nature (HSPN) and named Nature Without Garbage, began in 1996. Travellers to Greece who are interested in participating in this programme are invited to contact HSPN in Athens at 01 322 4944 or fax 01 322 5285.

OSE trains directly serve many hiking trails – and provide quick, easy access to others. This book will describe several such points but readers should consult a specific guide, such as Lonely Planet's *Trekking in Greece,* for more detailed maps and walks beyond the scope of this book.

History and archaeology
Greece's history is so long that this book cannot do it justice, though it will point out highlights visible or imaginable through the large train windows. Those interested in further historical background are advised to consult the *Further Reading* section. A quality series of locally produced archaeological guidebooks is available from Athenian Editions at Omirou St 11, 10672 Athens, or possibly by mail order at (0)1 360 8911.

Accommodation
The full range of accommodation is available, from ultra luxurious multistar palaces where guests pay to be pampered to the bunkbed-equipped hostels that would cheer a Spartan's heart. Only recently has the concept of quality bed-and-breakfast type accommodation in architecturally significant, renovated old buildings begun. Enterprising locals in villages lacking much tourism infrastructure often offer rooms for rent. These come in all sizes, types and prices. The rent room phenomenon is supposed to be controlled by the Ministry of Tourism, although at times the niceties of innkeeping are lost on proprietors who can't help noticing the quality of a traveller's accoutrements before setting a price. Individual travellers seeking one night's lodgings are savagely discriminated against. It seems the price of washing one sheet far outweighs the benefits accruing from such a rental.

A word about urban noise is in order. Most accommodation is quality rated, not by amenities offered but by its resistance to noise. Greeks are night people and tend to circulate until quite late. Most cheaper hotels located on major urban arteries are subjected to an all-night barrage of roaring exhausts, screeching tyres and loud, rambunctious voices that lasts until near dawn. A good night's rest is rarely possible. When seeking lodgings in these establishments ask to see the room and ascertain the decibel level for yourself. Try to obtain a room away from the street.

It should also go without saying that the small picturesque towns scattered throughout Greece, like Pylos and Koroni in the Peloponnese, simply cannot accommodate the quantities of summer tourists. Rooms fill fast and last-minute arrivals must go elsewhere.

Those with a strong objection to the behaviour of an innkeeper can seek advice from the proper authorities such as the Greek Consumers Institute (INKO) or the EKPIZO consumers association as listed below.

OSE trains, in time-honoured railway tradition, permit comfortable overnight travel on selected routes in six-bed couchette cars or wagon-lit type sleepers, but can also be responsible for some of the worst overnight rail travel possible in modern Europe. The best and worst will be discussed in the appropriate chapter.

Food and drink

Greeks still follow a seasonal style of cuisine. Summer means tomatoes and other fresh fruits and vegetables while winter offers soups and heartier meat-based oven-cooked dishes. Fresh baked bread, sheep's milk based white cheese (Feta) and fat-fleshed olives (from Kalamata) form the basis of the cuisine with olive oil serving as the main cooking fat.

Restaurants – called *estiatoria* – serve prepared foods that should always be visible behind protected glass shields in heated areas. Grilled meats are served at *psistarias*. Normally, grilled meats are not served in *estiatoria* and vice-versa but both can often be had in *tavernas*.

Pastry shops called *zacharoplastia* offer an astounding array of delectable sweets while *kafenio* – coffee shops – serve the ubiquitous small cups of thick coffee or refreshing frothy iced coffee drinks called *frappés*.

Coke and other fizzy drinks are available as is a range of locally and internationally bottled beers. Wine in Greece is a revelation – little known outside a select coterie of aficionados. As the ninth largest producer of wines in the world, Greece offers to the oenophile and casual drinker alike an extremely wide array of dry, sparkling or sweet white, rosé and red wine. Since the mid-1980s young Greek wine makers, mostly French trained, have left the large companies and struck out on their own to create an extremely broad selection of fresh and fragrant wines based on high-quality local grape varieties long ignored in favour of the ubiquitous French varieties.

Fine wine regions are located throughout Greece (150,000ha of agricultural land is planted with vines) and OSE rail lines pass near many of them. Wine aficionados and casual drinkers alike are catching on to the quality revolution sweeping the 3,000-year-old Greek wine industry. Where possible this book will describe wine-tasting excursions available near OSE stations.

OSE trains usually all operate with a snack bar car (with table service) resembling a typical loud, smoky village *kafenio* and serve hot and cold drinks, pre-packaged sandwiches, or fresh grilled squares of meat (lamb or pork) on a skewer called *souvlaki*. The newer and more rapid InterCity (IC) trains propose a more extensive menu with meals at your seat in addition to café car service.

OSE rail stations can be a revelation in the diversity and quality of food and wine they offer. Thessaloniki's massive station offers a great range of prepared and grilled food while small country stations, such as at Edessa, are locally noted as having the best *psistaria* grills – and outdoor settings – in Greece. At some stations, like Diakofto, café tables crowd the platform and it seems almost possible to order out of the train windows. Stations with exceptional food and drink offerings will be noted in the text. Major stations with IC service, such as at Xanthi in Thrace, are seeing their food and beverage service upgraded to correspond with the better quality of rail transport offered.

Tourist protection

Accession to the European Union has meant that Greece needs to adhere to a whole range of directives pertaining to the protection of consumers. In response to this, a Greek Consumers Institute (INKA) has been set up in collaboration with the Tourist Protection Service and the development ministry. INKA's purpose is to offer legal advice on difficulties with tourism-related services (overcharging, reneging on agreements on goods and services, poor telecommunications services). This organisation has its main office in Athens (Poseidonos Avenue 31, 17561 Paleo Phalero, Athens; tel: 01 98 29 152, fax: 98 25 096) but it has agents throughout the mainland and the islands: in Northern Greece at Thessaloniki (031 272 163, fax: 238 061), Kavala (051 834 534, fax: 238-061), Alexandroupolis (0551 37 843); in Central Greece at Volos (tel/fax: 0421 20 833), Larissa (tel/fax: 041 538 080), Ioannina (0651 31 932, fax: 30 970); in Western Greece and the Ionian Islands at Arta (0681 28 014), Corfu (0661 48 234, fax: 45 072); in Southern Greece at Patras (061 424 298), Kalamata (0721 23 003, fax: 81 556); in Piraeus, Athens, Attica and Saronic Islands (01 98 29 152, 36 29 569, 38 05 853, 41 31 186); on Crete (Agios Nikolaos: 0841 24 183, Iraklion 081 281 891, 0821 50 603); on Rhodes (0241 39 581, fax: 25 143).

Travellers should also note the existence of a tourism watchdog consumers organisation, The Quality of Life (EKPIZO), that provides free legal assistance for tourists and travellers who believe they have been taken advantage of by rapacious taxi drivers, bus or airline companies or tour operators, or feel they have been overcharged for goods and services. EKPIZO functions from 1 July until 30 September. Volunteers staff a kiosk at Athens airport and in Athens at Syntagma Square from 11.00 until 15.00. EKPIZO also provides a legal hotline in five locations around Greece. Legal counsellors are available to answer queries on weekdays from 10.00 to 14.00. These services (in English, French or Greek) are free. The five locations are: Athens, 43-45 Valtetsiou St, 01 330 4444; Irakleion (Crete), 1 Milatou St, 081 240 666; Kavala, 3 Hydras St, 051 221 159; Patras, 213b Corinthou St, 061 272 481; Volos, 51 Hatziargiri St, 0421 39 266.

Chapter Two

The Hellenic Railways Organisation (OSE)

INTRODUCTION

All Greek railways, with the sole exception of the Athens–Piraeus Electric Railway (ISAP), are administered by the Hellenic Railways Organisation (OSE) founded in 1971.

For the rail traveller, a train trip in Greece is an adventure unlike any other in modern Europe. Four different track width gauges: standard (1.43m), narrow (1m), 75cm and 60cm, comprise the 2,484km rail network of mostly single-track railway. The OSE system only began to see extensive infrastructure renovation (better signalisation, double track rights-of-way and major tunnelling work) and modern new locomotives and passenger rolling stock in the late 1980s.

It is still necessary to change trains when travelling between many major destinations because incompatible track widths prohibit the through passage of trains, though in some significant instances like Athens–Kalambaka (for Meteora, Ioannina and the Epirus Mountains) and Thessaloniki to Corinth, an infrastructure rationalisation is under way that will permit through service. It is often still necessary to travel on older rolling stock, some of it hand-me-downs from more advanced European networks, on isolated branch lines where the equipment is not entirely appropriate.

But given the lack of interest by Greek transport authorities for several decades that have prevented track realignments and roadbed strengthening but which have made rail travel such a smooth ride in other parts of the world, a train trip in Greece often evokes an era of relaxed, less time-sensitive travel. For the rail fan, Greece is a definite must, especially since it has embarked on an ambitious programme of restoration of steam-hauled passenger services, using recently rebuilt original locomotives and vintage passenger cars running over some of the most attractive stretches of track in Greece: the Diakofto to Kalavrita (75cm cog and adhesion or rack and pinion) railway in the Peloponnese, the Thessaly Railways 60cm Pelion branch in Central Greece and the main-line Drama to Xanthi segment through the dramatic Nestos Canyon gorge in Western Thrace.

HISTORY

Greece was among the last European nations to develop railways. The first iron wheel rolled over an iron rail in Greece (from Piraeus to Athens) in 1869, more than forty years after the British Stockton and Darlington line opened. Lines in northern Greece opened in Macedonia and Thrace shortly thereafter (in 1872 the line from Thessaloniki to the present FYRO Macedonia border and into Alexandroupolos from Edirne was opened). The first intercity railway opened in the Peloponnese in 1882 and in Thessaly the same year. These last two lines and their networks were funded by the new Greek State. Railways in Northern Greece are there as a result of an industrialisation policy: the fading Ottoman Empire trying to link together the last bits of an increasingly divisive and disruptive empire in Europe.

If we take a brief historical overlook at the development of railways in Greece, we can put the modern OSE and ISAP systems in perspective. Railways in Greece radiated out of the three major population centres: the Piraeus/Athens area to the north, east and west; Volos towards Epirus and the west as well as up to the Pelion peninsula in the Volos hinterlands; and in all directions radiating from Thessaloniki in northern Greece. .

Two different ideas dominated local thinking about railways. One, espoused by Prime Minister Alexander Koumoundouros in the late 1860s, saw the railways acting as a land-bridge line between Western European markets and Near-Eastern sources of raw materials. The other approach, led by Harilaos Trikoupis, favoured the internal development of Greece's internal transport infrastructure as a prerequisite for inclusion in the international railways scene.   ·

In practical terms, this meant the internationalists preferred building a more expensive standard gauge network while domestic proponents leant towards a cheaper narrow gauge railway. In 1881, Koumoundouros signed four contracts for standard gauge railway construction fanning out from Athens. One year later Trikoupis cancelled them and signed four others calling for a narrow gauge network commencing in the Peloponnese peninsula.

Harilaos Trikoupis deserves a special mention. Originally from Messalongi in western Greece, he spent fourteen years in London during the 1860s and 1870s. He saw the railways develop in Britain and understood that they could be of value to the emerging Greek nation. He was first appointed Prime Minister in 1875 and struggled with political reform and economic development, led by railway construction, until his death in 1896. Because of his selfless efforts, Trikoupis is considered the outstanding Greek politician of the nineteenth century.

Contracts for the construction of the first 700km were signed in 1882 and provided for the initial Peloponnese metre gauge system of 417km with two major arteries: one from Athens to Corinth, Patras and Pirgos with a branch from Pirgos to Katakolon; and the other from Corinth through Argos to Nafplion with a branch from Argos to Mili. Plans also entailed the construction of 202km for the basic metric gauge system of Thessaly, from Volos through Farsala, Karditsa, Trikala and Kalambaka with a branch from Velestino to Larissa. Finally, they included the 76km Attica system, from Athens' Omonia Square to Lavrion with a branch from Iraklio to Kifissia. Bit by bit, these lines opened for circulation between 1883 and 1890.

Greece fell foul of the Great Powers in the mid 1880s. This led to a military blockade of the Port of Piraeus and proved the strategic value of land transportation. Trikoupis pushed his railway plans by signing new contracts between 1887 and 1891 for an additional 1100km of rail lines, of which 441km would be built to conform to international specifications to connect Athens to its then border with Northern Thessaly at Larissa, 600km to complete the Peloponnese system, and 62km more for the Attica line.

Very few of these planned railway extensions were eventually built. Renewed warfare with Turkey in 1887, Europe's upswing and Greece's precarious financial situation with its third bankruptcy in its short sixty-year history truncated its railway dreams.

Between 1900 and 1902 railway efforts were re-established to complete Trikoupis' ambitions by Prime Minister George Theotokis. They were brought on line piecemeal until 1909, bringing the national network to a total of 1600km. Then the First Balkan War erupted.

It took 25 years and fully 50% of all Greece's financial investments, other than for agriculture, to build this network. Unlike Western Europe where railways were instrumental in satisfying demand for transportation services, the Greek system created that demand. Railways linked isolated regions that had never had roads or even much contact with their neighbours beyond the next hillock. Because of this, some economists call railway spending the greatest financial investment ever in Greek history.

During the Greek State's deployment of rail infrastructure, the Ottoman Empire proceeded with its own railway schemes in the north. A series of rail lines were developed to all points on the Ottoman compass from Thessaloniki, then the second city of a fading empire known as the "Sick Man of Europe". The first tentative links were from Edirne (formerly Adrinople) on the Bulgaria–Istanbul main line to the Aegean port of Alexandroupolis (then known as Dedeagac) in 1872 and then fanning out from Thessaloniki: north to Gevegeli (1872) and Yugoslavia (1888), east to Florina (1894), northeast to Strimon (1895), then east through Serres and Drama to Xanthi, Komotini and Istanbul (1896). These lines were designed to supplement Austro-Hungarian rails laid from Vienna through Belgrade and Sofia to Istanbul.

After the First Balkan War (1912), Greek rails pushed north from Larissa through the Vale of Tempi to Platy in 1916. This 89km rail stretch linked Greece to the Ottoman-built Macedonian system and permitted Greece to join Europe's international system. Once again Greece's railway ambitions were thwarted with planned lines from Kalambaka to Kozani and beyond Agrinion towards Albania left unbuilt (though with surveys done and some right-of-way and infrastructure work like bridges and tunnels completed).

From that time until the creation of OSE in 1971, no major work was undertaken to expand Greece's rail infrastructure, other than line straightening, an extension of the rail line from Isthmus to Loutraki (1954) and the Florina line from Amindeo to Kozani in 1957, and several new stations like Larissa (1962) and Thessaloniki's monolithic station in 1967. The most important achievement of this era was possibly the rail extension from Strimon to Bulgaria (1966).

World War II saw the decimation of Greece's industrial infrastructure and the post-war period was devoted to rebuilding the existing though severely damaged rail system. Highway construction was emphasised under American directed rebuilding after the Greek Civil War in the late 1950s and the railways began fading from the public consciousness as an effective method of public transport. From the post World War II era to the 1960s, the railways' share of passenger traffic plummeted from more than 50% in 1950 to below 4% in 1967.

The modern railway era began when the various Greek railways were consolidated into OSE in 1971. By way of comparison, France dates the beginning of its modern railway revolution to the creation of the French National Railways Society, the SNCF, in the 1940s. The Greek administration's move was accompanied by various rationalisations that led to the closing of branch railway lines throughout the country. Many observers believe that OSE was founded, much like Amtrak in the United States, to oversee the dismemberment and ultimately the closing of most of Greece's railways. In any case, the decade of the 1970s saw massive dieselisation of motive power but also a gradual though definite retrenching with line closings and reductions in frequencies the rule.

Greece's membership in 1981 of the European Economic Community, later to become the European Union, was a shot in the arm for the ailing railway system. This allowed Greece to participate with its Northern European neighbours in the pro-railway development Community of European Railways. Concretely this has meant the security of long range planning (rare in Greece), new investments in rolling stock and heavy infrastructure developments as part of the EU Delors II package, and a general revival of interest in railway redevelopment. Schedules have been speeded up between Athens and Thessaloniki and closed branch lines have been reopened in the Peloponnese from Isthmia to Loutraki and from Argos to Nafplion.

Another significant event occurred in 1983. An Athens–based but broadly followed popular consumers' group, the Hellenic Association of Railway Friends, was founded. This group of devoted friends of the railways has done immeasurable good in promoting railways and railway travel in Greece.

An increased awareness of the benefits of the railways and intensive investments in new rolling stock, improved tracks and signalisation and a general refurbishing of Greece's railway stations, many of which are authentic 19th-century architectural gems, has led to a railway revival whose practical aspects are only now, in the mid-1990s, being seen. With the summer timetable changes of 1996, the fastest Athens–Thessaloniki schedule on the 510km route is 5 hours and 50 minutes. This is the fastest schedule ever on this route. When all the infrastructure projects from tunnels to bridges to signalisation and double tracking throughout the line (with one extremely difficult segment excluded) are concluded and the line is electrified early in the 21st century, travel time will drop to 3 hours and 30 minutes. At that time, when new urban heavy rail systems are put in service in Athens and Thessaloniki, Greece's main population corridor will be equipped with a Northern European style quality railway.

RAILWAY TRAVEL INFORMATION
Stations
Most Greek rail stations date to the era of railway building in Greece. As such, they are seen as an important part of modern Greece's architectural heritage. Only a few significant big city stations (Thessaloniki, Larissa and Kozani among others) were built in the mid-to-late 20th century. The older stations, notably in Volos and a great many in the Peloponnese, date to the 19th century and resemble those of their Central European builders. Northern Greek stations on the French-built railway from Thessaloniki east to Alexandroupolis look much like French country stations. Most are well preserved and feature large, well tended gardens and obviously all necessary passenger services. Many offer complete cafés and restaurants serving excellent grilled meats (Edessa comes to mind) or home baked pastries (Thessaloniki). Rail travellers are strongly advised to give Greek stations, built of stone and well faced with brick, a long look before boarding trains or leaving the station area.

Greek railway stations are also the subject of a fine recently published coffee-table book called *Stathmoi – Greek Railway Stations*, that is recommended. It is listed in the *Further Reading* section at the end of this book and can be ordered directly from the publisher.

Types of trains
OSE offers new, air conditioned, all reserved, limited or no, stop trains called InterCity (IC) on most routes with the exception of the route south of Corinth through Argos. Express (Taxeia) trains using late model rolling stock featuring a diesel locomotive pulling six or more passenger cars and making limited stops operate on all routes except where Suburban Services (Topiko) using new permanently attached rail diesel cars operate: Athens to Chalkis and Athens to Loutraki. Local (Topiko) trains making all stops on selected routes also use diesel hauled rolling stock. Note that all trains except the Athens to Chalkis Suburban Services have both first and second class seats.

Ticket prices

These are based on kilometres travelled and are summarised on pages 60 and 164.

A return ticket purchased from an OSE counter entitles the traveller to a 30% reduction on the single one-way ticket. Also, a journey can be broken en route at an intermediate stop for 48 hours by announcing it to the ticket clerk at the intermediate station immediately after arrival. The clerk will provide a form for the traveller to present to the on-board train staff. If travel is to be continued aboard an IC train the entire supplement must be repaid.

OSE ticket offices close five minutes before departure time for a specific train. After ticket offices close prospective travellers are advised to present themselves to the on-board OSE ticket inspector for ticket purchase. Those not doing so are liable to be assessed a fine above and beyond the ticket price.

Supplements

InterCity trains require payment of a supplement based on distance travelled. On the Athens–Thessaloniki–Athens route, travel supplements are as follows:

up to 150km :	700Dr
from 151 to 250km:	1,100Dr
from 251 to 400km:	2,200Dr
from 401 to 760km:	3,600Dr
from 761km:	4,000Dr

The new non-stop Athens–Thessaloniki IC-Hermes train has a flat 4,100Dr supplement but this includes a full meal and all beverages.

On the Thessaloniki–Alexandroupolis–Thessaloniki route, IC supplements are as follows:

up to 100km:	400Dr
from 101 to 150km:	650Dr
from 151 to 250km:	1,000Dr
from 251km:	1,500Dr

On the Piraeus–Kyparissia–Piraeus route, IC supplements are as follows:

up to 100km:	400Dr
from 101 to 150km:	650Dr
from 151 to 230km:	1,000Dr
from 231km:	1,500Dr

On the Thessaloniki–Kozani/Florina–Thessaloniki route there is a flat 500Dr IC supplement.

Night trains

These operate between Athens–Thessaloniki and return, and Athens–Thessaloniki–Alexandroupolis–Ormenio and return. The Athens–

Thessaloniki and return trains (504/505) feature first and tourist class sleeping cars with single and two bed rooms in first class and one, two, and three bed rooms in tourist class. Four and six bed second class couchette cars also operate on the two above listed routes. Supplements for sleeping car space are as follows:

First class (air-conditioned sleeper-cars):
    one person in a single room: 7,700Dr
    per person in a double room: 4,800Dr
Tourist class (1, 2 and 3 berth compartments):
    one person in a single room: 5,400Dr
    per person in a double room: 3,700Dr
    per person in a triple room: 2,500Dr
Couchettes (4 and 6 couchettes):
    per person in a four-bed room: 2,100Dr
    per person in a six-bed room: 1,400Dr

It is possible to hire a whole compartment by paying the price of all places available in the compartment. However, in the compartment, the number of passengers travelling should not exceed the designated number of places.

Motorail trains

These operate on the internal Athens–Thessaloniki–Athens route. There are both a pair of night trains (504/505) and a pair of day trains (500/501) that offer this service. Supplements according to the size of the vehicle transported are as follows:

    smaller than 3.81m: 8,130Dr
    from 3.81 to 4.42m: 9,380Dr
    larger than 4.42m: 11,250Dr

Loading of vehicles should take place at least 60 minutes prior to departure at special installations near the passenger platforms of the Piraeus, Athens and Thessaloniki central stations. Motorail space is limited and advanced bookings are strongly recommended.

International connections

International trains originate and terminate only in Thessaloniki:

- Trains 334/335 Thessaloniki–Budapest and return: direct coaches to/from Belgrade, Moscow, Prague and Bratislava. Connections to/from Germany and other European countries
- Trains 392/393 day train Thessaloniki–Belgrade and return: connections to/from Budapest and Vienna
- Trains 602/613 Thessaloniki–Dikea and return: direct coaches to/from Istanbul
- Trains 614/613 Thessaloniki–Dikea and return: direct coaches to/from Sofia and Bucharest (summer only)

Reservations

Electronic on-line seat reservations are available through a network of 25 terminals to the following travel destinations: Athens–Volos, Athens–Larissa, Athens–Thessaloniki.

Seat reservation from other locations for other lines is still done by hand using paper car-diagrams and small, rectangular ticket chits. This system has been in use since railways began in Greece. Old brass, hand-cranked chit printing and stamping machines in excellent condition are on display in the Volos Railway Museum. In the rest of Greece similar machines are still in use.

Intermediate stations are allotted a certain number of seats. Unexpectedly large numbers of passengers on a particular day can throw the system off kilter, but those holding reservations do have priority over others boarding trains without them. Also, seat-backs on trains are not marked by OSE personnel to indicate a reservation. Given that most Greek travellers take a nonchalant attitude to the whole thing, its easy to understand the pandemonium that occasionally breaks out with the vigorous hand-waving gesticulations and excited cries that Greeks employ when someone is occupying their place. Practically, what this system means is that obtaining a seat on particularly busy travel days without previously reserving can occasionally be a hit or miss affair.

Luggage

Checked luggage is carried on most long distance trains, as is a variety of farm animals, big and small, and motorcycles. Left luggage is accepted at most stations for a fee of 280Dr per bag per day. Note that days begin at 00.00 and go to 23.59. This means that passengers arriving in Piraeus from an inter-island ferry at 23.00 and planning on departing on a morning train for Patras will have to pay for two days per bag.

Special offers

A number of special passes are available to non-Greek travellers. Holders may travel at no extra charge on IC trains, the Diakofto-Kalavrita rack and pinion railway, the Athens–Nafplion–Athens route and the Chalkis and Loutraki local trains:

Vergina Flexipass A combination of rail travel and hotel accommodation, cruise or excursions to archaeological sites and Athens sightseeing. It offers unlimited rail travel in Greece for 3, 5 or 10 days in first class and for 5 or 10 days in second class. Prices range from US$263 to US$550, with special prices for children aged 4–12.

Greek Flexipass Unlimited first class rail travel in Greece, for 3 or 5 days within one month (US$86 or US$120; children 4–12 reduced price). There are no restrictions on the day of the month travelled.

Greek Flexipass Rail 'n Fly This is a combination of rail travel and flights to the Greek islands. It offers unlimited rail travel in first or second class in

Greece for 3 days within one month from US$143 to US$202. Single or return flight coupons for journeys to any Greek island serviced by Olympic Airways' domestic flights are included in the price; additional flight coupons are available at US$66 each (one way); children under 11 reduced price. Airport taxes are not included and must be paid locally.

All other OSE special offers for Greeks (families, senior citizens, groups and children) are available to tourists as well. All Eurail, Eurail Flexipasses and Interrail passes are also valid in Greece. It may be cheaper to purchase the Euro Domino Pass when in Greece. Passes are available at the railway office (not the railway station) in Athens, or at the international ticket window at Thessaloniki. Care should be taken with Flexipasses because Greek railway travel is such good value that with the exception of a full-length cross country trip (Athens–Alexandroupolis for example) the use of a Flexiday for rail travel is often not warranted.

Passes are available from the following agents:

Australia Adventure World/Tracks, 73 Walker St, North Sydney, NSW 2060; tel: +61 2 9955 5000; fax: +61 2 9954 5817, +61 2 9956 7707

Touchdown Tours, 476 High St, Northcote, Victoria 3070; tel: +61 3948 25215; fax: +61 3948 25216

France Rail Europe Australasia, 24 Rue de Londres F-75009, Paris; tel: +33 1 53 32 81 90; fax: +33 1 49 70 09 51

Greece Hellenic Tours, Ermoy 23-25, Athens; tel: 324 3715-9; fax: 323 4947

Airtour Greece AE, Theseos 330-176-75, Athens; tel: 939 5000; fax: 939 5303

Carlson Wagons Lits, Stadiou 5, Athens TK 105-62; tel: 324 2281; fax: 322 0397

Israel European World Tour Representatives, 2 Shmaryahu Levine St, PO Box 4476, Haifa 31043; tel: +9724 616444; fax: +9724 671380

Italy Hellenic Products & Services, Piazza Tomaseo 4, 34121 Trieste; tel: +39 40 363 242; fax: +39 40 779 7097

Netherlands Celtic Travel, Fregat 57, 1113 EE Diemen, Amsterdam; tel/fax: +31 2069 56612

New Zealand Jet Age Marketing and Travel Ltd, Travel House, 6 Walls Rd, Penrose, Auckland 6; tel: +64 952 52360; fax: +64 952 52227

South Africa World Travel Agency (Pty) Ltd, 8th Floor, Everite House, 20 De Korte St, Braamfontein, 2001 Johannesburg; tel: +27 11 403 2606; fax: +27 11 403 1037

UK British Rail International, Victoria Station, London SW1V 1JY; tel: 0171 922 9875; fax: 0171 922 9874

USA Rail Europe Inc, 500 Mamaroneck Ave, Harrison, New York 10528; tel: +1 914 682 2999; fax: +1 914 682 2821

DER Rail Services, 9501 W Devon Ave, Rosemont, IL 60018-4832; tel: +1 847 692 4141; fax: +1 847 692 4506

CIT Tours Corporation, 342 Madison Ave, 207 New York, NY 10172; tel: +1 212 697 2497; fax: +1 212 697 1394

Stay-Drive Package This is a new programme introduced by OSE in conjunction with Carlson Wagonlit Travel (Athens: Skoufou 6, 10557 Athens; tel: 01 32 32 546, fax: 01 32 44 196. Thessaloniki: Tsimiskis 23, 54624 Thessaloniki; tel: 031 236 293, fax: 031 229 539). This offer is currently only available to travellers from Thessaloniki bound for Athens aboard IC trains and planning on staying three nights in Athens. It includes accommodation in the Novotel Hotel and a rental car during the stay (plus free parking). If the Athens test proves successful it will be extended throughout Greece.

Schedules

Timetables normally change once a year on or near 1 June. OSE issues a yearly timetable in a handy multicolour shirt-pocket size format as well as a trade paperback size. The little booklet will usually be available at timetable change dates, but the larger and more complete book is usually not available until two months later. The little booklet (only in Greek) is available at most stations but tends to be out of stock by the following spring. It only lists major schedules and has a way of even omitting some principal trains. The bigger Timetable Indicator (in English as well as Greek) is only available at the OSE headquarters skyscraper (room 607) at Karolou 1 near Omonia Square in Athens. This tome is available all year round.

Otherwise, schedules are available in the monthly red-covered *Thomas Cook European Timetable* that can be purchased at major Thomas Cook UK Travel shops (£8.40) or by mail order directly from Thomas Cook (£9.60 in the UK, £11.90 in Europe or £13.30 (overseas air mail) from Thomas Cook (TPO/FE), PO Box 227, Peterborough PE3 6PU, UK; or by telephoning 01733 505 821 or 268 943. Timetable information is also available in the UK from TIM (tel: 0891 700600), Mon–Fri, 0900–1800.

Occasional changes, some major, occur between timetable publication dates. The only way to know about them is to look at the posted timetables then ask at railway information counters. Rail travellers planning on really "doing" the Greek rails should also consult the Hellenic Association of Railway Friends at the Athens-based Railway Museum on Siolou Street.

Promptness

OSE trains are generally on time. Great strides have been made to ensure that schedules are kept. Chronic tardiness is observed on only one line: the scenically spectacular Argos–Tripolis–Kalamata metre gauge line in the Peloponnese. The other rail lines run more or less to schedule. Reasons for delays can be put into two categories: those due to extensive infrastructure-rebuilding programmes such as on the Athens–Thessaloniki standard gauge main line and those due to the weather. Hot summer temperatures approaching 40° combined with high tourist-season loadings conspire to make slippery track conditions for extra long trains especially on the many mountainous segments of railway. Otherwise, IC operating crews receive a substantial financial bonus when they meet on-time performance standards.

Major OSE sales and reservation offices

Alexandroupolis: Travel Office No 6, 1 Megalou Alexandrou Str (Mon–Fri 08.00 to 14.30), tel: 0551 27906

Athens: Travel Office No 1, 6 Sina Str (Mon–Sat 08.00 to 15.00), tel: 01 36 24 402-6

Travel Office No 2, 1 Karolou Str (Mon–Sat 08.00 to 15.00), tel: 01 52 24 302, 01 52 22 491

Travel Office No 7, 17 Fillelinon Str (Mon–Fri 08.00 to 15.00), tel: 01 32 36 747, 01 32 36 273

Information: 1 Karolou Str, tel: 01 52 40 601, 01 52 40 646-8

Larissa Central Station, tel: 01 82 37 000

Peloponnese Station, tel: 01 51 31 601

Kalamata: Central Station, tel: 0721 22 555, 0721 23 904

Kyparissia: Central Station, tel: 0761 22 283

Komotini: Travel Office No 9, 50 Nikolaou Zoidi Str (Mon–Fri 07.30 to 15.00), tel: 0531 26 804

Larissa: Railway Station, tel: 041 23 6250

Travel Office No 3, 14 Deli Str (Mon–Fri 08.00 to 20.30 & Sat 08.00 to 14.30), tel: 041 22 2201

Loutraki: Railway Station, tel: 0741 22 277

Patras: Central Station, tel: 021 22 1311, 021 27 7000

Thessaloniki: Central Station, tel: 031 51 7517-8, 031 51 9519

Travel Office No 4, 18 Aristotelous Str (Mon & Sat 08.00 to 14.30 and Tues–Fri 08.00 to 21.00), tel: 031 27 6382

Volos: Railway Station, tel: 0421 23 712, 0421 25 759

Travel Office No 8, 42 Iassonos Str (Mon–Sat 08.00 to 14.30), tel: 0421 25 759, 0421 28 555

Train to ferry connections

Though each appropriate section will cite rail station and ferry port link-up, the following list gives places where information can be obtained on train to ferry connections.

City (phone code)	OSE rail station	Port police
Piraeus (01)	46 12 734	41 72 657
Patras (061)	221 311	341 002
Kylini (0623)	33 234 (Kavassila)	92 211
Kyparissia (0761)	22 283	22 039 (regular police)
Kalamata (0721)	22 555	22 218
Chalkis (0221)	22 386	83 333 (tourist police)
Stylis (0238)	0231 61 061 (Lianokladi)	22 223 (regular police)
Volos (0421)	23 712	38 888
Thessaloniki (031)	517 510	531 504
Drama (0551) for Kavala (051)	22 444	223 716
Alexandroupolis (0551)	26 395	28 734

SUGGESTED ITINERARIES

The number of possibilities is limitless. Three suggested itineraries appear in *Chapters Sixteen–Eighteen,* starting on page 220:

- Athens to Epirus and the Ionian Islands
- Athens to Thessaloniki and Alexandroupolis by rail, then by ferry to the islands of Samothraki and Thassos and to the port of Kavala, with a return to Thessaloniki and Athens (directly by rail or through the Sporades and Volos)
- Athens to the Peloponnese, then Crete and the Aegean Isles and back to Athens

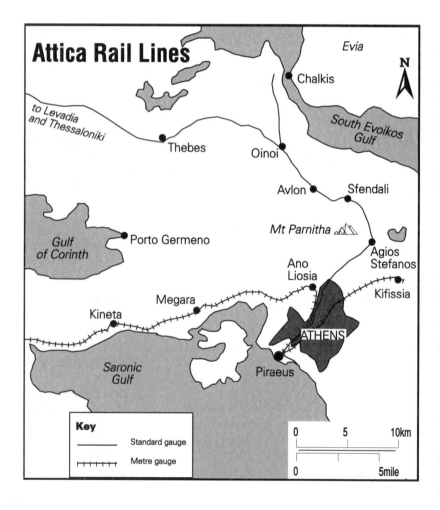

Part Two

ATTICA BASIN RAILWAYS

This section will treat the railways serving the capital and largest city in Greece – Athens (population: 3.5 million) – with its major port Piraeus (population: 500,000), and the other urban areas in the Attica Basin (population: 2,000,000). There are essentially three different railways dealt with here: The Piraeus–Athens–Kifissia standard gauge metro system (third rail electric – ISAP), the standard gauge line Piraeus–Athens–Chalkis and the narrow gauge Peloponnese line from Piraeus as far as Elefsina. The remainder of this line will be treated in the Peloponnese section.

With the exception of the ISAP line, these rail lines are not normally considered urban railways. But because of multiple daily frequencies on both lines, it is possible to use them both for day excursions from Athens by leaving the city early in the morning and returning late in the evening.

Chapter Three

Piraeus–Athens–Attica

INTRODUCTION

Cosmopolitan Athens is Greece's administrative capital and its major city. Piraeus is Athens' most important seaport (Rafina and Lavrion are the others) and one of the most important shipping centres on the Mediterranean. Together Athens and Piraeus account for almost half of Greece's total population. Though independent of each other in political and governmental matters, the two cities are linked intimately by history, culture, trade and a railway line. Greece's first railway line opened in 1869 and appropriately connected two cities which since then have grown to become a single metropolitan region containing close to five million people.

They have been linked since antiquity – glorious Athens, the birthplace of Democracy, depended on maritime wealth accumulated by commerce through the Port of Piraeus for the freedom to create its eternal legacy. Such was the bond between Pericles' Athens and Old Piraeus (planned by architect Hippodamos of Miletus) that twin, parallel walls were built by Conon in 394BC to protect the road binding the two cities.

During the heady days after the War of Independence (1835), communication between the two cities was assured by over 500 horse-drawn coaches daily.

Building a rail link between the two seemed a natural choice at the time, but 22 years were to pass between the date initial plans were announced and the signing of the first contract. Another ten years were to elapse before the first rails were laid. Two years later, in 1869, the first steam-powered trains ran over the single-track line between Piraeus and Thission. This was Greece's first railway. In all, it took 34 years to lay these 8.5km of rail line. At the time, track was being laid in the Western United States at the rate of 17km per day.

From an initial frequency of eight daily steam-powered trains schedules now operate every 5 to 10 minutes from 05.00 to midnight on the double-track electrified (third rail) line.

The line was extended from Thission to Omonia in the 1890s. Railway construction led to major archaeological discoveries. It exposed the exact site of the ancient Agora. The line was extended on to Attica in 1926. Work to extend beyond to the isolated village of Kifissia began in March 1948. This work followed the existing right-of-way of an old steam-powered country railway from the centre of Athens to the then far reaches of rural Attica. This old railway (1882–1938) is still affectionately known as the "wild beast".

From its modest beginnings, the line now counts 22 stations over 26km and has 195 rail cars on its roster – all built after 1985. It carries over 80 million passengers annually. After several name changes the line is now known as the Athens Piraeus Electric Railway SA (ISAP) or the "Electric" ("O Electrikos").

Locals know and use this convenient link to commute and avoid the notorious double daily auto gridlock that chokes Athens. But, despite the large windows, locals and visitors alike are largely ignorant of the charms of a rail system where a round-trip ticket to ride costs less then one pitta-wrapped souvlaki sandwich. The system is divided into three zones with travel in one zone costing 75Dr; and 100Dr in two or more zones. The honour system is practised with passengers expected to punch their tickets in the little yellow boxes situated at the entrances to each platform. Failure to do so could result in a 1,500Dr fine (payment is due immediately or the fine augments greatly).

The ISAP Piraeus terminal station (built in 1884) is a substantial brick building – the most impressive railway structure in the contemporary Athens metropolitan area – situated directly on the shore of the Great Harbour of Piraeus. The building has never been properly cleaned since the end of World War II and scars from Nazi attempts to destroy Piraeus transport facilities during their 1944 withdrawal are still evident along the platforms.

It is a short walk (to the right down the main ramp facing the harbour) to OSE's Peloponnese rail station and only several minutes further (around the Great Harbour past the OSE Peloponnese station) to OSE's recently restored main-line station. Ferries to most Aegean and some Ionian islands dock directly in front of the ISAP terminal. Late departing passengers have a choice of several travel agencies, situated directly inside the barrel-vaulted building. A personal preference is the Central Travel Agency on the left facing the port. In addition to providing for domestic sailings, it gives direct access to the reservation offices of Hellenic Mediterranean Lines for passage to Italy from Patras.

Automatic ticket dispensing machines and manned ticket windows are situated along one side of the building (by the park); and access to the several platforms is open under a large banner with a transliterated announcement inviting "owners of tickets to validate them". Passengers bound for points beyond central Athens stations should check individual train boards for their destinations as many trains – especially during rush hours – do not go from end-point to end-point.

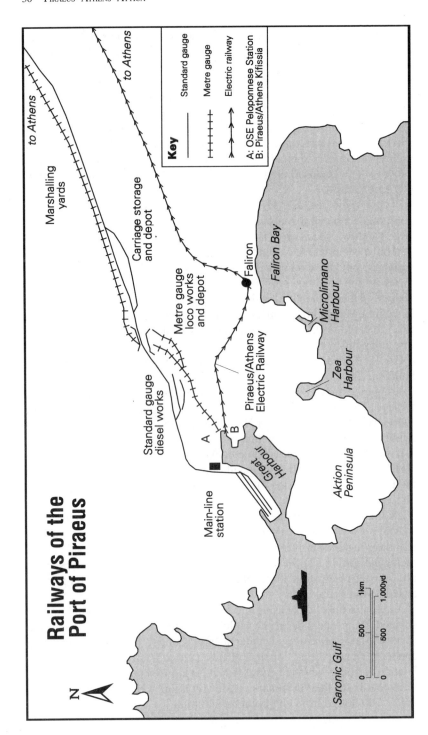

Railways of the Port of Piraeus

Key
— Standard gauge
—|—|—|— Metre gauge
↑↑ Electric railway

A: OSE Peloponnese Station
B: Piraeus/Athens Kifissia

to Athens

to Athens

to Athens

Marshalling yards

Carriage storage and depot

Metre gauge loco works and depot

Standard gauge diesel works

Main-line station

A

B

Piraeus/Athens Electric Railway

Faliron

Faliron Bay

Microlimano Harbour

Zea Harbour

Aktion Peninsula

Great Harbour

Saronic Gulf

N

0   500   1km
0   500   1,000yd

PIRAEUS

Piraeus (population 600,000), Greece's third largest city, is probably as well known as Athens, but only as a transit point with over 60 ferry and hydrofoil departures daily to most of the Greek Aegean islands and some Ionian isles as well. (Cyprus, Turkey, Israel and Egypt are also served but only seasonally and usually only weekly.) In addition, over 650,000 people per year embark aboard cruise ships from Piraeus – making it the Miami of the Mediterranean. Over 6.3 million people passed through the port of Piraeus in 1992 making it the world's third most important passenger port.

But, above all, Piraeus is the nerve-centre of the formidable Greek merchant marine fleet. Despite the great number of idle vessels at anchor, over 3,100 cargo and tanker ships representing 16% of world and 44% of European tonnage belong to Greek shipowners – some of whom like Onassis and Niarchos are household names, while others like the discreet George P Livanos possess more ships than the combined merchant fleets of France and Germany.

History

Piraeus's history is long and chequered. Its three major natural harbours – the Great Harbour (Kantharos of the ancients), the circular Zea (Trireme base in Antiquity), and Mikrolimani (still known as Turcolimani or Munychia of the Classical period) – have been known and respected for close to 3,000 years. With the rise of Athens, Piraeus became the major naval base under Themistocles and was fortified after the Battle of Marathon (490BC). Pericles decreed that a city be laid out to complement the harbours. Hippodaumos created the grid plan still followed today – though precious little of what the intrepid 3rd-century AD traveller Pausanius described as a beautiful city has been found (apart from the trireme sheds in the Zea Harbour).

During the four-century-long Ottoman hegemony, Piraeus was known as Porte Leone, but its importance dwindled until it was a meagre village of several hundred inhabitants at the end of the Greek War of Independence (1835).

The opening of the Suez Canal (1862) and the coming of the railroad (1869) brought about a belated period of industrialisation helped immensely by the completion of the Corinthian Canal (1893) and the final conversion of the Greek fleet to steam (1900). The population boom began with the depopulation of the outer islands during the Independence struggles (Chios); and was completed by the First Balkan War (1912–13) and the catastrophe of the Smyrna Adventure (1922) when a major negotiated population exchange brought almost one million refugees from Greek settlements in Asia Minor to Greece proper. Piraeus boomed.

World War II virtually destroyed the city and port with over 75% of structures severely damaged. It wasn't until the American-sponsored Marshall Plan took effect in the mid-1950s that Piraeus got back on its feet. Piraeus's best known modern personality is the late Melina Mercouri. She came to public notice in the 1960s as a film star portraying a Piraeus streetwalker in the acclaimed *Never On Sunday* then rose to political power as Greece's Minister of Culture in the 1980s.

What to see
Piraeus today is a very busy, polyglot, workmanlike city. Other than the dozens of colourful ferries at quay, which by themselves create the aura of a bustling port, Piraeus has plenty to occupy a day. Parts of the Walls of Themistocleos are still visible on the quay of the same name. The Zea yacht marina containing the ancient trireme ship sheds and the Microlimani fishing fleet and seafood restaurants are wonderful places to stroll. The twin sports stadiums of Peace and Freedom (1985) where the major Olympiakos Club plays football, basketball and volleyball before always enthusiastic crowds, and the two major museums of Archaeology (Harilaou Trikoup 31, tel: 01 452 1598, Tues–Sun 08.00–15.00, admission 500, 400, 300Dr) and Maritime History (Akti Themistocleous, Freatida, tel/fax: 01 451 6822, Tues–Sat 08.30–14.00, Sun 09.00–13.00, 400Dr, Sat free) should well occupy visitors. The Maritime Museum, with its scale model reproductions of famous naval battles, is a good preparation for visits to Salamis, Nafpaktos and Navarino (Pylos).

Where to stay
Hotels include: the Santorini (Trikoupis 6, tel: 01 45 52 147); Castella (Vasilissis Pavlou 75, tel: 01 41 14 735); and the more upscale Cavo D'Oro (Vasilissis 19, tel: 01 41 22 210). This rather short list should make its own statement that Piraeus is a working port that caters to sailors and seafarers with limited accommodation for tourists.

Travel information
Port police: 01 41 72 657, EOT (01 41 35 716, inconveniently located at the Zea Marina yacht harbour; it is better to use the central Athens Syntagma Square facility).

Rail travel tips
For those travellers based in Thission or Monastiraki and planning onward passage to Central, Northern or Peloponnesian Greece, it is often easier and cheaper to descend aboard ISAP trains to Piraeus then walk to one of the major OSE rail stations for departure. Narrow gauge Peloponnesian trains for Patras almost always originate in Piraeus, main-line trains to the North usually don't, but OSE has begun to use its Piraeus main-line station more and more.

Those travellers coming into Piraeus on early morning ships from the Islands and not planning on staying in Athens should use the Piraeus OSE stations. All Patras-bound trains originate in Piraeus. This means seats are normally available; and midday, mid-August temperatures that approach 40°C can be avoided. The attractive main-line Agios Dionysious station has been spruced up and a motorail service is planned. This means that passengers with cars can leave overnight ferries coming from Crete and board Thessaloniki-bound trains without leaving the port area.

Rail fans and train spotters should enjoy the action at the three Piraeus stations. They offer the widest array of rail activity anywhere in Greece.

PIRAEUS TO KIFISSIA BY RAIL

Departing from Piraeus aboard an ISAP train, travellers should be able to spot traces of the ancient walls built to protect the way between Piraeus and Athens (right side). Then comes the Faliro Station which provides easy access to the two Peace and Friendship sports stadiums (indoor and outdoor) and the charming Microlimani harbour seafood restaurant mecca that Athenians so cherish. (While facing Athens descend under the platform,

PIRAEUS–ATHENS–KIFISSIA ELECTRIC RAILWAY (ISAP)

Station	Travelling time in minutes
Kifissia	2
KAT	2
Maroussi	5
Irini	3
Iraklion	2.5
Neo Ionia	1.5
Pefkaki	1
Perissos	2.5

Ano Patissia	1.5
Agios Eleftherios	2
Kato Patissia	1.5
Agios Nikolaos	3
Attiki	2
Victoria	2.5
Omonia	1

Monastiraki	4
Thission	2
Petralona	2
Tavros	3
Kallithea	3
Moschato	3
Faliro	3.5
Piraeus	

Fares

One or adjacent zones

Basic	75Dr
Student	45Dr
Pupil	35Dr

Travel through all three zones

Basic	100Dr
Student	60 Dr
Pupil	45 Dr

------- *Zone limit*

ATHENS-PIRAEUS ELECTRIC RAILWAY

turn right, continue along the underpass to the end, once on the surface turn right in front of the indoor sports stadium, follow along to the traffic lights, then go left and follow the canal shore to Microlimani.) Current transport plans call for two additions: a second metro line that will eventually link Faliro to Piraeus via Microlimani and the Akti Peninsula where the bulk of Piraeus' population lives, and a fast ferry link to the coastal towns down towards Cape Sounion.

After a brief halt at the Faliro Bay/Peace Stadium, the line curves sharply – this is the boundary between Piraeus and Athens. From here the rail line continues close to the sea along the site where Thrasybule and his Army of Athenian Democrats defeated Critias and the Thirty Tyrants (403BC). The train passes over a wide concrete-lined open culvert – it is what is left of the ancient Kephisos River which separated the two cities. Here the line leaves Piraeus and enters Athens.

ATHENS

The Greek capital is world-renowned for its legacy to art, architecture, philosophy and the democratic principals which are at the basis of modern Western political society. It is also widely known as a busy, hectic, crowded urban agglomeration cursed with a severe pollution problem, due in part to its particular geographic setting in a large basin.

Essentially Athens is situated on the wide, westward sloping Attica Plain at the end of the peninsula stretching southeast at the base of the Balkan Peninsula. The Attica Plain is bounded on the southwest by the blue waters of the Saronic Gulf on one side and high mountains on the other three sides: Hymettos (1,026m), Pendeli (1,109m) and Parnitha (1,413m). There are at least eight hills that play prominent roles in the city, most notably Lykavettos (277m), the Acropolis (156m) and Philopappos (148m). The summits of the Acropolis and Lykavettos are excellent viewpoints and should be the first places to visit, for the vistas of the city surrounded by mountains on the Attica Plain; and for the beauty of the Classical era buildings on the Acropolis and the bird's-eye view of the Acropolis from Lykavettos. Lykavettos, by the way, is equipped with a funicular railway (daily except Thurs: 08.45–00.45, winter until 00.15; Thurs: 10.30–00.45, winter until 00.15; 500Dr; tel: 01 72 27 065). This classic 220m-long funicular was built between 1958 and 1965 by the Austrian Waagner Biro AG company and is the only funicular in Greece. Both of these hills are visible from most of Athens. Locals bound for the city centre always talk about going down to Athens. In reality, they are descending from the higher plain on the slopes of the mountains towards the sea.

Athens reached an apogee of power, influence and wealth about 500BC. Since, its history can be characterised as being one long, slow decline that began roughly 2,000 years ago. It may be unfair to caracterise Athens thus, considering that in even the lowest moments of its history it was a coveted destination. There is not enough space here to do the city justice. Interested readers are advised to consult other books as listed in the *For Further Reading* section.

History

The Acropolis, supplied with freshwater springs and providing commanding views of all possible seaward approaches, besides being protected by its mountains, has been peopled almost continuously for over 7,000 years. The Mycenaeans (1600–1200BC) established a fortified palace on the Acropolis. The Dorians, Phoenicians and various dynastic Greek clans continued the city's development until it reached its greatness under Pericles in the 6th century BC. This classical period, called Hellenic, evolved with Macedonian Greek rule, called Hellenistic, being supplanted by Roman domination. The Roman Emperor Hadrian enjoyed visiting Athens.

The city's decline began with the advent of Christianity and accelerated with the division of Christian theology between Eastern churches (based in Constantinople) and Western churches (based in Rome). Decline proceeded apace with the ignominious conquest by renegade Franks from the piratical Fourth Crusade. They were replaced by Catalans, Sicilians, Florentines and Venetians until Ottoman Sultan Mehmet II took the city in 1456. Then began almost four centuries of domination by Ottoman Turks (the Turcocratia) during which time Athens and Piraeus declined into little more than villages serving large military garrisons. Though he was writing in the 12th century, Michael Acominatus' comments apply to all this period: "All Athens' glory is dead. Not even a trace can be picked out."

The classical monuments were partially destroyed. The Parthenon, crowning the Acropolis, was blown up in a Genoese artillery attack (1685) against a Turkish ammunition depot callously stored within; and Lord Elgin carted off large segments of the sculpted frieze encircling it in 1802. These "Elgin Marbles" are a perennial source of contention between Greece and Great Britain. They are still controversially ensconced in a purpose-built chamber in the British Museum in London. Athens' darkest hour was arguably on Independence Day in 1835 when little Nafplion in the Peloponnese was chosen as capital of the new Greek State.

Bavarian and Danish architects, notably Edward Ziller, employed by the appointed foreign monarchs began the restoration of the city in the mid-19th century. They built grand boulevards (Stadiou, Panepistimiou and Vasilissa Sofia among others) and monumental buildings in a Neo-classical style. Allied troops occupied the city during World War I, but the turning point came with the signing of the Treaty of Lausanne in 1923, calling for a massive population exchange with Turkey. Over a million people came to Greece and more than half settled in the metropolitan Athens/Piraeus area. This was the beginning of the outward and upward sprawl. The 1940s

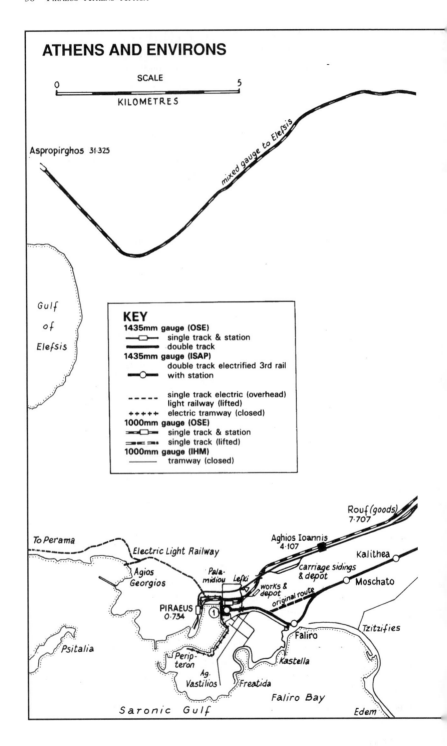

ATHENS AND ENVIRONS

SCALE

0   5

KILOMETRES

mixed gauge to Elefsis

Aspropirghos 31·325

Gulf
of
Elefsis

KEY
1435mm gauge (OSE)
— single track & station
double track
1435mm gauge (ISAP)
double track electrified 3rd rail
with station

single track electric (overhead)
light railway (lifted)
+ + + + electric tramway (closed)
1000mm gauge (OSE)
single track & station
single track (lifted)
1000mm gauge (IHM)
tramway (closed)

Rouf (goods)
7·707

To Perama

Electric Light Railway

Aghios Ioannis
4·107

Kalithea

carriage sidings
& depot

Agios
Georgios

Pala-
midiou   Lefki

Moschato

works &
depot

original route

PIRAEUS
0·734

Tzitzifies

Faliro

Psitalia

Perip-
teron

Kastella

Ag.
Vastilios   Freatida

Faliro Bay

Saronic Gulf

Edem

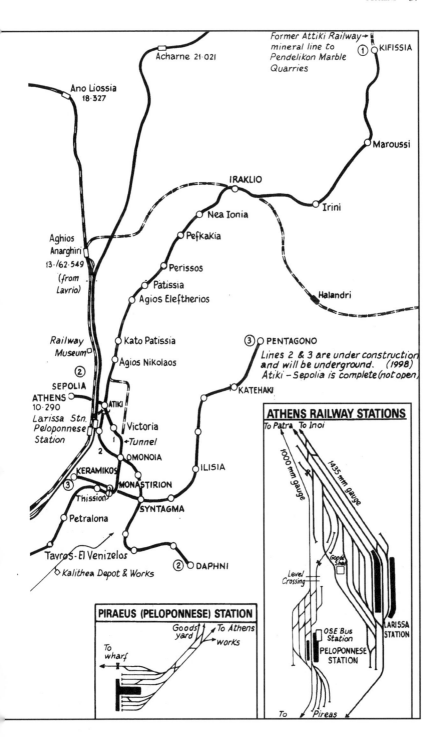

Former Attiki Railway →
mineral line to
Pendelikon Marble
Quarries

① ○ KIFISSIA

Acharne 21·021

Ano Liossia
18·327

Maroussi

IRAKLIO

Nea Ionia

Irini

Pefkakia

Aghios
Anarghiri
13·/62·549
(from
Lavrio)

Perissos

Patissia

Agios Eleftherios

Halandri

Railway
Museum

Kato Patissia

③ ○ PENTAGONO

Agios Nikolaos

Lines 2 & 3 are under construction
and will be underground.   (1998)
Atiki – Sepolia is complete (not open)

②
SEPOLIA

KATEHAKI

ATHENS
10·290
Larissa Stn.
Peloponnese
Station

ATIKI

Victoria

←Tunnel

1

2

OMONOIA

ILISIA

KERAMIKOS

③

MONASTIRION

Thission

SYNTAGMA

Petralona

Tavros – El Venizelos

② ○ DAPHNI

◇ Kalithea Depot & Works

ATHENS RAILWAY STATIONS

To Patra   To Inoi

1000 mm gauge

1435 mm gauge

Goods
Shed

Level
Crossing

OSE Bus
Station

LARISSA
STATION

PELOPONNESE
STATION

To Pireas

PIRAEUS (PELOPONNESE) STATION

Goods
yard

To Athens

works

To
wharf

brought a decade of severe penury during and after World War II and the protracted Civil War that followed. Peace in the 1950s brought rapid industrialisation and massive migration from the islands and the surrounding countryside. The tragic dictatorship of the 1960s was followed by a swing to the left with the rise of the Socialist PASOK party in 1982.

Since the restoration of Democracy in 1974, Greece and Athens have embarked on a 20-year period of peace and prosperity unknown in the 20th century. At this point began the beautification of Athens. Concerted tree-planting and the conversion of many streets to pedestrian-only use began to alter the image of Athens as a brutal concrete jungle.

Getting around

The automobile was the undisputed king of transport until the 1980s. Then severe air pollution in the late 1980s, due in part to unseasonably high summer temperatures during several consecutive years, was the last straw. It created an urgent political and environmental crisis (following many deaths and other protracted pollution-related health problems) and gave impetus to long-stalled plans to build an underground metropolitan-area rail system. Construction of two new rail lines finally began in the early 1990s and is scheduled for completion in the spring of 1998. This system will double existing urban and suburban rail trackage. Urban planners state that the opening of these lines, along with dissuasive policies to limit car use (and possibly trams in the historic centre), will lead to a city with the least air pollution in Europe.

While that remains to be seen, Athens merits a visit for its monuments and its museums but also for its charming and convivial neighbourhoods which remind visitors that in a nation of villages, Athens is the biggest village of all.

Maps and information

Athens information and maps can be obtained from two free sources in Syntagma Square: at the Athens City kiosk on the corner of Ermou and Stadiou or the EOT window in the National Bank one block away at Stadiou and Karageorgi Servias. Banks and ATM machines abound in this square as does a large post office. Ask for a free copy of the handy 112-page, multicolour *Athens General Information* booklet.

What to see

After a hot morning gathering information and running errands at Syntagma Square, travellers should relax in the fine **National Gardens** and **Zappeion Park** across Amalia Avenue next to the Parliament House (not open for visitors): about a two-minute walk. Here, in one of the coolest parts of central Athens beneath some of the largest trees in Greece, it is actually possible to unwind and prepare for a visit to the city. It also possible to learn more about the rare plants at the **Botanical Museum** inside the gardens. Open Tues–Sat 07.30–15.00, Sun 08.30–15.00; admission free. Other attractions are listed under the relevant rail stations.

Cinemas

Summer cinephiles should take advantage of the great many outdoor walk-in cinemas in the Athens area. These comfortable venues, experiencing a major revival, project first and recently run films on large screens. Foreign films are in the original language and subtitled in Greek. City centre cinemas include: *Cine Paris* (01 32 22 071) in the Plaka, *Dexamini* (01 36 23 942) in Dexamini Square behind the Roman cistern in chic Kolonaki, the *Riviera* (01 38 37 716) 46 Valtetsiou St and the *Vox* (01 33 01 020) at 82 Themistocleous. The last two are in Exarchia behind the National Archaeological Museum. Check the English language daily *Athens News* or the weekly *Scope* for the full list of cinemas. There are two showings of the same film per night.

Museums

Museums abound in Athens. Besides those listed in the ISAP route text below are the following, although the list is by no means exclusive.

National Gallery (50, Vass. Constantinou Ave; open: Mon, Wed–Sat: 09.00–15.00, Sun 10.00–14.00; admission 500Dr; tel: 01 72 35 937)

Museum of the City of Athens (7, Paparigopoulou St-Klathmonos Sq; open: Mon, Wed, Fri–Sat: 09.00–13.30; admission 400Dr; tel: 01 32 30 168)

Historical and Ethnological Museum (13, Stadiou Ave; open: Tues–Sun 09.00–13.30; tel: 01 32 37 617)

Greek Folk Art Museum (17, Kydathineon; open: Tues–Sun: 10.00–14.00; admission 500, 400, 300Dr; tel: 01 3213 018)

Byzantine Museum (22 Vass. Sophias; Open: Tues–Sun 08.30–15.00; 500, 300Dr; tel: 01/72 31 570)

Museum of Cycladic Art (4, Neo. Douka; open Mon, Wed–Fri: 10.00–16.00, Sat: 10.00–15.00; tel: 01 72 28 321)

War Museum (2, Rizari St & Vass. Sofias Ave; open Tues–Sun 09.00–14.00; tel: 01 72 90 543).

The **National Archaeological Museum** is covered in greater detail on page 42; and the **Hellenic Railways Museum** on page 45.

Historic sites

The **Acropolis** is mentioned on page 40. Other sites are covered in relation to the stations via which they are best approached.

CONTINUING TO VICTORIA

The next stop on the ISAP train after Athens is Moscato. From here to Kalithea, much recent urban landscaping (new walkways, lighting and greenery) can be seen from the right side of the train. This presages the expanding network of pedestrian streets that is making much of central Athens and adjoining towns in the metropolitan area, like Maroussi in northeastern Attica, a stroller's delight.

After the Petralona station riders should prepare for one of the most dramatic sights on any urban rail line: the ancient **Agora** crowned by the **Acropolis** and its monuments easily visible between the Thission and Monastiraki Stations. Open-cut digging to extend the line beyond Thission in the 1890s revealed the exact site of Athens' ancient Agora. It was finally excavated in the 1960s.

Visitors to the **Acropolis** should get off the train at Thission, turn right on exiting the tiny, country-style station, then either take a taxi or stroll for ten minutes up to the gates of the ancient sanctuary (site tel: 01 3214171, Mon–Fri 08.00–18.00, Sat–Sun 08.30–15.00; Mus. tel: 01 3236665 Mon 12.30–18.00, Tues–Fri: 08.30–18.00, weekends 08.30–15.00; on full-moon summer nights, open 22.00–01.00, admission free; otherwise: 2,000, 1,500, 1,000Dr). Pay particular attention to the Propylaea entrance-way which opens dramatically on the Parthenon; the view from the temple of Athena Nike; the harmony of the Parthenon created in part by its columns whose lines are slightly curved, creating an impression of perfection; and the unusual, asymmetrical Erectheion (its two porches have no architectural relationship to each other) with the six Caryatids supporting the roof on the south porch.

The **Philopappos Hill** with its 2nd-century AD Roman monument is further along. It is where, in season, recorded sound-and-light shows and live Greek folk dances are performed by the members of the Dora Stratou troupe (call 01 32 46 921 for exact times, venues and languages).

Those in no hurry should consider a halt at the little square of **Thission village** halfway up the hill towards the Acropolis where there are at least 16 traditional and more modern, chic café/bars. The Thission outdoor cinema (01 34 70 980) at 7 Apostolou Pavlou is one of Athens' best, with the Acropolis plainly in view.

Visits to the ancient **Kerameikos Cemetery and Museum** (open Tues–Sun: 08.30–15.00; admission 500, 400, 300Dr; tel: 01 34 63 552) are also possible from the station. Visitors should turn left on exiting the Thission station, then cross Ermou Street, turn left and continue along to the main gate of the cemetery that stopped being used in AD330. Probably named for potters living on the banks of the Eridanos River that flows through the site, Kerameikos gave its name to ceramics. The ancient Kerameikos was on the northwest fringes of ancient Athens and extended both within and without the city walls which now traverse the site. Two of Athens' most famous gates, the Dipylon and the Sacred Gate, are on the site. The Sacred Way from the Acropolis to Elefsina passed through here as well. It is also a nationally protected bio-diversity area where massive turtles waddle unhurriedly about.

The always lively **Monastiraki Flea Market** is directly across the street from the Thission station.

Continuing along the rail line to the next station (Monastiraki), visitors will first glimpse, immediately after exiting the tunnel from the Thission station, the **Temple of Hephaestus** (449BC) to the right. Built by Iktinos, as part of Pericles' rebuilding programme, it is considered the finest Doric Temple in Greece. At the western edge of the Agora, it was the site of many foundries and metalworking shops. Hephaestus was the god of metalworkers. Is it ironic that a temple to his name overlooks the ISAP railway line? The variety of the old stones of the Agora on both sides of the tracks along this stretch of track belong to the unreconstructed Stoa of Basileios (Royal Stoa) and the Stoa Poikile (painted Stoa). For excellent views of the **Parthenon** crowning the Acropolis, it is best to look out of the right side of the train.

A quick glimpse of the restored (1953) **Stoa of Attalos** (built in 159–138BC) which contains the Agora Museum signals arrival at the busy Monastiraki station. Passengers detraining will ascend to a worn station that opens on to a whirl of activity. An Ottoman-era Mosque of Tzistarakis (1759, minaret razed after 1821, now closed) directly across Areos Street gives way to a wall of the ancient **Roman Library of Hadrian** which leads the eye further up to the right to the Acropolis above the island-like Anafiotika sector of the Plaka. Hawkers, buskers and hustlers abound. Pandrossa Street to the left of the closed mosque leads to the Plaka district while Ifaistou Street around to the left of the station leads into the hectic Flea Market. Those wanting to visit the Athenian **Agora** are advised to turn right on Areos Street then right at the first corner (Adrianou Street), then proceed for several minutes until just past the Stoa. A short bridge over the rail line leads to the Agora entrance (tel: 32 10 185, Tues–Sun 08.30–15.00; admission 1,200, 900, 600Dr). Rail fans might want to rest at the tree-shaded *kafenion* at the corner of Adrianou and Vrissakiou overlooking the Monastiraki Station, although the bridge to the Agora entrance provides better perspectives for viewing the ISAP line.

Most of the open ground in front of the Monastiraki station is now closed for construction of a junction station, with new metro line 3 scheduled to open in 1998 or 1999. Several worthwhile budget hotels in this area include: the Hermion (Ermou 66c; 01 32 12 753); the Pella Inn (Ermou 104; 01 32 50 598) and the Hotel Tembi (Eolou 29; 01 32 13 175).

After a tour in Monastiraki, a rail traveller can continue: underground now beneath busy Athinas Street and its colourful markets to **Omonia**

(Concord) Square. This modern, frenetic and always bustling area reminds one of Times Square, New York, and leaves few feeling ambivalent. Modern author Vassilis Alexakis writes in his recent novel *The Mother Tongue* that the particular odour of Omonia Station reassures homesick Greeks that they are back in Athens. Surrounded by hotels, restaurants and cafés, Omonia is far from charming, though extremely useful with several post offices and banks scattered about. Street-level Omonia is crowded with people and heavy construction for the metro line 2 junction station with the ISAP line.

Around the corner of 28 October/Patission Avenue is the small Lavrion Square. From here ran a meter gauge railway to the Aegean seaport of Lavrion. A great deal of public support exists to reopen the line from Lavrion in through the new airport site at Spata in Attica to connect at new metro line 3 at Stavros. Community leaders at Markopoulo in Attica have completely renovated the railway station there and volunteers from HARF are clearing the line and actually operating a small rail diesel car over part of the line. Hotels here include: the Dorian Inn (Pireos Street 15-17; tel: 01 52 23 460, fax: 52 26 196); the Odeon Hotel (Pireos 42; tel: 01 52 39 200, fax: 52 32 778).

The next stop, Victoria – named for the queen of England – is the last major tourist stop as well as the last underground station. A variety of gritty hostels and cheap and mid-priced hotels surround the leafy square where mandolin players vie with hawkers promoting local lotteries.

Visits from Victoria Station

Those bound for **OSE railway stations** should turn on 3 Septembriou Avenue towards the still visible Parthenon, walk down the street, then take a right two blocks later on Ipirou Street for the 10-minute walk to the railway stations. Two fine relatively new hotels near the Larissis Central Station include: the Oscar Hotel (Filadelphais 25; tel: 01 88 34 215, fax: 82 16 368) and the Novotel (Michail Voda 4-6; tel: 01 82 50 422, fax: 88 37 816).

Others bound for the National Archaeological Museum should continue along 3 Septembriou past busy Egyptou Square (the terminal for buses to Cape Sounion and the Aegean seaports of Rafina and Lavrion) for three blocks then turn left. The massive neo-classical building is directly before them.

National Archaeological Museum

This museum (open Mon: 10.30–17.00, Tues–Fri: 08.00–17.00, weekend: 08.30–15.00; 1,500, 1,000Dr; tel: 82 17 724, fax: 82 13 573), opened in 1874, should be on the itinerary of all visitors to Athens. In almost 50 rooms of exhibits on two floors, the NAM opens the world of Ancient Greece to both the casual and the most passionate of visitors. Several excellent guidebooks, on sale in the gift shop, detail the many exhibits, but any must-see list should include: the large Poseidon of Artemision bronze statue, the miniature statuette of Zeus, the Demeter and Persephone relief from Elefsina, the Golden Mask of Agamemnon, and the frescos from Minoan Santorini that make up the Thera Exhibition. (For other museums in Athens see page 39.)

Rafina, Lavrion and Sounion

From busy Victoria Station, excursions are possible by coach through eastern Attica, to Athens' secondary ports of Rafina and Lavrion then south to the evocative Cape Sounion peninsula. This area was Athens' fruit and wine source from antiquity. Now, severe population pressures have pushed the boundaries of the metropolitan area into the fertile plain. Spata, once an important agricultural centre, will soon be the site of Athens' second international airport. Some prescient people, like Assimina Frangou (tel: 01 66 33 940, fax: 66 32 087), have taken important steps to preserve Spata's wine-producing past. She has recently restored her ancestral 18th-century stone cellar and is beginning to produce fine wines representative of the quality possible in the local area.

Rafina, 28km from Athens, has developed into a major port and weekend beach resort for Athenians. Ferries from Rafina radiate out to many of the same destinations as from Piraeus, but without the hassle and crowding seen there. Once a quaint, though important, fishing port, Rafina has redefined itself as a port of some consequence. Ships (ferries, hydrofoils and catamarans) sail daily for the Cycladic ports of Andros, Tinos and Mykonos, as well as Evia; several times weekly for Kavala via Limnos and even Thessaloniki. Sailings, however, are not listed in the weekly EOT departure sheets issued to tourists. It is best to contact the Rafina Port Police (0294 22 888) for full details.

Several hotels in Rafina provide accommodation: the Akti (0294 24 776), the Rafina (0294 23 460) and the slightly more upscale Avra (0294 22 781, fax: 23 320). North and south of Rafina are important beach resorts that are increasingly becoming the summer residences of Athenians. These include Nea Smyrna, founded by refugees from Smyrna on the Turkish coast, Zouberi on the north coast, and the popular though crowded Loutsa south of Rafina.

Lavrion, some 45km from Athens, is the port for the Athenians' favourite nearby island of Kea (or Tzia), only three hours from Platia Egyptiou. Lavrion was known in antiquity for its silver mines and is still a busy mining town. Once again, ferry departures are not listed by EOT. The Lavrion port police (0292 25 249) will provide details.

On the way to Lavrion through the hilly, green Mesogio Valley, rail enthusiasts should discern the rail right-of-way easily visible to the left of the road beyond Markopoulo. HARF members have restored part of this line and operate short excursions from Markopoulo south to Keratea. In fact, Markopoulo has restored its rail station and displays rail equipment in the station yard. Markopoulo also counts two tiny chapels, Agia Paraskevi and Agia Thekla, with attractive 17th-century frescos. One of Greece's largest and best-respected wine producers, Kourtakis (0299 22 311, fax 23 301), has its state-of-the-art winery in Markopoulo.

The two rail stations at Lavrion have been restored as well and are now music cafés. Greek rail activists, as well as community leaders along the route, would like to see the rail line reopened to connect with the terminus of the Attiki Metro at the suburb of Agia Paraskevi and extended down to Cape Sounion. Such a move would also provide rail service to the new international airport under construction at Spata.

Isolated stony beaches separate Lavrion from Cape Sounion. Two fine campsites are here as well: Camping Bacchus (0292 39 262) and Sounion Beach Camping (0292 39 358).

Cape Sounion, on the edge of the Sounion Peninsula, has enchanted people for centuries. All ships sailing from Piraeus south to the islands pass this evocative spot which the ancients cherished as a major landmark. The Athenians, led by Pericles, built the 5th-century Doric Temple of Poseidon (daily; 10.00–Sunset; 600Dr). This is as good a spot (despite the hordes and tour buses) to watch the sunset as any in Greece. Below Cape Sounion is a fine isolated hotel: Hotel Aegion (tel: 0292 39 200, fax: 39 234).

Returning to Athens along the Saronic Gulf, the road passes Athens' Hellenikon Airport as well as the booming chic beach communities of Voula, Vouliagmeni and Glyfada on what has become known as the "Apollo Coast". These glistening suburbs full of international boutiques, expresso bars and terraces remind one more of France's Côte d'Azur than they do of Greece.

Victoria to Kifissia

After Victoria, the rail line comes back to the surface for the remainder of its thirty-minute run to Kifissià. Its main interest now is in the glimpse it provides of modern Greek life: urban, suburban and rural. Massive construction visible to the left at the Attiki Station signals another junction station – this one for new metro line 2 (which, after leaving Omonia, has served the OSE rail stations before re-crossing the ISAP line). The ISAP line parallels Ionias Avenue. This modern avenue lines both sides of the ISAP right-of-way and shows what can be done with the massive six-storey apartment blocks quickly put up to accommodate the million refugees from Asia Minor who fled mostly to Piraeus and Athens as a result of the 1923 Treaty of Lausanne population exchange. Elsewhere throughout modern Athens they seem to create deep dark canyons.

Aficionados of Greek rail history might want to drop off the ISAP train at the pleasant Agios Nikolaos Station for the short walk to the **Hellenic Railways Museum** (under the tracks on exiting ISAP then straight along M. Koraka St to its end at Liosion (7 blocks), cross Liosion and proceed one block to the OSE tracks, turn right, and follow the street one block to the OSE rail grade crossing. This is Siokou – the OSE Museum is in the low-level white buildings directly opposite and across the tracks. (OSE Museum, tel: 01 52 46 580, open Fri–Sun 09.00–13.00, Wed. 17.00–20.00; admission free). The Hellenic Association of Railway Friends has its meeting rooms on the first floor. They meet most Wednesdays and in good weather, meaning most of the time, use the wide terrace overlooking the tracks into Athens' two railway stations.

The Agios Nikolaos station is also the gateway for travellers bound for the large KTEL intercity bus terminal for the north, situated close to the Railway Museum on Liosion Avenue.

From here stations become further apart and passengers have more time to contemplate two modern Greek phenomena: unfinished buildings and graffiti. Partially completed reinforced concrete structures can be found throughout Greece. They bear testimony to the Greeks' spendthrift desire to avoid debt – buildings are finished when funds are available, not through borrowing. But these unsightly scars also indicate an unwillingness to pay taxes. Levies are not due until the structure is completed. Graffiti in striking red, green and blue hues covering the cemetery wall on the right and the old stadium on the left between the two Patissia stations are visible reminders of the Greeks' two main passions: politics and sport. Before the 1990s, red indicated support for one of the two Communist parties in Greece; now it refers to the colours of Piraeus' Olympiakos sports club. Green meant loyalty to the PASOK social democrats; now it indicates support for the Panathnaikos sports empire. Blue was the colour of the centre right New Democracy Party, little supported in this neighbourhood.

Smoothly rolling trains on well-ballasted track on this part of the line can easily lull riders to doze – and some locals do; though they always seem to sense the presence of a church or some other sacred spot along the right-of-way, awakening to cross themselves before dozing off again. The constant clacking of Komboloi worry beads also soothes, as do passing impressions of many lemon–laden trees and the red-tiled roofs of traditional houses. Each train seems to have a resident busker which adds to the atmosphere.

Look for a large EMI sign on the left after the Ano Patissia Station. The show-biz giant has its Middle-East headquarters here in what are some of the oldest recording studios in Greece (1929). Older Greeks still remember the legendary singer Sophie Vembo. Her hits recorded here in the late 1930s encouraged and inspired Greek troops during the 1940 campaign against the Italians in Albania and Epirus. They are still played on October 28, *Oxi* Day – Greece's commemorative national holiday celebrating the firm "No" given to an Italian ultimatum to surrender.

Broad vistas across to high **Mount Pendeli** and back across the Plain of Attica to the sprawl of modern Athens can be seen after the Iraklio Station. From here a metre gauge railway (now abandoned) branched off to serve the ancient marble quarries at Pendelikon on Mount Pendeli. This marble was prized in antiquity for its fine grain and brilliant white colour. It was used on the Acropolis and many other notable public buildings.

Then the multi-platform station of Irini signals arrival at the grand **Olympic Sports Complex** with the most modern stadium in Europe. With a capacity of close to 80,000 and multiple electronic scoreboards, it is hard to miss. Easier to miss at Irini is a train, as they are often turned here to trundle back to Piraeus. Outward-bound passengers are forewarned of the risk of finding themselves on the way back to central Athens.

Kifissia-bound trains continue beyond Irini on a recently built overpass through the shady central square of the charming town of **Maroussi**, whose name should be familiar to readers of the works of Henry Miller. In the marble-tiled park below the exit from the elevated station is a bust by Tombros (1961) of local shepherd Spiros Louis – winner of the first modern Marathon during the 1896 Olympics. As the story goes, this selfless shepherd was showered with offers of financial rewards after his great victory but only accepted a young donkey and a new cart for his produce.

From here, through the major accident hospital complex at the new (1989) KAT station to line's end at Kifissia, tall plane trees alternate with full pines to provide shade for new villas and old stone farms. Tilled fields give way grudgingly to single family dwellings and concrete, multi-storey apartment buildings.

Kifissia

This leafy, green suburb – long associated with easy living and tenderly rendered in oil by Vico Ghikas during the 1970s – maintains its charm. High-summer temperatures here are noticeably lower than in central Athens – explaining why Herodes Atticus had a villa here as well as it being the seat of the Orthodox Church for the region. A peaceful well-maintained green park lined with flower stalls separates the ISAP station from the chic shopping district along Kassaveti Street, up to its intersection with Kyriazi and Levidou Streets. The intersection where the park meets Kassaveti Street is known as Platanos, even though the large plane tree is long gone. Rail fans should note the presence of a steam-era water tower at the corner of Leoforos Kifissias and Irod. Attikou – it is now used to provide moisture for the park's greenery. Athens' most important annual flower show is held in this park during the spring.

Horse-drawn carriages leave from here and provide leisurely tours of the villas and neo-classical mansions. Kifissia–Athens express buses (A-7) also depart from this corner for the appalling ride down Leoforos Kifissias – a modern suburban sprawl as ugly as anything Los Angeles has to offer.

In a nook at the base of Kassaveti Street are four Roman Sarcophagi possibly from Herodes. Campers should note that a campground is situated two kilometres from the rail station. A major attraction in Kifissia is the Goulandris Natural History Museum and herbarium (250,000 items) housed in a large marble mansion (Levidou 13, tel: 80 86 405, fax: 80 80 674. open Tues–Thurs, Sat, Sun 09.00–14.30; admission 500, 100Dr). Seemingly modest, the collection contains good coverage of Greek butterflies, birds and endangered species like the sea turtle (*Caretta Caretta*) and monk seal (*Monachus Monachus*). For more information on protecting these endangered species contact either MOM – the Society for the Study and Protection of the Mediterranean Seal (Solomou 53, 104 32 Athens; 01 52 28 888) – or the Hellenic Ornithological Society (Emm Benaki St 53, 10681 Athens; tel/fax: 01 38 11 271). A café and book and gift shop in the museum provide the necessities for those planning to explore Greece's wild country. Those interested in actively pursuing environmental concerns in Greece should consider contacting Greenpeace (Zoodochou Pigis 52c at Dervinion in Exarchia, 10681 Athens; tel: 01 38 40 774, fax: 01 38 04 008) which in the last few years has taken a more positive approach to environmental action.

Kifissia was the summer home for Athens' upper class during the nineteenth century and many eclectic villas are still visible, amongst the anonymous 1950s-era concrete blocks. Even though on few tourist agendas, Kifissia merits a visit – if only to see how the other half lives.

Two campsites are located near Kifissia at Nea Kifissia: the Dionissioti (tel: 01 80 71 494) and the Acropolis (tel: 01 80 75 253).

Soon, the transport map of Athens will radically change. When the two new Metro lines open later in this decade, ISAP will become a part of a modern urban rail network. Those who ride ISAP from Piraeus to Kifissia today should realise that the city is moving inexorably out to the Plains of Attica.

The time to discover a fast disappearing Athens is now – and what better way to do it than aboard modern ISAP trains?

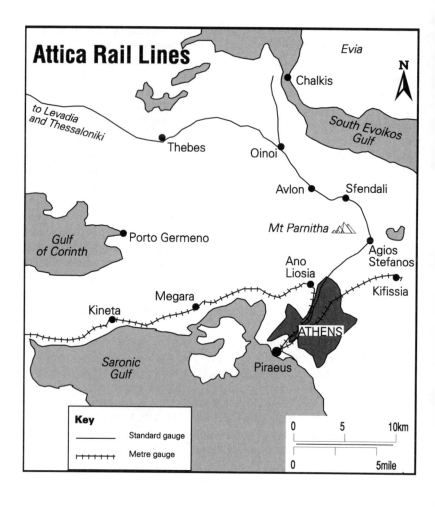

Attica Rail Lines

Evia

N

Chalkis

to Levadia and Thessaloniki

South Evoikos Gulf

Thebes

Oinoi

Avlon

Sfendali

Mt Parnitha

Gulf of Corinth

Porto Germeno

Agios Stefanos

Ano Liosia

Kifissia

Megara

ATHENS

Kineta

Saronic Gulf

Piraeus

Key

Standard gauge

Metre gauge

0   5   10km

0   5mile

Chapter Four

Piraeus/Athens–Chalkis

INTRODUCTION

Strictly speaking this 93km line is not a suburban railway. But because it sees 17 daily round trips (not including the main-line trains that call at Oinoi), single-day excursions to the island of Evia (Euboia) and its main city of Chalkis are possible. OSE operates two-car rail diesel sets from Athens Larissis Station from 04.11 to 22.50. At present only four trains initiate this route at Piraeus but plans are to have more trains begin from there. The full route requires 90 minutes and there are 13 intermediate stops. There are no food and drink services on any of these trains. As previously stated this busy line is destined for electrification, improved signalisation to allow for 30 round trips daily, park-and-ride parking lots at major stations and possibly new tilting technology trains to reduce travel time.

This route permits the discovery of the relatively unpopulated and agricultural Attica highlands, as well as the large island of Evia. The terminus of the line is 50m across the unusual Evripos tidal channel from Evia; so this train truly goes to an island.

ATHENS TO AGIOS STEFANOS

Leaving Athens from the Larissis station, trains use the main Athens–Thessaloniki double-track rail line until Oinoi, then leave it for the 22km around the Evripos Bay to Chalkis.

Soon after passing the Hellenic Railways Museum (no stop), the rail line curves to the right and immediately starts climbing up and out of the Athens populated area. It passes through the stations of Pyrgos Vasilissias, Acharne and Dekelia, before reaching Agios Stefanos. Acharne and Dekelia are villages just beyond the Kifissia suburb. Here the attractive Attica countryside is most evident. Buses return from both villages to Kifissia. It is thus possible to rejoin the ISAP line at Kifissia from Acharne or Dekelia.

Rail enthusiasts should be particularly attentive to the marshalling yard tracks at **Acharne**. In addition to all the major track laying equipment stored on the many tracks is a massive Breda steam locomotive. This is an example of one of the biggest types of steam locomotives ever to operate on European railways.

The railway continues to climb while curving steadily to the left around Mount Parnitha. The Agios Stefanos station is on the top of a long gradient. The attractive small stone Agios Stefanos station is served by all the Chalkis trains as well as the two Stylis/Lamia round trips and the Larissa local. From here visits to the Marathon Lake, the battlefield of Marathon and the Semeli Winery are possible.

Marathon

Here, ten thousand soldiers from Athens and Plataia defeated a Persian invasion force of almost 25,000 infantry and cavalry. Athenian general Miltiades purposely weakened the centre of his infantry line while reinforcing his flanks. The Persians easily broke through the centre but were crushed by the reinforced wings. They broke ranks and, while fleeing to their ships, many drowned in a large marsh in the plain. This battle temporarily ended the Persian threat to Athens. The runner Phidippides, supposedly sent to Athens to announce the victory, collapsed and died shortly thereafter. This is the origin of the marathon race. Over 6,400 Persians died compared with only 192 Greeks. The Greek dead, rather than being repatriated to their families as was the custom, were honoured with cremation and burial on the battlefield. A large mound, called the Solos, visible today, marks the spot where the Athenians were buried. It also provides a panoramic view of the area (open Tues–Sun: 08.30–15.00; admission 500, 400, 300Dr; tel: 0294 55 155). The Solos of the Plataians, excavated in 1969–70, is nearby. A five-room museum in Marathon (same hours as above) has finds from the site as well as commemorative trophies to the victory.

The impressive dam (built between 1925–31) at **Lake Marathon** has the distinction of being the only marble-faced dam (from Mount Pendeli) in the world. It is 285m long, 47m wide at its base and 4m wide at the top; and provides a part of Athens' water supply. At the downstream side is an exact marble replica of the Athenian Treasury at Delphi. It serves as an entrance to the inspection station and is quite a pleasant spot to picnic; there is a tourist pavilion on the spot.

From Lake Marathon it is possible to take a bus via the **Cave of Pan** (a place of cult worship from Neolithic times to the Bronze Age; revived in the sixth century BC until the late Roman era) to the battle site in the **Plain of Marathon** (490BC). The Roman-era Greek benefactor Herodes Atticus was from the settlement at Marathon.

South of Marathon is the fine beach of **Shinias** with an in-season campground (tel: 0294 55 587). Northeast of Marathon, 15km below the isolated and evocative headland near the village of Agia Marina, is the ancient port of **Rhamnous**. The name is derived from a prickly shrub that still grows in the isolated area. Among the ruins on the headland is a Doric **Temple of Nemesis** (open daily: 07.00–18.00; admission 500, 400, 300Dr; tel: 0294 63 477) built in 435BC to the goddess of happiness and misery. It is said that the invading Persians, who landed here, took a marble block to commemorate their impending victory. Nemesis punished them for their hubris with defeat in battle.

The Semeli Winery

The winery (visits by appointment; 01 62 18 119, fax: 01 62 18 218), situated in the village of Stamata, is one of the most progressive wineries in Greece. It has shown what can be done with the Savatiano variety of white grape. Most Greek wine-makers use this variety as a base wine by adding resin from the Aleppo pine tree to create the lively resinated Retsina imbibed with abandon in Athenian taverns. Semeli is fresh, fragrant and dry: perfect as an aperitif. In addition to the Savatiano, Semeli makes other white wine from the Chardonnay variety and rosés and reds from Agiorgitiko and Cabernet Sauvignon. Call in advance and someone from Semeli will meet you at the station, or give directions.

AGIOS STEFANOS TO CHALKIS

Beyond Agios Stefanos the rail line takes on a decidedly rural and at times mountainous nature as it heads towards the limit of Attica. It passes, on a narrow terrace with several tunnels, the northeastern extremity of Mount Parnassos. There are excellent views on the right. Afidne, Sfendali, Avlona, Ag Thomas and Inofita stations follow.

The Sfendali station should be of particular interest to hikers planning to stroll around **Mount Parnitha**. This heavily forested mountain has always been one of Attica's and Athens' major green areas. There has long been a tuberculosis sanatorium on top and the summit has recently been declared a national park. The ascent from the railway station should take about four hours. It is considered easy and gradual, but allows an appreciation of the wide range of rich flora and fauna that surprisingly exists so close to sprawling Athens. The trail begins about three hundred metres out of the railway station.

Ancient records state that residents of **Avlona** (present day population 6,700) were professional charcoal burners on Mount Parnitha. After crossing the Asopos river, the rail line enters the ancient region of Boeotia. The 12th-century church at **Agios Thomas** incorporates much ancient material from Tangara. At **Inofita**, the Athenians won a battle over the Thebans in 457BC.

The **Oinoi** station is the first stop made by main-line expresses bound for the north after leaving Athens. Those heading to Thebes or further north should change here from the local trains. For those continuing on to Chalkis, there is usually enough time at Oinoi station to drop off the train and visit the snack bar. In antiquity, Oinoi was an important border outpost protecting against the city-state of Thebes in Boeotia to the north. The scant remains of this site are located approximately 3km from the railway station.

Beyond the Oinoi station the railway line to Chalkis leaves the main line, crosses under the Athens–Lamia toll road and begins its passage through rolling wheat fields to the coast. There are stunning views (right) down to the coast and across to southern Evia from here.

Trains stop at the three hamlets of Kalochori, Avlis and Steno. After the Avlis station look out to the right for the ruins of ancient **Aulis** where the **Temple of Artemis** (excavated in 1956–61) is visible. Here Agamemnon slew Iphigeneia. **Steno** is the stop for a large cement works. After the Steno stop, the line ducks under the new suspension bridge (1993) to Evia, then circumnavigates the large Evripos Bay before coming to a halt at the station under **Karababa**, the 1688 Turkish fort that protected the area. This fort, the Evripos Channel and Chalkis are all visible in the distance on the right after passing under the new (1993) suspension bridge.

Evia and Chalkis

Evia, at 150km in length, is the largest Greek island after Crete. In fact, it once was part of the mainland, as the 40m-wide Evripos channel makes clear. The legend claims that a lightning bolt from Poseidon separated the island from the mainland, creating the channel. No-one yet knows why this channel is tidal. The current changes directions every few hours and those walking across the bridge can easily see the fast flowing water underneath.

Although Evia is an island, it is tightly connected to the mainland with bridges and at least seven ferry crossings along its length. It is so large that its southern end is closer to Athens than Chalkis. Evia is agriculturally wealthy – the ancient name Euboia means "rich in cattle". It is also rich in minerals; primarily lignite and magnesite. The east coast is rough, inaccessible and full of ominous cliffs, but the west coast is gentler. The centre is largely occupied by a tall mountain range with Mount Dirfis (1,745m) being the highest point.

Historically, Evia was populated by colonists from Thessaly in the north, Ionians from Attica and Dorians from the Peloponnese. The island was divided into seven independent city-states that eventually coalesced into the two most important of **Eretria**, now a small fishing port, and **Chalkis**, a city of nearly 55,000 inhabitants. These two were rivals for the fertile Plain of Lelantine. Chalkis was also a coloniser, sending people to Thrace, Italy and Sicily. It passed from Athenian to Theban to Macedonian and then to Roman control, before becoming a Byzantine possession. By 1366

Evia had become Venetian and the name was changed to Negroponte. Under the Venetians it was classified as a kingdom and its flag was one of the three flown in St Mark's Square. The Turks occupied the island in 1470, and it remained theirs until 1830. The **Archaeological Museum** in Chalkis (Leoforou Venizelos 13; open Tues–Sun: 08.30–15.00; admission 500, 400, 300Dr; tel: 0221 76 131) contains finds from the city's ancient past and is worth a visit.

The railway station's neighbourhood contains the **Karababa fort**, hotels and a tourist information office. Chalkis, across from the Evripos channel, seems like a typical Aegean island city with its long, wide inviting seaside promenade. The old Ottoman Kastro neighbourhood (turn right just across the Evripos bridge) contains an old mosque and fountain and is still home to a handful of Turks, Gypsies and Jews. Other assorted Venetian and Turkish ruins, like a **Venetian city tower** at Balalaiou St 43, the **Venetian Governor's Palace** and the arcaded **Turkish aqueduct**, all attest to the area's importance.

The island has much to offer, but is not often visited by tourists or travellers. Those desiring an alternative route to the north of Greece other than the standard route through Thebes and Larissa should consider passing through Evia. It is possible to take a ferry from Rafina to the southern island ports of Karistos or Marmari then traverse the length of the island to Orei or Pefki in the north for another ferry to Volos. Or, it is possible to take the train to Chalkis then a bus north to Orei or Pefki for the ferry to Volos. A warning though: Evia has become an extremely popular summer weekend resort for Athenians. Day-trippers should have no difficulties but those wishing to stay overnight in the more popular resorts should consider midweek trips during July and August..

Excursions to the village of **Steni**, at the base of **Mount Dirfis**, provide good jump-off points for the climb to the summit. Excursions to Vasilika on the northeastern shore permit walks to **Cape Artemision** where the Greek fleet first encountered the Persians in 480BC. The famous bronze Poseidon, now in the National Museum, was found offshore near here in 1928. Excursions to the south should begin at ancient **Eretria** which was destroyed during the Mithridatic War between the Roman Sulla and the king of Pontos in AD87. The little museum (open: Tues–Sun: 08.30–15.00; admission 500, 400, 300Dr; tel: 0221 62 206) has finds from this era. Beyond Eretria the road winds through villages including Amarinthos to the junction of Lepoura for **Kimi** on the east coast or **Karistos**, with its lovely Psili Ammos sand beach and waterfront fourteenth century Venetian castle, on the south coast. **Kimi** has a free folklore museum (daily: 10.00–13.00, 17.00–19.30) and a monument to Dr. George Papanikolaou, the inventor of the "pap" smear. **Karistos** has a free archaeological museum (Tues–Sun 08.30–15.00; tel: 0224 22 471). Kimi also has hydrofoils and ferries to the Sporadic Isle of Skyros.

Where to stay

Hotels in Chalkis are plentiful and rooms should not be difficult to obtain
once there; try the Lucy (0221 23 831) on the promenade, the Hara (0221
25 541) near the Karababa Fort or John's (0221 24 996). The tourist police
(0221 77 777) can also help.

Chapter Five

Piraeus/Athens–Elefsina

INTRODUCTION

This is the first 36km of the metre gauge ex-SPAP rail line that connects Piraeus, Athens and the Peloponnese. This mostly double-track segment serves the western end of Attica and all trains on this line call at Elefsina. There are 17 daily trains in all: 4 IC, 8 Express and 5 locals. The main advantage of the train to Elefsina is that it is much less congested than the unbelievably clogged national road, and therefore much more rapid. It also permits broad views of western Attica.

PIRAEUS TO ATHENS

Leaving the tiny, efficient and almost serene SPAP Piraeus station, trains first roll through the metre gauge railway repair shops where everything from cleaning to light rebuilding to heavy overhaul is done. Buildings in these shops date from the late 19th century construction of the line. Roundhouses for locomotives (left) and long buildings where all sorts of mechanical repairs and complete rebuilds are undertaken (right), all built of brick, will be of great interest to rail aficionados. Trains then roll through old neighbourhoods and wasted industrial lands before shuffling through the major standard gauge tracks and yards to Athens' domed **Peloponnese station**.

The Peloponnese station is located, appropriately, on Railroad Street. This full-service passenger station, designed by the noted Bavarian architect Edward Ziller, was built in 1893, and restored in 1980. Note that to access the main-line Larissis station it is necessary to exit the Peloponnese station, turn left, walk about 200m, turn right, cross the street, then go over a large iron bridge. The large Larissis station can be seen from the top of the bridge on the left side. As all main-line trains do not originate in Piraeus, this station changing manoeuvre is a necessary and obligatory one if planning to travel from Piraeus up the main line.

Please note that OSE does not guarantee connections and does not transfer baggage from the Peloponnese to the Larissis station. OSE plans call for construction of a major Athens rail passenger terminal, which will replace the two older facilities, to be located somewhere near the two present stations. This project will commence when the metro is completed and operating.

ATHENS TO ANO LIOSIA

Departure from the Peloponnese station means paralleling the double main-line tracks for about 3km. The SPAP metre gauge track is the furthest on the left. From the Hellenic Railways Museum terrace, good views of this operation are possible. Beyond the railway museum (no stop), the two rail corridors diverge with the main-line north bearing towards the right. After the triangular-shaped park at the point where the two rail corridors diverge, passengers should look to the right. At the first major street on the right, about one hundred metres from the tracks is a colossal olive tree. The tree trunk is 10m in diameter and the tree is estimated to be over 2,500 years old. Neighbourhood residents banded together in the spring of 1996 to protect this tree. This action is all the more significant because it represents another step in the evolution of Greek environmental consciousness. As urban Greeks become more financially comfortable, they are beginning to evaluate the quality-of-life issues that others in Northern Europe have been confronting for several decades. This is one example of many.

After a brief halt at the **Agios Anargiri** station (which is OSE's metropolitan-area only rail container terminal), the rail line runs north through the ever haphazard suburban developments typical of all emerging countries. The line starts curving to the southwest. Here there is much evidence of track work. The most astute of rail observers will note that there are three rails, not the normal two, on the right-of-way. OSE is rebuilding this rail line into a double track, standard gauge configuration from Athens to Corinth initially, then on to Patras. The third rail is an intermediate step in the transformation.

Ano Liosia (right on the southern slope of Mount Parnitha) is the next stop. This station is the highest point on the Peloponnese line to Patras and around to Kyparissia. Ano Liosia has the rather dubious distinction of being the site of the main rubbish landfill for all of Athens and Attica. Local public officials have taken to unilaterally closing the landfill in the spring to protest against what they rightly see as a lack of interest by the powers-that-be in dealing properly with the rapidly deteriorating Athens rubbish disposal situation. When a plan was announced in the spring of 1996 to locate a new landfill in the village of Avlona, located on the rail main line north of Agios Stefanos, Ano Liosia locals closed their saturated landfill. Avlona residents rose up as one, and blocked the OSE main line and the Athens–Thessaloniki toll road. These two actions paralysed Athens for a week and created, excuse the expression, quite a stink.

ANO LIOSIA TO ELEFSINA

Beyond a large military transport depot (left) the rail line traverses a narrow valley, passing through a gap in an ancient westward-facing defensive wall called the Dema (the link) or the **Aigaleos-Parnes Wall**. This rampart follows an undulating course along the watershed. The southern two-thirds were built in 53 short sections separated by 50 sally-ports and two gateways, in various styles of masonry. Further north on the higher slopes of Mount Parnitha the wall is crude and continuous. The wall is military and may date from the sixth century BC. A house dating from the fifth century was excavated to the right of the railway in 1960. This lightly populated agricultural valley, surprisingly so close to Athens, is dotted with little wooden beehives.

The **Aspropirgos** village rail passenger shelter denotes entry into the **Thriasian Plain**. Traces of the Sacred Way are visible to the left. This 14.5km-wide plain stretches from the Saronic Gulf up to the foothills of Mount Parnitha. In mythology, the Thriasian Plain is associated with the Rarian Plain, the first to bear crops. Here Demeter made the ground lie fallow while his daughter remained in the underworld. Today, this plain is the most industrialised area in Greece. Trains pass through enormous oil tank farms. Luckily, the heavily used road is away at a distance (left). The island of **Salamis** (left) is often obscured by dust, and, as rail passengers will confirm, by sulphur and carbon monoxide fumes.

Views to the left and behind the train reveal the **Scaramanga shipyard complex**, one of two on this coast. The Scaramanga complex, built by shipping magnate Stavros Niarchos, on the site of naval yards destroyed in World War II, contains some of the biggest docks in the Mediterranean. Excess capacity here is used to assemble rail passenger rolling stock. All Peloponnese IC and suburban trains to Chalkis are finished here.

The next stop is the growing industrial city of **Elefsina** (population 23,500) which also symbolises the western limit of Attica.

Elefsina

The ancient city of Eleusis, birthplace of Aeschylus (525–456BC), and home of the **Sanctuary of Demeter** and of the **Eleusinian Mysteries**, was situated on the eastern slopes of a low rocky hill (63m) that runs parallel with and not far from the shore. The ancient ceremonial road, the **Sacred Way**, ran directly to the sanctuary. The site and museum (open Tues–Sun: 09.30–15.00; admission 500, 400, 300Dr; 01 55 46 019) are of great interest to archaeology buffs; the Sanctuary of Demeter was, after Delphi, the most important sanctuary in the ancient Greek world. Sacred rites, called the Mysteries, were performed here for close to 1,500 years. The cult of mystery surrounding these rites was incredibly well followed because not one initiate ever revealed what happened here. During the height of Athens in the 5th century BC, up to 30,000 people came here annually, using the sophisticated Sacred Way, to participate in the ceremonies. The rituals began on the Acropolis and continued here. Today, the site is difficult to comprehend. A visit should be preceded by a careful study of the scale models of the buildings found in the museum. The most prominent edifice is the **Telesterion**, the windowless Hall of Initiation.

A visit to Elefsina by rail could be combined with a return trip to central Athens by bus via the **Monastery of Daphni**; or northwest, on an intercity bus to Thebes on a modern secondary road, which was a continuation of the Sacred Way that eventually led all the way to Delphi. The continuation by rail to Corinth and the Peloponnese will be dealt with in *Part Three*..

Buses ride on the modern highway which parallels and at times is built upon the ancient Sacred Way. This paved road with well developed rain gutters and curbs was lined with statues and votive monuments. Today the modern road is the most congested in Greece. Plans have recently been announced to build an outer ring road from the Thessaloniki toll highway connecting directly to the Patras toll road, thus avoiding this section of highway. It would then be rebuilt and beautified, re-establishing the ancient Sacred Way to a semblance of its glory. As Henry Miller stated: "One should not race along the Sacred Way in a motor car – it is a sacrilege. One should walk, walk as the men of old walked, and allow one's whole being to become flooded with light."

Where to stay
Those wishing to stay in Elefsina could try reserving a room at the Melissa Hotel (tel/fax: 01 55 46 547) which is located east of the OSE rail station.

By road from Elefsina
Returning to Athens, visitors can stop at the **Daphni Monastery** (daily; 08.30–14.45; admission 500Dr) – considered the finest example of Byzantine architecture in Athens. Originally established in 1070, it has been destroyed and rebuilt several times. Now it is no longer occupied as a monastery. The mosaics in the classical Greek cross octagon are considered among the greatest of the era. The park near the church is the venue for a rather hedonistic wine festival which lasts all summer.

Continuing along the ancient road to Thebes, it is possible to leave the Sacred Way for the little resort of **Porto Germeno**, situated on the far northeast extremity of the Corinthian Gulf. Near here are located stretches of **Megara**'s outer defensive walls (see *Chapter Six*). These are considered some of the best preserved classical walls in Greece. Look for the twin 12m-tall towers and the Classical era fort of Aegosthena. Back on the Thebes road just past the Porto Germeno turn-off is another well preserved 4th-century BC fortress (open and free), to the right above the largely abandoned village of Eleutherai. This fortress of Eleutherai stands at the entrance to the pass over Mount Kyhairon. In mythology the baby Oedipus was left to perish on this mountain. Further along and 5km left from the Erithres turn-off are the scant remains of **Plataia**, the courageous city-state that sent its entire 1,000–soldier army to help the Athenians at Marathon.

Thebes will be dealt with in *Chapter Ten*.

SAMPLE FARES: THE PELOPONNESE

TICKET FARES, PELOPONNESE

1. class

From \ To	ELEFSINA	MEGARA	ISTHMOS	LOUTRAKI	KORINTHOS	KIATO	XYLOKASTRO	DIAKOPTO	KALAVRYTA	EGHIO	PATRA	K. ACHAIA	LECHENA	KAVASSILA	GASTOUNI	AMALIADA	PYRGOS	KATAKOLO	OLYMPIA	KRESTENA	ZACHARO	KYPARISSIA	ARGOS	TRIPOLI	ZEVGOLATIO	KALAMATA
ATHINA	450	630	1100	–	1170	1260	1350	1350	2400	1350	2370	2580	2990	2990	2990	3120	3240	3690	3690	3690	3690	3840	1560	2250	3080	3240
ELEFSINA		320	770	–	810	1080	1140	1140	2080	1140	2010	2250	2670	2780	2780	2880	3080	3120	3150	3150	3240	3690	1290	1950	2780	3080
MEGARA			480	–	560	840	900	1030	1910	1030	1800	2060	2460	2580	2580	2670	2880	2990	3080	3080	3120	3690	1220	1710	2580	3240
ISTHMOS				–	160	450	480	860	1520	860	1520	1650	2060	2160	2160	2250	2460	2580	2670	2670	2880	3080	770	1400	2250	2580
LOUTRAKI					260	550	580	960	1620	960	1620	1750	2160	2260	2260	2350	2560	2680	2770	2770	2980	3180	870	1500	2350	2680
KORINTHOS						320	480	820	1460	820	1470	1620	1950	2060	2060	2160	2460	2580	2670	2580	2780	3080	770	1350	2160	2460
KIATO							160	630	1330	630	1230	1470	1760	1600	1600	1950	2160	2370	2460	2370	2500	2800	900	1500	2370	2670
XYLOKASTRO								1220	1200	540	1220	1290	1650	1710	1710	1860	2060	2160	2250	2250	2460	2670	1130	1650	2460	2780
DIAKOPTO									640	115	770	900	1260	1290	1290	1470	1610	1760	1800	1800	1950	2250	1470	2060	2990	3150
KALAVRYTA										570	1330	1400	1790	1850	1910	2010	2230	2400	2430	2430	2590	2890	1980	2700	3500	3790
EGHIO											340	540	870	870	870	950	1030	1140	1200	1160	1200	1520	1100	1580	2160	2270
PATRA												320	770	840	840	980	1230	1260	1290	1290	1470	1760	1920	2670	3690	3690
K. ACHAIA													480	590	590	770	980	1170	1230	1220	1260	1560	2160	2880	3690	3840
LECHENA														160	160	280	480	770	770	770	900	1230	2580	3150	3930	4290
KAVASSILA															160	160	480	630	770	770	900	1220	2580	3150	4100	4290
GASTOUNI																160	480	560	770	690	890	1220	2670	3240	4100	4490
AMALIADA																	320	480	480	770	1100	2780	3690	4100	4490	
PYRGOS																		160	350	220	480	810	2990	3690	4290	4680
KATAKOLO																			160	160	350	750	3080	3690	4490	4680
OLYMPIA																				420	690	900	3120	3750	4490	4860
KRESTENA																					220	590	3120	3690	4490	4860
ZACHARO																						480	3150	3840	4680	5160
KYPARISSIA																							3690	4100	4860	5270
ARGOS																								890	1620	1920
TRIPOLI																									1080	1260
ZEVGOLATIO																									480	900
KALAMATA																										480

Prices do not include supplements for special services
(Intercity, sleepers, couchettes, etc.).
These supplements are listed in following pages.
To the prices containing journeys to the Diakopto-Kalavryta line.
To the prices involving the Argos-Nafplion line
a supplement of 300 drs. has been added.

TICKET FARES, PELOPONNESE

2. class

From \ To	ELEFSINA	MEGARA	ISTHMOS	LOUTRAKI	KORINTHOS	KIATO	XYLOKASTRO	DIAKOPTO	KALAVRYTA	EGHIO	PATRA	K. ACHAIA	LECHENA	KAVASSILA	GASTOUNI	AMALIADA	PYRGOS	KATAKOLO	OLYMPIA	KRESTENA	ZACHARO	KYPARISSIA	ARGOS	TRIPOLI	ZEVGOLATIO	KALAMATA
ATHINA	300	420	730	700	780	840	900	900	1600	900	1580	1720	1990	1990	1990	2080	2160	2460	2460	2460	2460	2560	1040	1500	2050	2160
ELEFSINA		210	510	500	540	720	760	760	1390	760	1380	1850	1850	1850	1920	2050	2050	2080	2100	2100	2160	2460	860	1300	1850	2050
MEGARA			320	300	370	560	600	690	1270	690	1200	1370	1640	1720	1720	1780	1920	1990	2050	2050	2080	2460	810	1140	1720	2160
ISTHMOS				100	300	320	570	1010	570	1010	1100	1370	1440	1440	1500	1640	1720	1780	1780	1780	1920	2050	510	930	1500	1720
LOUTRAKI					205	400	420	670	1110	670	1110	1200	1470	1540	1540	1600	1740	1820	1880	1880	2020	2150	610	1030	1600	1820
KORINTHOS						210	320	550	980	550	980	1080	1300	1370	1370	1440	1580	1720	1780	1720	1850	2080	510	900	1440	1640
KIATO							105	420	890	420	820	980	1170	1240	1240	1300	1440	1580	1640	1500	1720	1920	600	1040	1580	1780
XYLOKASTRO								360	800	360	810	860	1100	1140	1140	1240	1440	1500	1500	1500	1640	1850	600	1100	1640	1850
DIAKOPTO									430	75	510	600	840	860	860	980	1070	1170	1200	1200	1300	1500	980	1370	1990	2100
KALAVRYTA										230	360	580	580	580	630	690	760	800	770	840	1010		730	1050	1440	1520
EGHIO											230	510	560	560	580	630	690	760	800	770	840	1010	730	1050	1440	1520
PATRA												210	510	560	560	650	650	650	780	820	810	840	1040	1440	2460	2460
K. ACHAIA													320	390	390	510	650	780	820	810	840	1040	1440	2460	2460	2560
LECHENA														105	105	185	320	510	510	510	600	820	1720	2100	2620	2860
KAVASSILA															105	105	320	420	510	510	600	810	1720	2100	2730	2860
GASTOUNI																105	320	370	510	460	590	810	1780	2160	2730	2860
AMALIADA																	210	320	320	510	730	1850	2460	2730	2990	
PYRGOS																		105	230	145	320	540	1990	2460	2860	3120
KATAKOLO																			105	105	230	500	2050	2460	2990	3120
OLYMPIA																				280	460	600	2080	2500	2990	3240
KRESTENA																					145	390	2080	2460	2990	3240
ZACHARO																						320	2100	2560	3120	3440
KYPARISSIA																							2460	2730	3240	3510
ARGOS																								590	1080	1280
TRIPOLI																									720	840
ZEVGOLATIO																									320	600
KALAMATA																										320

Prices do not include supplements for special services
(Intercity, sleepers, couchettes, etc.).
These supplements are listed in following pages.
To the prices containing journeys to the Diakopto-Kalavryta line.
To the prices involving the Argos-Nafplion line
a supplement of 300 drs. has been added.

Extract from OSE Timetable 1996-97

Part Three

THE PELOPONNESE

Background

If Greece is the birthplace of Western Civilisation then the Peloponnese is the birthplace of Greece. With the prehistoric city-states of Mycenae and Tiryns, the classical Greek city-states of Corinth and Sparta, the Byzantine refuges of Mystra and Monemvasia, the timeless athletic sanctuaries of Olympia and Nemea along with the medieval bastions of Nafplion, Moroni and Koroni, as well as majestic mountains, isolated valleys, high plains, secluded peninsulas and pristine sand beaches, the Peloponnese exerts a perennial fascination for travellers seeking history, nature and adventure in a relatively compact area.

The name means Pelops' Island after the legendary king of the autonomous region of Elia in the western Peloponnese and for the fact that this southernmost extension of the Balkan Peninsula resembles an island (*nisos*). It is, in fact, an island. The building of a canal in the late 19th century across the narrow Isthmus of Corinth cut the Peloponnese from the mainland. Some still use the medieval name – the Morea (mulberry tree) – so called either because it has the shape of a mulberry leaf or, more likely, because so many mulberry trees grow in the fertile soil.

Geography

The Peloponnese looks like a random blot surrounded by three seas: the Aegean to the east, the Sea of Crete to the south and the Ionian Sea to the west. The Gulf of Corinth, contained mostly by Cape Drepanon opposite the city of Nafpaktos, makes up the northern boundary. The Southern Peloponnese extends to three long prongs flanked by the Laconian and Messinian Gulfs, with Cape Malea in the East, Cape Matapan in the centre

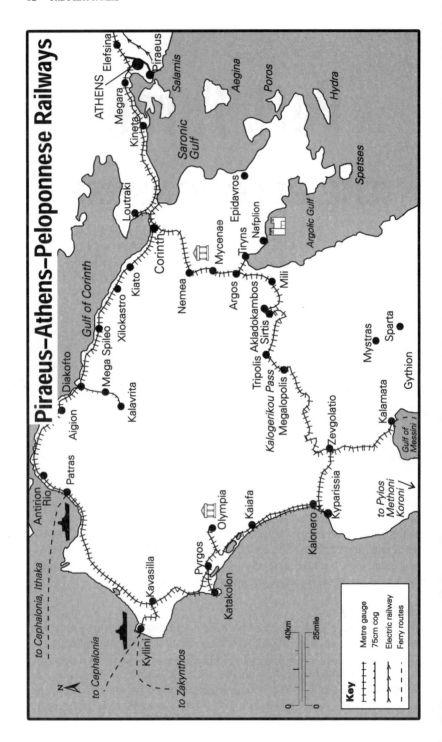

and Cape Gallo in the West.

In all, it is roughly 132km long by 134km wide with a total land area of close to 22,000km.

The backbone of the Peloponnese is mountainous with cultivable lands confined mostly to the coasts, the high plain around Tripolis and many narrow, isolated valleys between the rugged peaks. The highest mountain is Agios Ilias (2,408m) in the southern Taigetos range. Several other central mountains extend over 2,300m: Zereia (2,378m), Helmos (2,355m) and Erymanthos (2,322m). These peaks encircle the legendary area of Arcadia. Mount Panakaikon (1,929m) rises behind Patras in the northwest while Parnon (1,940m) and Artemission (1,772m) close off the east.

Seven modern administrative districts (called Nome) coincide rather closely with the ancient regions: the Argolid in the east, Laconia in the southeast, Messinia in the southwest, Elia in the west, Achaia in the north, Corinthia in the northeast and Arcadia in the centre.

Economy

Besides its archaeological and natural riches, the Peloponnese is an important agricultural area where olives, grapes and a full range of fruits with their oil, wine and juice-extracts make up the core of the economy. It is also a major shipping centre. Patras, Pyrgos, Kalamata and Gythion are major ports that serve the many islands encircling the peninsula as well as permitting the export of local produce.

Railways

The railways came very late to the Peloponnese. The first line, of the metre gauge, was built by the private SPK Company in 1881. It connected the western market town of Pyrgos to its port at Katakolon (12km). This was the first railway in free Greece after the Piraeus–Athens line.

In 1882, the construction of an ensemble of publicly-funded metre gauge lines was decided upon. This track width was chosen because it could be built less expensively and more quickly in the rugged terrain than the so-called wider standard gauge. Speed was not an issue. Before the railways came, produce and people went to market on donkey or horseback along narrow dirt trails or the ancient flagstone paths of the ancients. In 1884, the Piraeus–Athens–Peloponnese Railway Company (SPAP) was founded. The Piraeus–Athens–Corinth line reached Corinth in 1885. Patras was connected on 22 December 1887. The Patras–Pyrgos segment came on line early in 1890 while the line was extended south to Kalonero and Kyparissia later in the decade. The branch line from Pyrgos to Olympia was inaugurated on 29 April 1891. A private company built an unusual 75cm line from the SPAP main line at Diakofto near Aigion 22km up through the rugged Voraikos River gorge to Kalavrita.

While SPAP was furiously building from Piraeus to Kyparissia, another company, the Mili to Kalamata Railway (ESME), began the 172km railway from the then important port of Mili in the eastern Peloponnese south of Argos through Tripolis and Zevgolatio to Kalamata. This was opened in 1892.

Early in the 20th century, SPAP completed the Mili–Corinth link with a 12km branch line from Argos to Nafplion. It also built the Kalonero to Zevgolatio link as well as several other branch lines.

In essence, the single track, metre gauge Peloponnese railway is circular. It is possible to travel from Corinth to Kalamata via Patras to the west or via Argos and Tripolis to the south. Several branch lines complete the Peloponnese rail network: the previously mentioned Pyrgos to Katakolon and Olympia, Diakofto to Kalavrita and Argos to Nafplion lines, then Kavassila–Vartholomio–Kilini (16km), Lefktron–Megalopolis (5.3km) and Asprohoma–Messinia (4.7km). All these lines with the exception of Asprohoma–Messinia are open and have regular service. Only Lefktron–Megalopolis does not have passenger service. The Asprohoma to Messinia line could reopen soon as it serves the Kalamata area airport.

For the purpose of this book, the 100km-long metre gauge Piraeus–Athens–Elefsina–Megara–Isthmus (and Loutraki)–Corinth line, with the exception of the Piraeus–Elefsina corridor, will be treated as part of this Peloponnese chapter. The Piraeus–Elefsina corridor is discussed as part of the Attica chapter. The rail lines are discussed as follows:

(Piraeus–Athens–Elefsina)–Megara–Isthmus (Loutraki)–Corinth
Patras–Pyrgos (Olympia)–Kalonero (Kyparissia)–Zevgolatio–Kalamata
Patras–Rio–Aigion–Diakofto (Kalavrita)–Xylocastro–Kiato–Corinth
Corinth–Argos (Nafplion)–Tripolis–Kalamata

This order has been selected to reflect personal observations of foreign travellers' use of the Peloponnese rail network. Kalamata will be the base for excursions to the three southern Peloponnese Capes as well as for trips to Sparta, Mystra and Monemvasia.

Chapter Six

Piraeus–Corinth

Piraeus/Athens/Elefsina–Megara–Isthmus (Loutraki)–Corinth

For the Piraeus–Athens–Elefsina segment see *Chapter Five*.

ELEFSINA TO MEGARA

Beyond Elefsina there are 15 daily trains for Corinth, but if the destination is Isthmia there are 18 because three branch off there for Loutraki (Train 1432 for Corinth departing Piraeus at 15.44 runs combined with Train 1314 for Loutraki). Four IC trains make one stop at Megara, eight expresses make limited stops and the three others make all stops. This metre gauge rail line is basically a single track with long passing sidings at all stations. Signalisation between Elefsina and Corinth is by old-fashioned hand-delivered orders and semaphore signals. The line is close to traffic saturation and some trains have to wait while others pass. IC trains have priority and normally do not wait.

OSE infrastructure-rebuilding plans call for reconstructing the railway to the international standard gauge with double tracking where possible. Current funding levels preclude laying double tracks immediately but the new right-of-way will permit double tracks in the future.

This route is the transition between the modern Athens urban metropolis and the more tranquil Peloponnese where the largest city – Patras – is not much bigger than the centre of Athens. Seascapes and mountains predominate in this major transportation corridor. Passengers should sit on the left side of the train for the best views.

After departing the Elefsina OSE station the rail line skirts the municipal football stadium, another large oil tank storage facility and the large **Elefsina shipyards**.

These money-draining shipyards, among the biggest in Europe, have been at the centre of controversy and labour unrest for several years. They were incorporated into the public portfolio during the first years of the 1980s' PASOK socialist rule; and the current government needed to divest themselves of the giant dry dock facility in order to qualify for European

Monetary Union membership. Closing the yards was out of the question; but buyers were scarce, especially given labour's strong position against job rationalisation. The controversy was eventually quelled by the usual Greek methods of deferral to Brussels. In reality this means that little was done to change the situation. In addition to major ship dry-dock repairs, many OSE goods wagons are built at Elefsina.

Beyond the shipyards, the rail line climbs a steep grade on a new, more direct though curving embankment. The old sinuous rail line is visible on the right, then again at the crest on the left. The many ships visible at anchor in the narrow straits (left) are a sign of the world-wide shipping crisis that has particularly affected Greece. Beyond in the haze is the long island of **Salamis**. Here, in September of 480BC, near the shore visible from the train, the Athenians under Themistocles, with help from their eternal rivals Corinth and Aristides, hastily repatriated from exile for his opposition to Themistocles, surprised and defeated a larger Persian force. This is considered one of the world's most decisive battles as it extinguished the Persian leader Xerxes' plans of western expansion by conquest.

At this point the railway runs close to the sea along a rail line carved from the mountain. The occasional stone pillbox can be seen. These are from an era before the multi-lane road (visible occasionally high up on the right) was cut into the mountain. This stretch of railway passes through the jagged **Trikerato** at the southeast end of the Pateras Mountain range. In ancient times this was the boundary between the regions of Attica and Megara and was called "kerata" or horns. Small coves and inlets alternate with rocky promontories. Early morning passengers can see fishermen in colourful painted wooden boats tending their lines far below the railway.

The rail line descends from the Trikerato into a cultivated region – the **Plain of Megara** – planted with olives and grapes. The next stop, Nea Perama, serves the small community (population 6,500) founded as a refugee settlement and now serving as the Greek military's main commando and artillery schools.

After several minutes of fast street running past the apartment blocks of Megara, the train enters the Megara station.

Megara

Megara (population 22,000) is a large country town that rises along the slopes of two small hills – Karia (270m) and Alkatoos (287m) – visible on the right. This town, often associated with Attica, was an early rival of Corinth and Athens. But, like Sparta, it fell from power, absorbed by its larger neighbours. Never a great military power, it counted both on its position in the medium-sized plain between the Trikerato to the east and the Yerania Mountains (1,370m) to the west and on its two harbours to develop into a trading power like Corinth. But Megara, which means "big houses", became a coloniser (750BC). A rapidly expanding population in the plain, double today's number, forced Megara to send emigrants to Sicily (Megara Hyblaea), the Halkidiki Peninsula near Thessaloniki and Thrace near the Bosphorus. Late in the 7th century (630BC), the dictator Theagenes took power, establishing a pattern of oligarchic rule that was upheld by the elegiac poetry of Theogenes (570–485BC), who lamented the rise of the common man. Megara eventually allied itself with Sparta and quarrelled with Athens over Salamis. Pericles' decree in 432BC excluding Megara from Attic harbours and markets was one of the prime causes of the Peloponnesian War. The city eventually fell into severe decline leaving little of distinction.

Today, few remains of ancient Megara survive. The major site is the **Fountain of Theagenes**, on Krinos St, above and to the right of the **Platia Iroon**, which is built over the ancient agora. Sections of the 4th century wall are visible on 28 October Street near the rail station and segments from a **Temple of Athena** on the slopes of the Alkatoos hill are incorporated into small churches there.

MEGARA TO CORINTH

From Megara the rail line re-enters the mountains, sinuously winding its way through the outer appendages of the **Yerania Mountains** and passing through tunnels and shelters to protect against falling boulders. There are magnificent views of the Peloponnese from here (left). This area was the natural boundary that protected Corinth from Athens. Rail travellers will note the difficult trace of the railway and the two roads, the old far below and the new far above. The ancient road passed on a narrow ledge high on the cliff. OSE plans to widen and double-track the railway from Athens to Corinth will be blocked by this 18km segment – it will most probably always remain single track.

Once again the rail line descends into a plain. A long fine segment of sandy beach announces the stop of **Agios Theodoros**. The station is located several hundred metres above the beach. This area is known for its candied fruits.

The rail line continues along across the **Plain of Sousaki**. This area contains oil refineries and tank farms but also provides excellent views across to the Peloponnesian mountains. The limestone outcrop of the isolated Acrocorinth mountain is also visible. The Saronic Gulf begins to narrow and snatches of the entrance to the Corinth canal can be seen along with the Peloponnese seaside village of Kenchreai. The tiny port of Kalamaki, on the site of the ancient Schoinous, is the next stop, and signals the approach to the Isthmus of Corinth.

The rail line curves to the left, giving good views of the wide modern toll road. Then, after a short, steep climb comes the station of **Isthmus**. Some trains split here with one segment going to the nearby casino-equipped beach resort of Loutraki, and another heading over the Corinth Canal to the Peloponnese.

The Isthmus rail station is a short walk from the road bridge crossing the canal (from the tracks turn left on Loutraki road in front of the station, right on the main road to Corinth and proceed along 100 metres to the bridge. A sturdy pedestrian walkway separated from the roadway allows worry-free canal viewing). All trains to the Peloponnese except IC trains stop at Isthmus. It is possible to alight, visit the canal, then reboard a train for Corinth. Alternatively, a local bus coming from Loutraki stops after negotiating the turn from the road in front of the OSE station. This will deposit people at the grade crossing 20 metres west of the Corinth station.

The Corinth Canal

The Corinth Canal is a wonder of the world and in its time was an unequalled engineering feat. The Isthmus of Corinth is a barren tract of limestone 16km long and 6.5km wide. The ancient Corinthians developed a paved and grooved trackway called the Diolkos. Ships were unloaded, then placed on a wheeled platform and winched from Poseidonia on the Bay of Corinth to Schoinous on the Saronic Gulf. (Could this be considered the prototype for the modern railway?) Control of the Diolkos contributed to Corinthian power. This system was used until the 12th century. Parts of the Diolkos and traces of the ancient dock are still visible at Poseidonia, across the sinking bridge that replaced the car ferry, west of Loutraki.

Periander was one of the first to contemplate digging a canal. The Roman Emperor Caligula had the isthmus surveyed and Nero actually began to dig in AD67. Work halted due to an insurrection in Gaul only to be taken up again by a French company in 1881–1893. The canal, cut 87 metres through the rock below the surface of the isthmus, is 6.5km long, 25m wide and 8m deep. Both ends are protected by breakwaters but there are no locks. There is a current of 1–3 knots through the canal. Comparatively large ships can pass through, as do all ferries and cruise ships bound from Piraeus to Corfu and beyond. Historically, this canal changed shipping patterns in the Aegean, turning Piraeus into a major port. But it also affected the railways. After the coastal shipping lines switched to steam power in the 1930s, they could effectively compete with the little metre gauge railway. Piraeus to Patras and beyond to the near Ionian Island of Cephalonia by steamer took a little more than eight hours. The railway schedule just to Patras took eight hours. This competition forced the railway to re-equip most Patras passenger trains with self-propelled diesel equipment, which reduced the schedule to near four hours, about where it is today for non-IC trains.

Visitors intrigued by the canal have a variety of cafés, restaurants and shops at their disposal or they can visit Ancient Isthmia. This was also a sanctuary – the Sanctuary of Poseidon – and the site of the Pan Hellenic Isthmian games which ranked with those of Olympia, Delphi and Nemea.

The site is near the village of Kryavryssi where visitors can roam the ruins or tour the museum (open daily 08.30–15.00; free; 0741 37 244). This is also where Philip of Macedon succeeded in uniting the Greek city-states for the first time, in 337BC. The idea of Hellenism dates from this episode. Before, Greeks, though speaking the same language, identified themselves with their city-state.

Loutraki

Loutraki, 6km from Isthmus, is a popular beach town which, despite being at the epicentre of the 1981 earthquake, offers an appealing alternative to staying in Corinth. Besides its beaches Loutraki is a major centre for bottled mineral water production and soothing hydrotherapy with thermal spas, whirlpools and the like. Those interested can contact: The Hydrotherapy Thermal Spa, G. Lekka St 26, Loutraki; tel: 074 22 215. Rail fans will appreciate the long stretch of street running to the centre city station. Gamblers should enjoy the 24-hours-per-day casino. Loutraki (population 11,000) is also a staging base for a visit to the village of Perahora and the Lake Vouliagmeni lagoon around Cape Melangavi. **Ancient Perahora** below the modern town is magnificently located on a small sandy cove. The identifiable ruins of two sanctuaries – Hera Akraia and Hera Limenia – as well as parts of the submerged port make the area appealing. Fishermen at Loutraki will take people to the site.

Where to stay

Hotels in Loutraki include: Hotel Brettagna (0744 02 348); the Madas Hotel (0744 22 575, fax: 0744 22 791) or the Agelidis (0744 21 490). These are open all year. The tourist police (0744 65 678) can suggest others.

Corinth

After crossing the Corinth Canal (at a very slow speed, better for viewing), the rail line swings sharply to the right and parallels the canal (right) until its end at Poseidonia (no stop) then parallels the Corinthian Bay into **Corinth**. The beach fronting Loutraki below the crags of the Yerania mountains is visible to the right. Station tracks on the left and well built stone water towers and other steam traction facilities on the right signal arrival at the Corinth station. Most trains continuing on from here stop to exchange crews and/or divide the train. Travellers have enough time to visit the kiosk set up next to the station.

Modern Corinth (population 30,000) is a good base to explore the immediate area – the Ancient Corinth archaeological site and the Acrocorinth citadel – and to prepare for travel to the Argolid in the south. Hotels and all tourist services are available but modern Corinth has little intrinsic charm. It sits on an earthquake-prone fault and is often touched by massive tremors like that in 1981 which levelled the town. In fact, modern

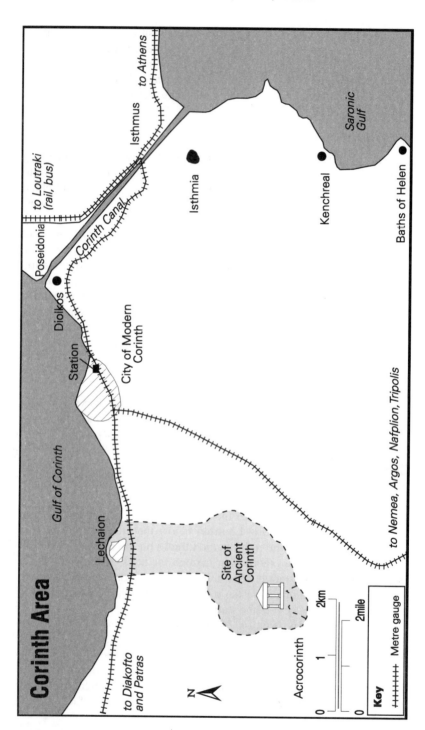

Corinth dates from 1858 but it in turn was wrecked in 1928. Ancient Corinth was finally destroyed by an earthquake. One of the mainstays of the economy since antiquity is the preparation and export of Sun–dried grapes: currants or raisins. The name currant derives from Corinth. The elaborate, fluted column used in most later Greek and Roman temples called Corinthian was developed here.

History

Ancient Corinth was once extremely wealthy, strategically controlling, as it did, the sea routes east and west and the land routes from Macedonia to the Peloponnese. It was a prime colonising power sending emigrants to Corfu and the coast of what is now Albania. The population ebbed and flowed up to an incredible 750,000 (this includes slaves and foreigners) during the classical period. It was also the main rival of Athens, even supplanting it to be the chief city of the Roman province of Greece. Apparently Corinth was an extremely decadent place during the Roman era when local women were considered very beautiful; local merchants traded in them and worship at the Temple of Aphrodite on the Acrocorinth with its sacred courtesans was well attended. St Paul spent 18 months proselytising in the city to little avail. Two major earthquakes in AD521 and 550 completely depopulated the area.

What to see

The **archaeological site and museum** (open daily 08.00–19.00; admission 1200, 900, 600Dr; tel: 0741 31 207) offer insights into Corinth's grandeur: even the Roman city was a megalopolis with over 15km of walls. The major survival of the Greek period is the stirring 5th-century Doric **Temple of Apollo**. Near this is the extensive agora and the foundations of the stoa. Look for the Roman-era **Fountain of Peirene**, which occupies the site of one of two of Corinth's natural springs. Waters from this spring still course through the ancient cisterns and serve the modern town. The shelter for the fountain was a gift of Herodes Atticus, the wealthy Athenian friend of the Roman Emperor Hadrian who contributed many buildings to Athens. Standing on the Temple of Apollo what is most evident is the considerable distance from the sea, attesting to the size of the city.

The **Acrocorinth** (open daily 08.00–15.00; free), looming (574m) up behind Ancient Corinth, is the finest natural fortification in Greece and possibly in Europe. Considered the key to control of the Peloponnese, its 2km of thick walls, paths and towers were built by successive conquerors and are attributed to Greek, Roman, Byzantine, Frankish, Venetian and Turkish overlords. A walk to the top of the citadel requires stamina and good shoes, but the views stretching to near Patras in the west and Athens in the east with Delphi on the slopes of Mount Parnassos to the north are worth the effort. Corinth's other natural spring is here – the Upper Peirene

Spring – but hidden in a corner of the upper citadel. It is easy to understand from the citadel, looking down at the rich agricultural plain surrounded by protective mountains, why Corinth prospered.

Hourly buses leave from modern Corinth to the archaeological site but no public transit ascends up the 4km road to the Acrocorinth. It requires a steady walk up, or taxis will go for a reasonable price. In any event the Acrocorinth merits a visit.

In the city is a **folklore museum** (daily, 08.00 to 13.00; free), several outdoor cinemas (in season), and enough travel offices to organise visits to the sites.

Where to stay
Hotels include: Acropolis (0741 22 430); Korinthos (0741 22 120); Belle Vue (0741 22 088). The tourist police (0741 23 282) can suggest others. Campsites are at the Blue Dolphin (0741 25 766; mid-May to mid-Oct) at Leheo beach by city bus.

• DISCOVER THE ATTRACTION OF GREECE BY TRAIN •

Chapter Seven

Patras–Kalamata

Patras–Pyrgos (Olympia)–Kalonero (Kyparissia)–Zevgolatio–Kalamata

This route which passes through three administrative districts provides access to the major archaeological site of Olympia and to long unspoilt sandy beaches as well as access to the little-visited city of Kyparissia. It also acts as a gateway to the historical sites around Cape Gallo: the Palace of Nestor on the Bay of Navarino at Pylos and the massive Venetian forts of Methoni and Koroni – the Eyes of the Republic – that guarded sea lanes in the Southern Peloponnese.

PATRAS

The sprawling white city of Patras (population 150,000 and 450,000 in the metropolitan area) spreading along the sea and up to the heights of towering Mount Panakaikon is often the first vision many travellers have of Greece. Lord Byron first set foot on Greek soil here in 1809.

Patras is Greece's second port after Piraeus and the major arrival point for ferries from the Italian ports of Venice, Ancona, Bari and Brindisi. It is home port for ferries to the Ionian Isles of Corfu, Ithaca, Cephalonia and Zakynthos.

Patras is also a major rail centre. There are eight daily trains for Corinth–Athens and Piraeus to the east and eight daily trains south to Pyrgos with seven continuing further to Kyparissia (two continue on to Kalamata). The small, modern station is conveniently situated on busy Amalias street between the international docks (a five-minute walk to the left when exiting the station) and the domestic ferry quays (a three-minute walk to the right).

All the boat and train activity along the long harbour makes for a lively port area. The main square to the right across Amalia Street from the OSE Station, the arcades along Agios Nicolas Street and the long promenade opposite along the harbour mole offer respite for those arriving from Italy the long sea passage. The café at the far end of the mole is an ideal spot to contemplate the massive ferries that seem never to cease gliding by, or to follow the slowly setting sun virtually at arm's length as it drops into the blue Ionian sea.

Though much maligned by travel guides and travellers weary after the long Adriatic Sea passage, Patras deserves a visit. In fact, travellers arriving from Corfu or other places on late afternoon boats would do well to consider Patras for an overnight stay to avoid arrival in Athens after midnight, when buses and trolleys have stopped circulating. A variety of hotels, cafés, restaurants and cinemas situated near the harbour offer a range of prices and services equal to any budget and should well prepare travellers for the next step of their Greek odyssey.

History

Patras is named for Patreas, chief of the Achaians, a member tribe of the Indo-European settlers who created the Mycenaean Civilisation. But, the city only dates its origins to the 11th century BC – much later than the apogee of the Mycenaean Culture. It didn't play a great role in political history until the 4th century BC, and fell to the Romans in the second century BC. Roman legionnaires were billeted there after Octavian defeated the armies of Anthony and Cleopatra in 31BC. These soldiers are credited with reviving Patras which had decayed in the waning years of Greek hegemony.

Patras was introduced early to Christianity by St Andrew who taught and preached there. It is thought that he was martyred in Patras in 68AD. Patras passed to the Byzantine empire; Justinian (527–565) was responsible for fortifying the Castle that enabled locals to withstand attacks by besieging Slav and Saracen pirates in 805. The city prospered under the Byzantine silk trade.

It was ceded to the Venetians in 1199 and continued to prosper under Frankish occupation (1205–1430). Ottoman Turks captured Patras in 1460 and it remained their possession until near the end of the Greek War of Independence.

Archbishop Germanos hailed from Patras and the castle was finally liberated by French forces under General Maison in 1828. The brief decade between the arrival of the railway in 1887 and the completion of the Corinthian Canal allowed Patras to grow exponentially.

It is now the leading port for Peloponnesian agricultural exports, notably olive oil, raisins and wine. If current EU infrastructure plans for widening and strengthening the railway to Athens to standard gauge are realised, Patras could rival Piraeus as Greece's major seaport.

What to see

Though few vestiges remain from the classical period, the castle and the museum offer glimpses into the past. **St Andrew's Cathedral** (recently built in 1979 and easily visible on the left from Pyrgos-bound trains) contains relics from Saint Andrew who was allegedly martyred on the spot, though it is most likely that the cathedral was built over a Temple of Demeter.

Wine lovers would do well to linger in Patras; the city is considered a major centre of modern Greek wine making. Two major wineries located in or near the centre should well entertain aficionados and casual imbibers alike (The Achaia Clauss Winery and the Patraiki Co-operative).

A Dionisian style pre-Lenten Carnival that is largely followed in Greece and which is gaining in international stature distinguishes Patras. Dates for this event follow the Orthodox Christian and not the Catholic calendar.

Night-life is centred on the port area where a variety of chic cafés, expresso bars and restaurants line arcaded Agios Nicolaou Street. Two cinemas are also located on the right side of the first block of Agios Nicolaou Street from the harbour square. Agios Nicolaou will be closed to traffic and turned into a full pedestrian arcade during the winter of 1996–97. Providing this happens, hotels situated on Agios Nicolaou should be quiet and comfortable.

Where to stay

The Mediterranée at Agios Nicolaou 18 (061 279 602) should prove to be popular. Busy Agios Andreas Street, which bisects Agios Nicolaou at the harbour side of Platia Triion Simahon, counts several acceptable hotels: the Galaxy at no. 9 (061 275 981), the Astir at no. 16 (061 277 502), Pension Nicos at 121 (061 623 757) and the El Greco at number 145 (061 272 931). There is a youth hostel at Iroon Politechniou 68 (061 222 707), a ten-minute walk northeast along the waterfront past the International Docks, and a campground (Kavouri 061 422 145) further along towards Rio along the same street. Other accommodation can be found by contacting the Tourism Office on the second floor of the International Port terminal building's main concourse.

PATRAS TO PYRGOS

From Patras, three IC (1h 35 min), four express (2h 03 min) and one local (2h 21 min) trains ply the rails of the main line daily to Pyrgos (100km) with all trains except one IC continuing on to Kyparissia (163km from Patras). Local trains shuttle along all the branch lines: from Kavasila to the old port of Kylini (for Zakynthos and Cephalonia) and from Pyrgos to its port at Katakolon and up to sacred Olympia.

After departing the OSE station, trains trundle past the main city square (left) and the domestic piers (right). They continue along the tree-lined right-of-way for several minutes before crossing the road to stop near St Andrew's Cathedral. Shortly thereafter the rail line passes between gigantic outdated cement vats which look as if they belong more to oil refineries than to wineries. They indicate the role grape growing and wine production plays in Patras' economy, that of the province of Achaia, and in fact that of all the Peloponnese.

Fully 25% of all Greek wine is produced in the Peloponnese, and the immediate Patras area accounts for over half that amount. The growth of Patras after the War of Independence and the ready access by rail to the markets of the capital created the modern table-grape and dried raisin industry that currently ranks near the top of world production. Gustav Clauss left his native Bavaria to take part in the mid 19th-century table-grape and raisin boom, only to convert to wine making with the founding of the Achaia Clauss Winery. His company is credited with being the first Greek firm to put wine in glass bottles. The Domestica label brand of white, rosé and red wines thus created has been a world standard for over a century now.

Vineyards, creating a sea of green during the summer ripening period, cover the plain from the Ionian Sea to the far distant mountains. Rail passengers have an impression of travelling directly through the vineyards. During the harvesting season in late August to early October many grape pickers use the early morning local to commute to their vineyards, creating quite a festive atmosphere aboard the train.

The morning local stopping every few minutes and the first express of the day provide the most colour, laden with shoppers to and from the Patras markets carrying fragrant bunches of basil and thyme, and offering tasty oranges or cakes to everyone aboard. Either side of the train will do, as the festive activity inside matches the lush green vines without. Railway personnel seem to know all the passengers and can point out the local sights to visitors. It is hard to believe that this region was known as a malarial swamp as recently as the 1940s.

Patras to Pyrgos (100km) by the morning local or express presents a microcosm of rural Western Peloponnesian life in an area where few foreigners tread, unlike the eastern trains to the archaeological sites. More often than not trips on these trains quickly turn into facsimiles of village life with locals discussing their events in a lively manner. The only major stop along this stretch is Kavasila, for the short, bumpy l6km ride to the ramshackle port of Kylini.

Kylini, the medieval Glarentza, was at one point the chief port of the Frankish realm of the Morea, as well as containing the mint and government records. It was destroyed in 1436 by the last Byzantine Emperor Constantine Dragatsis and has been declining ever since. Above the town, accessible from the village of Kastra, is the 13th-century castle of Clermond, built by Geoffroy de Villehardouin (who also built Mystra) to survey the straits between the mainland and Zakynthos. It is considered the finest Frankish fort in Greece. Kazantzakis romanticised during his visit that the Clermond was so impregnable that if the Franks had been thrown out of all the Morea, they could have reconquered all their lost territory from within its walls. Excellent vista across to the isles of Zakynthos, Cephalonia and Ithaca are possible from the ramparts. Regular ferries from Kilini serve Zakynthos and Cephalonia. The helpful tourist/port police (0623 92 211) can assist in finding accommodation and onward passage.

After Kavasila the railway briefly skirts the coast at Agios Ilias before finally turning inland for Pyrgos in the Nome of Elia.

Pyrgos

A major junction station for Katakolon and Olympia, Pyrgos (population 22,000) has an architecturally significant railway station. It was designed by Edward Ziller, the Bavarian architect known for the Athens University buildings on Panepestimiou Street. He is also responsible for the neo-classical railway station in Olympia and inspired the local Pyrgos market building now under reconstruction as a museum. The station building itself contains, along with all the usual railway amenities, a convivial and excellent vine-covered terrace café perfect for those interested in observing the railway action on the platform.

Apart from these few structures the city of Pyrgos is less appealing than the railway station. It takes its name from the tower (*pyrgos*) built by John Tsernotas (1512–1520). But it is a modern market town which was devastated in the early days of the Greek Civil War (1947–1949) when most of the town endured vicious street fighting and was nearly levelled.

As a railway junction, Pyrgos offers two destinations: west towards the port of Katakolon on Greece's first railway line (five trains per day during the summer tourist season – 24 minutes) and east to the sanctuary of Olympia (five trains per day – 36 minutes). Pyrgos is also an important bus junction with several coaches per day from the KTEL station nearby for the quaint villages of mountainous Arcadia and Tripolis across the Peloponnese. These are treated in the Tripolis section of this chapter.

Those bound for Katakolon should contemplate a visit to the **Ktima Mercouri winery** for a visit (by reservation only; tel: 0621 41 601). This renowned family winery was established in 1860 and has recently gained international acclaim. In the sea near the Agios Andreas church, a thirty-minute walk north from the Katakolon beach, can be seen the remains of **ancient Pheia**. This lost seaport permitted the independent city-state of Elia to profit economically from the fame of Olympia

PYRGOS TO OLYMPIA BY RAIL

Most travellers will change at Pyrgos for trains to Olympia. Through Katakolon–Olympia trains operate during the summer season. During the winter, reduced schedules are in effect with only one through Katakolon–Olympia train.

Travel by train to Olympia resembles an idyllic stroll through the lush garden of Elia. The railway passes over the fabled Alpheos River and its tributary streams. This river is the subject of a legend which claims that its waters disappeared under the sea to surface elsewhere. Here, it seems that Alpheos pursued the nymph Arethousa and re-emerged at the Arethousa spring in Sicily. Trains veer inland at the Alpheos OSE West Coast main-line station. Passengers bound to Olympia from the south can change trains at Alpheos station but they should note that there are no services here and that the shelter is rudimentary.

After serving the small settlements of Pelopion and Platanos, trains call at the Olympia Station. Here the small diesel locomotive is run around the two car trains and heads back to Pyrgos. Arrival at Olympia for many passengers means a quick exit and a dash up the single street to the fabled archaeological site and museum. But the charming, recently restored rail station and the equally renovated steam locomotive depot across the tracks merit a visit. The steam locomotive barn and its approach tracks have recently been converted into a delightful outdoor/indoor video café/disco bar with a good view on to the neo-classical rail station designed by Edward Ziller.

Despite this charm, the fabled athletic sanctuary should remain the main focus of a visit to Olympia.

Olympia
History
It must be remembered that Olympia was never a city. It was a sanctuary established in the bucolic countryside of Elia. The calm and pleasant leafy spot is unlike much of Greece. The modern town grew in the early 20th century to service visitors to a place that, with Delphi and Mycenae, expresses the idea of Hellenism. The significance of Olympia relates to its being the host of Pan Hellenic sporting events every four years for over 1,000 years (776BC to AD394). City-states throughout the Greek world from Magna Grecia in Europe, Asia Minor, the Black Sea and the Sea of Azov sent athletes for the five-day-long event. The city-states were bound by a sacred truce (*Ekeheiria*) lasting three months not to make war during the contests.

Olympic events included sprints, the Pentathlon, the Pancratinon (a no-holds-barred confrontation similar to today's Ultimate Combat) and chariot races. This gathering of peoples and nations also acted as the occasion to negotiate treaties and mercantile contracts. The tradition was strong enough to be maintained through the Roman era when the prize – an olive wreath – was replaced by monetary awards; subsequent corruption occurred under Roman emperors like the nefarious Nero.

Though its origins are clouded in myth and legend, Olympia seemed to have flourished during Mycenaean times as a local festival, then developed by association with Pelops, ruler and god of Elia before Zeus and Hercules, himself an early victor. Games and conduct were codified by the Oracle of Delphi and respected by Iphitos and Lycurgus rulers respectively of Elia and Sparta in the 9th century BC. Elia – militarily weak – stayed away from politics but profited economically from Olympic truces.

Suppressed by newly converted Christian Emperor Theodosius I as part of a general elimination of public pagan festivities in 393AD, Olympia slowly sank into obscurity. Buildings, temples and statuary were destroyed, carried away or buried under several metres of silt whenever the Kladeas and Alpheos Rivers changed course.

The site was first excavated by a French archaeological expedition led by Abel Blouet in 1829. Then it was systematically worked by the German Institute of Archaeology from 1875 to the present.

The Olympic spirit was revived in 1896. Athens hosted the first games in its newly restored marble Pan Athenian Stadium. Olympiads still occur every four years, but the games, much expanded since antiquity, no longer adhere precisely to their ancient starting time at the first full moon following the summer solstice.

What to see

It is important to note that the site does require imagination and planning to convey its significance. It would be wise first to visit the archaeological museum and look at the maquette (tel: 0624 22 742, fax: 22 529; open Mon 11.30–18.00, Tues–Fri 08.00–18.00, Sat-Sun 08.30–15.00; admission 1,200, 900, 600Dr), before continuing on to the archaeological site (tel: 0624 22 517; open Mon–Fri 07.30–18.00, Sat-Sun 08.30–15.00; admission 1,200, 900, 600Dr). The recently opened Historical Museum of Olympic Games (tel: 0624 22 544; open: Mon–Sat 08.00–15.30, Sun 09.00–16.30; admission 500Dr) also provides perspective. Early arrival at all venues is advised to avoid swarming tour groups and summer heat.

Certainly there is a bit more to see than during the time of Gustave Flaubert who saw "traces of huge walls, massive stones, the base of a fluted column". In the sacred precinct of the Altis, there are the Temples of Zeus and Hera, the Metroon, the Prytaneron, the Philippeion, the Treasuries and the Stadium. Outside are: the Palestra, the Gymnasium and Phidias' workshops which are partially covered by a 5th-century church. But there is more. Discover for yourself.

Spend a day or two – Olympia is a much better place for an overnight stay than Pyrgos – breathing in the atmosphere. Listen for the ancient echoes, then contemplate noted Greek writer Nikos Kazantzakis' comment that "in all of Greece there is no landscape more inviting, none that so gently and perseveringly invites peace and reconciliation". (*Travels in Greece* translated in 1965 by FA Reed.)

Plans exist to close the centre of Olympia to cars and buses, especially tour bus traffic, diverting it all to a ring road away from the sites. Rail advocates would like to close the area to tour buses which seem to be more and more numerous. Visitors would be required to take an especially designed train from Pyrgos up to Olympia. Local and national authorities are taking these ideas seriously, but the present situation should not change for several years.

Where to stay

For places to stay, check with the efficient local tourist information bureau (0624 23 100, open May–Oct: 09.00 to 22.00 daily, Nov–April: 11.00–17.00), or try: Camping Diana (0624 22 314), YHA Hostel (0624 22 580), Hotel Inomas (Class C, 0624 22 056), Hotel Antonios (Class A, 0624 22 348), Hotel Amalia (Lux, 0624 22 190).

Note for rail fans

1) Watch the quickness with which OSE operating crews shunt the locomotive around the short train.

2) Explore the café in the old steam loco shed and find the manual turntable outside in the weeds used to turn steam locos around. Try to guess how long it has been since it last functioned.

PYRGOS TO KALONERO (KYPARISSIA) BY RAIL

This 72km rail line south across flat delta land has little of archaeological interest but it does have magnificent beaches. This is the hedonist's line par excellence with the sea and long sandy beaches at arm's length from the railway throughout the trip. There are seven daily trains: one morning all-stops local, four expresses and two IC trains making up the passenger roster.

Minutes after leaving the tiny Alpheos junction station – bearing straight rather than curving left to Olympia – trains cross the wide, steadily flowing **Alpheos river** over a long, low iron bridge down-river from the Olympia branch rail bridge (visible in distance on the left). It is not hard to imagine the Alpheos easily shifting its course, as it so often has, in the flat fertile plain.

The countryside is even more rural here than between Patras and Pyrgos. Small isolated stone stations like Epitalion and Krestena are surrounded by irrigated fields. Rugged mountains (left) protect the high inland plains of the Peloponnese while the blue Ionian sea is always visible (right) in the distance.

When the rail line leaves the sea it is only momentary, curving behind pine trees and sand dunes where it is possible to camp in sight of both the sea and the railway. The stop at **Kaiafa** is one such place. The unmanned station (29km from Pyrgos) is conveniently tucked in between a small freshwater lake (left) and the sea (right) separated only by a tall tree-covered dune. Other interesting beach stops include **Zacharo** (all trains) several kilometres after Kaiafa, and Kakovatos (all except IC); with Zacharo having the most tourist amenities. Zacharo also serves many small villages (left) hidden high up in the folds of the escarpment. Once again, the morning local train comes into the scene stopping, it seems, anywhere.

Next is **Kalonero** (meaning good water) junction (56km from Pyrgos) for Kyparissia and Kalamata. The sea is but 500m away (right) and a small settlement around the railway buildings gives the area an oasis feel. Passengers on Kalamata-bound trains can drop off here, waiting 30 minutes while their train trundles down through endless olive groves to Kyparissia before immediately returning to Kalonero for the remainder of the trip to Kalamata.

But the short run to Kyparissia is worthwhile, with striking views of the **medieval castle** (l295) on the ancient acropolis (152m) always visible on the left as the train winds through the extensive olive groves to the striking stone OSE station at the end of the railway line.

Kyparissia

Kyparissia (population 4,520) is an attractive town whose name means City of Cypresses. It is a gateway by bus to the attractions south along the coast (dealt with in the Kalamata section) in the Nome of Messinia.

History

Kyparissia was founded by Epaminondas as the port of ancient Messene. Traces of the ancient harbour works can be seen on the seashore near the present fishing port. The city was known as Arcadia to Byzantines because so many Arcadians took refuge there during Slav invasions. It has a convoluted medieval history, passing repeatedly from Turkish to Frankish to Genoese and then Venetian hands only to be burned by Ibrahim Pasha in l825. There are, needless to say, few traces of its ancient past besides the round tower and arch on the commanding heights. Sunset views across to the islands of Zante, Zakynthos, Cephalonia and the Strophades are splendid and draw a crowd. The striking coastline visible as far as Kaiafa is just as remarkable. Rail fans will have no trouble following the miniature rail line from the heights as it winds its way through solid green olive groves to Kalonero.

Where to stay

A good, though expensive, campground (0761 23 491) can be found within easy walking distance near the beach where sea turtles often touch shore. The Ionian Hotel (0761 24 411) across the street from the OSE terminal and the Trifolia Pension (0761 22 066) in the town offer good lodgings for travellers in what is a little-visited but charming place.

Further afield

It is possible to continue on by bus from Kyparissia over the Aigleon Ranges to Nestor's Palace, by Pylos on Navarino Bay, and the massive Venetian strongholds of Methoni and Koroni. The rail ride skirting Mount Psykhro (1,116m) and Mount Sehkri (1,390m) along the Soulima Plain through the villages of Kopanakion, Dorion and Vasiliko to the Zevgolatio junction for

Kalamata and Tripolis is recommended. Two locomotive-hauled daily local trains travel over the little-touristed route.

Kalonero to Kalamata

The rail line crosses several interesting stone bridges: note particularly the elegant six-arch stone structure just after the Glikorizi shelter seven minutes after departing Kalonero (left). Some ruins have been excavated: a 14th century Venetian fort near Aitos and recently discovered Mycenaean Tholos tombs at Metsiki. The spectacular views of the Aigleon peaks (right) and the Pamisos Mountain chain (left) that define the valley keep travellers glued to windows. Amused locals use the trains to access the extensive Sunday markets at Kopanikon.

Zevgolatio is the main railway junction station but, though it is possible to change trains here for the east coast Peloponnese line, current schedules in this extremely rural area do not allow for convenient transfers. It is best to continue on to Kalamata and wait there. Travellers' destinations from Kalamata throughout the southern Peloponnese are dealt with in the Kalamata section of *Chapter Nine*.

Chapter Eight

Patras–Corinth

Patras–Rio–Aigion–Diakofto (Kalavrita)–
Xilokastro–Kiato–Corinth

INTRODUCTION

This 131km route offers some of the most striking sea and mountain vistas in all of Greece. There are eight daily trains: four IC and four express. This is the main railpass user's route to Athens. Note that Athens-bound train 305 departing Patras at 19.54 arrives in Athens well after midnight, when all forms of public transport have stopped circulating for the night. First-time visitors are at the mercy of aggressive hotel touts and sometimes rapacious cab drivers.

Most travellers use this route, the Peloponnese main rail line, solely to access Athens from Europe. Few take time to explore what are some of the best mountain areas of the Peloponnese. This is a rail line where epic history and dramatic scenery along the Gulf of Corinth have the upper hand over human contact. For rail fans and adventurous types, the spectacular 22km Diakofto-to-Kalavrita 75cm cog railway line up through the Vouraikos River gorge to Zachlorou is a must on any itinerary.

PATRAS TO RIO

Trains departing the Patras OSE station follow the docks 500 metres to just before the entrance to the International Port Mercuri Gate Six. Massive car ferries representing all the major shipping companies, like the ANEK Lines 3000 passenger Venizelos or the new red Superfast Patras–Ancona speedsters (20 hrs rather than 28), can be seen on the left.

After the port area, the rail line crosses the street diagonally to pass through OSE's repair shops and storage tracks. Here the classic old wooden narrow-gauge sleeping cars are stored: no longer used on Peloponnese overnight runs (306/307, 426/427) to the chagrin of voyagers. A variety of vintage railway rolling stock, including several types of steam locomotives that operated well into the 1960s, can also be seen.

Within minutes, trains pass near the Rio ferry to stop at the OSE Rio station.

Rio–Antirio ferry

Regular ferries have plied between the Peloponnese and mainland Greece at Antirio (45-minute trip 24 hrs/day) since the beginning of human civilisation in the region. Rail passengers wishing to cross the narrow channel will have to walk approximately 15 minutes down the hill from the rail station to the docks. Antirio (with its well preserved Venetian fort) is the transfer point for Western Greece. Messalongi of Byron fame, Prevesa, Parga and Igoumenitsa to the north as well as charming Nafpaktos and mythical Delphi towards the east are all accessible from here.

This ferry crossing should cease its several-millennia-long service in the next decade. The construction of a new multi-lane and multi-span suspension bridge, significantly reducing transit time, was approved by the Greek Parliament in April 1996. To be jointly funded by the European Union and Greece, the bridge will provide all-weather passage for pedestrians, cars, trucks and possibly a rail line. The only railway in Western Greece from Antirio up through Messalongi to Agrinion (vestiges of which are still visible) was abandoned in the late 1960s. The new bridge will contain two two-metre-wide pedestrian lanes as well as a two-lane service road that could possibly be used as a railway line. Whether this happens remains to be seen.

Where to stay

Rio has two campgrounds: the Rio Mare (061 992 263; May-Oct) and the Rion (061 993-388; April-Oct); and two small hotels: the Rio Beach (061 991 421) and the Georgios (061 992 627). For those who prefer a more peaceful setting than lively, rambunctious Patras, Rio is a recommended overnight stop.

RIO TO AIGION

From Rio the rail line plays tag with sandy beaches and the National Road to Aigion (40km). The coast here, through such beach-village stops as Psathopyrgos (thatch tower) and Neo Erineos, has many soaring cliffs plunging down to isolated sand beaches (left). The railway crosses innumerable rivers and streams leading down from the north slopes of Mount Panahaiko (right). The next major stop is Aigion. The leisurely approach to the OSE station along the brick-and-gas-lamp-lined sea front is so close to the water you can inspect fishermen's baskets and their catch from train windows (left).

Aigion

Supposedly named for a local goat that suckled the baby Zeus, this is a large (population 22,000) but ageing and severely earthquake-damaged commercial port and seaside resort. It is one of the oldest settled places in the Peloponnese. It is said that Agamemnon assembled the Achiaen League chiefs here before setting off for the Siege of Troy.

It serves as a ferry crossing to Agios Nikolaos (three trips daily). This crossing is geared more to motor vehicles than to independent travellers, as no buses meet ferries on the other side. It is, however, the closest crossing for Delphi.

The main part of the town is above the harbour. To go to the centre from the OSE station, visitors should leave the station behind them, turn right, cross the street, then turn left on the first street and follow that to the long series of wide and wavy stairs up to the town.

Despite the violent June 1995 earthquake, Aigion still possesses many 19th-century mansions, as well as several fountains. The Platia Psili Alonia, on the escarpment overlooking the harbour, is an attractive setting for sunset coffees with splendid views over the Gulf of Corinth. The old Market (1890) designed by Ziller was refurbished to house an extensive museum of local archaeological finds dating from the prehistoric founding of Aigion to the Roman era. It opened in the autumn of 1994 but was damaged in the 1995 earthquake. When it will re-open is anybody's guess.

Visitors to both Aigion and Kalamata, on the far southern side of the Peloponnese, will have a chance to compare major towns that suffered extensive earthquake damage. Kalamata has had a decade to recover from its 1986 cataclysm, while Aigion has had but a year. Both cities have had a chance to rebuild using modern structural methods that should avoid extensive damage the next time, and they also have had a chance to create an attractive and aesthetic urban environment worthy of their importance and physical setting. If Kalamata's successful efforts provide a guide, then Aigion – with its infinitely more appealing site – should evolve into an extremely pretty town.

Hoteliers are busy rebuilding their properties and most upscale hotels should reopen in 1997. Both Rio and Aigion make interesting overnight alternatives to busy Patras. They are both quieter, more traditional and much less frequented by tourists. Those interested in tasting local wines should telephone the Oenoforos Estate (0691 29415). The recently built winery is located in the nearly abandoned village of Ano Ziria.

AIGION TO DIAKOFTO

Leaving Aigion, the rail line crosses the Selinous river and enters a wide coastal region bounded by the Vouraikos River to the east where major archaeological finds are waiting to be unearthed. Somewhere here, near the 20th-century village of Eliki, the American School of Archaeology believes it has found the ruins of an important ancient city. On a winter night in 373BC, the prosperous town of Heliki was levelled by a violent earthquake. Then a massive tidal wave flushed away the remains into the sea. Heliki disappeared into oblivion.

A recent geological survey of the alluvial area, conducted by Greek and American archaeologists, indicated that in this area between the two rivers are two ancient habitation levels: the first is Roman and the second (at a depth of 7–12m) is classical, and contemporary with the lost city.

The rail line curves away from the coast at Eliki leaving the beach for a short while. The next stop is at the pleasant, important railway junction of Diakofto (53km). Diakofto offers many possibilities, not least of which is the unusual cog railway to Kalavrita.

Diakofto

This is a large and lively sea-facing village featuring attractive beaches, hotels and restaurants. It owes its prosperity in part to the two railway lines that figure so prominently in the geography of the village, and that permit trade with the high villages located in hidden valleys of the rugged Achaean Mountains rising so prominently behind the village.

Where to stay/eat

At least four hotels are open all year round both in the centre and at the beach, catering to a variety of tastes: in the centre are the Helmos (0691 41 236), or Chris-Paul (tel: 0691 41 715, fax: 42 128); near the beach are the Hotel Lemonies (0691 41 821) and the Panorama (0691 41 614) .

Restaurants and cafés abound. Costas Restaurant, on the main street leaving the railway station towards the mountains (across from the bakery and the attractive Illios rooftop outdoor cinema), has an attractive wall-size expressionistic oil painting of the Diakofto–to-Kalavrita rack and pinion railway. Rail fans will want to spend time at two specific cafés: the rail station café on the platform between the two rail lines, and the beach café situated at the extreme eastern extremity of Diakofto near where the Peloponnese main rail line makes a wide curve on an embankment overlooking the beach. Here a wooden gazebo is perched on a large rock and is perfectly placed for rail and sea photography below the railway where waves lap the track embankment.

DIAKOFTO TO KALAVRITA COG RAILWAY

This 75cm, 22km-long rail line is the only rack and pinion railway in Greece. For the uninitiated, rack and pinion means that the ascent of the precipitous Vouraikos River Canyon behind Diakofto up to Kalavrita is so steep that trains cannot propel themselves solely by adhering to the tracks, so they must help pull themselves up with the aid of a cog that drops from the train and fits into a third rail of steel teeth installed inside the double rails of the tracks. This system is often used in the mountains of Switzerland. It is, in fact, the invention of an Englishman, John Blenkinsop, but was refined by

Swiss civil engineers Niklas Riggenbach and Roman Abt who gave his name to the system employed in the Diakofto–Kalavrita Railway.

This railway was built by a French-Italian company between 1885 and 1895, using both the regular adhesion traction (gradient 1 in 28) and rack and pinion cog traction (gradient 1 in 7) to climb through the phantasmagoric Vouraikos River Canyon. The railway ascends from an altitude of 10m in Diakofto to 725m during its 22km length. There are three sections of cog railway for a cumulative length of 3.6km.

The original five steam locomotives built in the 1890s were progressively replaced in the 1960s by a unique diesel-fuelled system (traction coach, independent motor car, trailer car). In 1996 one of the original steam locomotives was completely rebuilt in the SPAP Piraeus repair shops. It, like the others, had been stored on display. It was near the Kalavrita station; the others are still near the Diakofto station (Patras end of station).

Leaving Diakofto, the rail line curves sharply away from the main Peloponnese line and runs relatively straight toward the seemingly impenetrable stone wall of the **Achaian Mountains** on a flattish stretch of track 6km to the station of Niamata. From here the line begins its climb through a plethora of long and short suspension bridges and trestles carved out of sheer limestone cliffs. The sites of two ancient cities, Bura and Kynaitha, invisible from the railway, occupy hilltops east and west of the entrance to the **Vouraikos gorge**. The railway braves a boulder-strewn river canyon so precipitous that it is difficult to fathom why it was ever challenged. **Triklia**, 4km beyond Niamati, is a wide spot on a shoulder of the mountain which permits a short passing track. It is an excellent spot for picnicking in the shade under the massive oaks. The delightful mid-route stop of **Zachlorou** is next.

Zachlorou

This village, 13km from Diakofto, counts on this rail line for its main direct link to civilisation. A dirt road penetrates to the upper half of the village, but the two café/inns in the lower village rely on the railway for provisions. This pleasant village is an important stopping point on the way to the 4th-century Byzantine Orthodox Monastery of **Mega Spileo** situated high on the slopes of Mount Helmes. The trail to the monastery begins to the left before the iron bridge over the Vouraikos River just beyond the Hotel/Restaurant Romantzo (0692 22 758). It is signposted; the ascent should take under an hour. Mega Spileo – the big cave – carved out of a sheer face of the mountain is a large monastery that contains a 60-bed hostel. A calamitous 1935 fire led to the complete destruction of the main building. It is said that a keg of gunpowder left over after the 1822 War of Independence exploded. The Monastery has been completely rebuilt and merits a visit for its vistas over the extensive Achaian Mountain range, and for its icons, relics and paintings. In 362AD the shepherdess Euphrosyne supposedly found an icon attributed to St Luke and known for miraculous powers. Various bodily appendages from Karalambos and Saint Theodore as well as the heads of Saints Simon and Theodore, the founders of the monastery, form a part of the reliquary. Byzantine-style expressionist paintings from the 19th century commemorate the courageous and active role played by Mega Spileo monks during War of Independence battles fought in the Peloponnese in 1822 and beyond. Attired in black, with long silver hair and beards flowing behind them and heavy crosses on their chests beneath crossed bandoleers, monks on horseback attack others on horseback wearing fezzes.

Besides the drama of Mega Spileo, the village of Zachlorou must be one of the most pastoral villages in Greece. It is a tiny hidden mountain respite where the soothing natural sounds of winds rustling through leaves and fast-running water splashing over and around immense boulders have no competition from cars and motorbikes.

Beyond Zachlorou, the canyon widens and the rail line passes the station for Kerpini; the village is hidden away on the right.

Kalavrita
History
Kalavrita, at the end of the rail line, does not hide the tragedy of its modern history. Directly across from the solid stone rail station is a large commemorative mural on the wall of the old primary school to the martyred towns of the world. Kalavrita was the site of unspeakable crimes during World War II. In early December of 1943, Austrian Nazi troops, enraged by losses to Greek resistance groups, machine-gunned and pushed off cliffs over 1,400 men and boys – the entire male population of the village. They then locked the women and girls in the school across from the rail station, set it and the village afire and left. The women were saved when someone opened a window. The clock over the church in the main square is permanently fixed at 2.34 – the hour of the massacre. A sombre trail, which begins to the left of the rail station, leads up to the execution spot.

What to see
No public transit exists between Kalavrita and the monastery of **Agia Lavra**. The eight kilometres can be walked or bicycled along the paved road; or taxis, usually waiting at the station, will take a carload to the monastery. The only disadvantage is that cabbies allow only thirty minutes to visit the monastery.

Nestled among ilex woods and cypress alleys, Agia Lavra is one of the great Greek national shrines. The crumbling but functional 17th-century chapel before the main building represents the site where, on March 5, 1821, Metropolitan Bishop Germanos of Patras proclaimed "freedom or death", and commanded Greeks to throw off their Turkish oppressors and defend their heritage. Germanos' banner, complete with a bullet hole in the forehead of an angel in the upper-left-hand corner, is on permanent display at the museum in the main complex. This monastery was also sacked and burned several times – most notably by Ibrahim Pasha in 1826 and by Nazis in 1943.

Where to stay
Abundant accommodation exists in Kalavrita, though reservations well in advance are strongly recommended during Greek national holidays. Try the Villa Kalavrita with its suites and rooms in the new building directly across from the railway station; tel: 0692 22 712 or 22 845 (or in Athens, call 01 58 13 272); Hotel Filoxenia, in the town centre, a five-minute walk from the station, tel: 0692 22 422, or 290, or 493. The basic Paradise Hotel is directly opposite the Filoxenia, tel: 0692 22 303.

Further afield
Kalavrita has good bus connections to Patras and adequate connections to Tripolis. Local buses bound for the villages of Kato Loussi, Kastria and Planitero will take you near to the Cave of the Lakes or Spilio Limnon (Mon-Fri 09.00 to 14.30, Sat-Sun 09.00 to 18.00; 800Dr; tel: 0692 31 588). These are small natural lakes formed underground when mineral-water-laden stalagmites built up dams, bottling the water's flow. Not all the caves are yet open to the public.

A burgeoning winter sports resort is situated nearby on Mount Helmos and OSE would like to build a 14km extension of the 75cm rail line to service it. Mount Helmos, at 2,341m, is only 60m below the summit of Mount Taigettos to the south. Walking up Mount Helmos from Kalavrita is less interesting than the ascent from the village of Solos behind the rail station at Akrata (see below).

Original plans called for the rail line to connect at Kalavrita with an extension of the existing line or of the normal Peloponnese metre gauge line to Tripolis. But the building of the first segment to Kalavrita proved so costly and took so long that the rest of the project was abandoned. As it is, the present rail line exists only because Zachlorou would be isolated and because it is slowly becoming a leisure location for local people. Leisure is a relatively recent phenomenon for a people where the struggle for subsistence has been a full-time pursuit up until the 1970s. Saving this railway was not a priority after the nearby highway was completed in the 1970s. The growing tourism potential and the awareness that it is a unique and significant civil engineering feat led to its preservation and expansion as a travel destination. Even without the railway line the Vouraikos River Canyon and gorges would attract admirers. With it, the canyon becomes a real, easily accessible, treat.

DIAKOFTO TO CORINTH

Continuing on past Diakofto, the rail line follows the Gulf of Corinth through the seaside villages of Akrata and Derveni. **Akrata** is the originating-point for a more attractive ascent of Mount Helmos than that from Zachlorou. A thrice-weekly local bus from Akrata to the end of its route at the village of Zarukra will lead to the trailhead. Or the dirt road behind the rail line can easily be walked. The five-hour walk up through the seasonally inhabited village of Solos leads to the **Mavroneri waterfall**, traditional source of the legendary River Styx. The souls of the dead had to cross this river to enter Hades.

Near the village of Derveni, the Nome of Achaia is left behind for Corinthia. The mountains protecting Achaia which cause the rail line to hug the coast recede (right), giving way to the fertile plains that helped make ancient Corinth prosper.

The next major stop is **Xilokastro** (wooden castle). This large village (population 5,000) is a popular seaside resort for Corinthians with several tavernas lining the tracks. The town, well located at the opening of the Sithas Valley, could possibly be situated over ancient Aristonauti – the seaport where the Argonauts touched sandy shore. Lofty Mount Parnassos, across the Gulf, makes quite an impression when seen from the shore. Buses leave from Xilokastro for Trikala and the trek up Mount Zirin.

Shortly after departing Xilokastro, an unmanned shelter marks a request stop for modern Sikyon. The ancient, partially excavated, city of **Sikyona** is nearby (right). It is reputedly one of the oldest Greek cities, dating to 1000BC. Always a loyal ally of Sparta, Sikyona was acclaimed during the classical period for its arts: bronze sculpture by Aristokles, Kanachos, Polykleitos and Lysippeos gained renown along with painting by Pausias and Pamphilos. It seems that sophisticated ancients also appreciated the quality of the shoes produced here.

Though the older city in the plain, its harbour and the Roman city that covered it have left little trace: outlines of the walls and other ruins can be found along the banks of the Asops River upstream from the rail line and the modern village. Of the ancient city, the ruins of the Agora, a temple, theatre and stadium can be discerned. The **Roman baths** have been repaired and converted into a museum where finds from the site are exhibited. The site is best visited from Kiato where six daily buses carry the few visitors who come. A short walk is needed from the bus stop to the museum and site entrance.

The flourishing port of **Kiato** situated in the midst of flourishing orchards is the next major rail stop. This large prospering town (population 9,500) has the remains of an early Byzantine basilica near the station. Besides the buses to Sikyona, others lead to Lake Stymphalia. Small boats at the harbour can be coaxed into taking passengers to visit Perachora across the Gulf of

Emerging from the Trachis Tunnel in high mountains between Lianokladi and Levadia on the main Athens–Thessaloniki line: southbound OSE train 411 Hellas Express *(AK)*

Above: *Crossing the Vale of Tembi north of Larissa on standard gauge Athens–Thessaloniki line: northbound OSE* Tempi (AK)

Below: *On the Kifaira Bridge descending towards the Plain of Thessaly, between Paleofarsalo and Lianokladi on the main Athens–Thessaloniki line (AK)*

Above: *Kalabaka station, the end of the Thessaly Railway narrow gauge line at the foot of the Meteora in the Pindos Mountains* (AK)

Below: *Mycenae station in the valley. All Greek stations have the name posted in both Greek and French.*

Left: *Ancient Corinth*
Right: *Train passing over the Corinth Canal*

Corinth.

After Kiato, the rail line leaves the coast for a fast, straight run through endless orchards and the small village of Braxati to Corinth. The imposing, multi-walled **Acrocorinth Castle** on its prominent, isolated, limestone outcrop is clearly visible away on the right. The site of Ancient Corinth at the base of the Acrocorinth is hidden in the orchards.

Soon the single track railway becomes double, and a succession of multi-storeyed apartment dwellings signal imminent arrival at Corinth.

From Corinth, rail passengers have a choice of routes: across the Isthmus to Athens or south through the Argolid to Mycenae, Nafplion, Tripolis and Kalamata. Fifteen daily trains serve Athens but only eleven stop at the Isthmus Station for a view of the Canal. Seven daily trains continue south to the Argolid; but if arriving at Corinth aboard Train 305, the southbound choices are limited. An overnight stay in Corinth is recommended for those planning on visiting the sights south of Corinth.

Chapter Nine

Corinth–Kalamata

Corinth–Argos (Nafplion)–Tripolis–Kalamata

INTRODUCTION

This is a 235km railway of superlatives and extremes. It is arguably the most archaeologically important railway in all of Greece with Nemea, Mycenae, Argos, Tiryns, Nafplion and Lerna along its line. In addition, the circumnavigation of Mount Tegea up through the valley to the high inland Arcadian plain at Tripolis ranks near the top of spectacular European mountain railroading.

In all, seven daily trains are listed in the timetables as expresses, but in reality only semi-express trains operate over all or part of this route: three as far as Nafplion and four on through to Kalamata. All serve Mycenae and Argos.

Given the difficult nature of the terrain and the long-term lack of serious infrastructure renovation, the ride beyond Achladokambos up to Tripolis is rather rough. In fact, this is the roughest-riding railway through some of the most remote country in Greece.

Tripolis is an important junction for the isolated mid-Peloponnese villages and for cross-Peloponnese bus connections. Kalamata, at the end of the railway line, is a lively provincial town which, though without great intrinsic historical interest, is an excellent gateway for discovering the pleasures of the three prongs of the Southern Peloponnese: Sparta–Mystra–Monemvasia to the east; the Mani in the centre; and Pylos in Navarino Bay, Methoni and Koroni to the west. Access to the islands of Kythera and Crete is available through the port of Kalamata or the more charming Gytheon.

All trains on this route run as combined trains from Piraeus and Athens to both Patras and Kalamata or Nafplion. They split at Corinth, with one section continuing west to Patras and the other south to Nafplion or Kalamata. Normal operating practice is to place the southbound section behind the westbound, but this can alter according to equipment availability and anticipated passenger loadings.

It is advisable to reserve space on southbound trains and to confirm where to board with station staff and with the panel attached to the side of each car. On-board ticket inspectors will usually advise passengers if they have made a mistake. The penalty for being on the wrong section is a hectic change at Corinth. If laden with heavy packs, alighting and changing trains quickly at the low-platform Corinth station can be stressful.

Trains bound for Argos and beyond continue along the main Patras rail line for several kilometres before veering sharply to the left. This rail line crosses under the present National Road to Patras and passes through massive construction work for an extensive interchange between the Patras and new Tripolis multi-lane highways. The rail line then runs southwest through vineyards and olive orchards. The Acrocorinth monolith leaps into view (right) and dominates all perspectives to the west.

CORINTH TO NEMEA

The rail line commences climbing and winding through a densely wooded valley between Mount Skiona (700m) on the right and the Oneia Hills (563m) on the left. The unmanned **Athikia** Station (11km) serves the village of the same name four kilometres distant where an archaic statue – the Apollo of Tenea – was found. It is now in Munich.

A road (left) near the Chilomodi station (18km) branches up to the **Pass of Agionori** which is guarded by a Venetian castle built by Morosoni. The Turkish General Dramali was ambushed here retreating north on 10 August 1822 while attempting to reach safety in Corinth after the battle at the Pass of Dervenakia.

Extensive reforestation south of Dervanaki hides the scanty remains of **Tenea**. This ancient city, inhabited mostly by Trojans, supplied most of the colonists for Syracuse in Sicily. Oedipus was brought up here by Polybus.

The next station is **Agios Vasilios** (26km). Above this village are the remains of a medieval castle and off to the east towards Klenia is the low hill of Zygouries where a Bronze Age settlement was unearthed in 1921–22. The rail line continues to wind through the ever-more-wild country. To the left, though out of sight behind Mount Fokes – the ancient Apesas (872m) – are the ruins of **Kleonai**. This city, on the prehistoric road from Corinth to Argos, is perched on an isolated hill overlooking the valley of the Longos river. It contains foundations of a Shrine of Hercules.

As the rail line turns sharply to the right after Agios Vasilios, riders should keep a sharp eye out of train windows on the left for a colossal white statue high on the forested hill. This is a memorial to General Kolokotronis, the victor in the 1822 battles over Dramali in this area.

The OSE Nemea–Dervenakia station (31km) is in a narrow defile at the summit of these hills. The old, two-lane Corinth–Argos road crosses the railway here. (The new multi-lane toll-road is hidden behind a series of hills.) The railway turns sharply to the left while the road to Nemea continues directly up the hill on the right. The road to Dervenakia, where the statue to Kolokotronis is located, is further along the Argos road after the railway crossing on the left.

Public transport to Nemea is extremely limited, as only local Argos–Nemea buses (two to three per day) now use this road. The most convenient bus passes this spot at about 13.30. Otherwise, hitchhiking or negotiating with a passing taxi remain the best ways to access Nemea from this isolated no-services railway station.

Nemea

This town is known as the place where Hercules slew a particularly tenacious lion as his first labour, wearing its pelt ever after. It is also known for its full-bodied, elegant red wine produced throughout the three-tiered valley; and as the site of an **Athletic Sanctuary** that rivalled Olympia in antiquity.

The intriguing though little-visited Sanctuary is located in the village of Ancient Nemea. This village was formerly named Iraklion. The entrance to the Sanctuary is on the right behind the English-language signpost announcing the village. The **Nemean Games** originated in 573BC and took place every two years. They were part of four ancient panhellenic competitions of which the biggest and oldest was, of course, at Olympia. The others were at Delphi and Isthmia. The remarkably intact and recently restored archaeological site is behind a fine **museum** (tel: 0746 22 739, open Tues–Sun 08.30–15.00; admission 500, 400, 300Dr) that contains artefacts from the site, and early visitors' comments and drawings on Nemea. The museum overlooks the Doric **Temple of Nemean Zeus**. It is possible to visit the original marble-floored locker room, and pass through the graffiti-inscribed athletes' tunnel into the horseshoe shaped stadium, complete with judges' benches and a grooved starting line ready for re-use.

A two-minute walk from the sanctuary in the centre of the village (left) is the **winery** and tasting room of the Pappaionnou family (tel: 0746 23 128, fax 23 368). These vintners are among the best wine producers in the region and in all of Greece. It helps that the local grape variety – the Agiorgitiko, cultivated here since antiquity – is also considered Greece's most noble red wine variety.

Five kilometres further along the same road is the modern town of Nemea (formerly known as St George's). The wine co-operative in this agricultural market town of five thousand people also produces excellent wine that can be tasted in the new tasting room without prior appointment.

Travellers returning to the rail line can use the same Argos-bound buses to return back to the Nemea–Dervenakia rail station; or they can board other buses from the same station (or hire a car in Nemea) to visit the inland marsh/lake of Limni Stimfalias. Situated in Arcadia, this was known to Hercules and the ancients as the Stymphalean Lake. It was considered in myth as the nesting ground of man-eating birds that Hercules grounded as another of his labours. This area can also be accessed by local bus from Kiato on the Patras rail line.

NEMEA TO MYCENAE

Beyond the Nemea–Dervenakia station the rail line follows a sinuous route through a closed-in canyon between the twin peaks of Mount Tretos. This **Pass of Dervenakia** – the ancient Pass of Tretos – is where Kolokotronis ambushed and smashed Dramali's army on 6 August 1822. The Turks left over 4,000 dead on the battlefield. The remainder split up and fled, making their separate ways to Corinth where they were evacuated by sea. This early victory by the Greeks encouraged them to continue their struggle for independence that was to last another decade.

The rail line begins to descend from the Dervenakia Pass where the mountains give way dramatically. The wide valley visible is the Argolid: the fabled **Argolid Plain** whose praises were sung in antiquity by Homer and others.

The craggy, barren slopes of Mount Tretos fall off to the left; then soon, as the train speeds through the upper folds of the Argolid Plain, a long double row of tall eucalyptus trees comes into view (left) in the near distance. This is the sign to prepare to leave the train for ancient Mycenae – at the Mycenae station (no station personnel or services).

Mycenae

The Mycenaean ruins (1500BC) are tucked high in the folds of the southernmost two of the three peaks visible to the left of the train. The twin peaks are Mount Ilias (750m) to the north and Mount Zara (600m) to the south. The roughly triangular-shaped Mycenaean palace, reputed to be Agamemnon's royal palace, is at 280m and is separated from the two mountains by a deep ravine. The site is not visible from the train or the station. From the station, travellers should cross the tracks at the grade crossing and either walk for two kilometres along the shady lane to the village below the ruins or hail a local bus.

From this village it is another two kilometres up to Agamemnon's fortress. This archaeological site (open daily 08.00–17.00; admission 1,500, 1,100, 800Dr; tel: 0751 76 585) is one of the most revered of ancient places. Its discovery in 1874 by the German archaeologist Heinrich Schliemann gave truth to the legends and myths recounted by Homer. As such, it is overwhelmed by visitors. Early arrival at the site, before the flotilla of tour buses, is strongly recommended.

In addition to the mysteries and subtleties of the Mycenaean civilisation visible from the majestic site, there are panoramic views of the entire golden Argolid Valley. From the closed-in end to the north (right) through to the medieval fortress protecting Argos (left) and the waters of the Argolic Gulf with that city tucked into a fold on its headland, the valley important to the ancients for its richness is visible. The rail line at the base of its lane of tall eucalyptus trees seems but a slight pencil mark far in the distance.

Where to stay
All food and lodging services are available: Agamemnon (0751 76 222); Rooms Dassis (0751 76 123); IYH Youth Hostel (card required; 0751 76 385); or Camping Mykines (0751 66 247).

MYCENAE TO ARGOS

After Mycenae, the train makes a beeline for Argos, crossing the Panitsa and the Xerias rivers: two major tributaries that provide the water necessary for the oranges and other fruit so long associated with the Argolid. Soon after leaving the village station of Koudsopodi, where the highway once again crosses the railway, the massive fortress on the summit of the citadel hill of Larissa (276m) comes into view (right). Many different fortifications have been placed on this hill during the almost six millennia of organised human settlement in the area. The citadel dominates all approaches to Argos and explains why the city has been continuously occupied since the prehistoric era.

Argos
Argos (population 21,000) is the most important market town for the Argolid. It was Agamemnon's base while Mycenae was his palace. It is also a railroad junction with a branch line to Nafplion and the main line on through Mili to Tripolis. It is ironic that the rail line to Nafplion is now considered the branch line. During the heady days of extensive rail building in the area, Nafplion was the SPAP terminus and Mili around the bay was the ESME terminus. Both railways counted on agricultural exports through their ports for revenue. The piercing of the Corinth Canal ended the long circumnavigation of the Peloponnese by ships, thus virtually eliminating Mili, but Nafplion as a sizeable and prosperous town survived.

History
After the invading Dorians supplanted the Mycenaeans, Argos rose to prominence in the Argolid, a hegemony it retained for over four centuries. The last great Argive king, Pheidon, was the first to introduce coinage and a new system of weights and measures to mainland Greece. The city-state's fortunes waxed and waned during the various wars fought alone, or in alliance with Athens, against Sparta for control of the eastern seaboard of the Peloponnese. At a particularly sensitive time the city was allegedly defended against the besieging Spartans by the poetess Telessilla. The city allied itself with Corinth in its war with Sparta (395–386BC). Christianity

came early and Argos was the site of a bishop by the 5th century and was elevated in 1088 to the rank of metropolis. It fought the Franks for seven years before succumbing in 1212. Thereafter its history is linked with that of nearby Nafplion.

What to see

Argos is another sizeable Greek provincial town that is mostly ignored by tourist and traveller alike. The ancients attached a great deal of importance to Argos. In Homer, Argive is a synonym for Greek. Today, Argos is a workmanlike town that caters to local farmers and fruit growers; the weekly market on Wednesdays is one of the best in Greece. But the discerning traveller would do well to visit Argos for the well-laid-out **archaeological museum** (open Tues–Sun 08.30 to 15.00; tel: 0751 68 819), and a major archaeological site containing an ancient Greek **amphitheatre** reputed to be rivalled on the mainland only by those at Dodoni, Megalopolis and Sikyona. With a capacity of 20,000, it is twice as large as the theatre at Epidavros. The **Church of St Peter** (1859) in Argos' centre is also worth a visit. These sights will well occupy a visitor's time, as will the winding ascent to the **Larissa Citadel**.

Renowned sculptors came from Argos. **Polykleitos** (452-412BC) was the best known. It was remarked that, though Pheidas made the best statues of gods, Polykleitos made the best of men. Today noted Greeks in Argos produce excellent fruits and fine wines. Wine lovers desiring to taste some of the best wines currently made in Greece would do well to visit the cellars of George Skouras. They are situated 2km along the road to Pirgelas that crosses the rail line just north of the station's northern perimeter wall. The tasting area is regularly open 08.00–14.30 on Mon–Sat, but visitors who want to meet the dynamic young vintner should call to confirm his presence, tel: 0751 23 688 or fax: 0751 23 159.

Where to stay

Given the market nature of Argos, it is full of busy hotels and lodging places. Those seeking a more calming location should continue along the railway line to Nafplion.

ARGOS TO NAFPLION

Trains for Nafplion leave the main line just south of the walled-in station complex. The rail line veers to the left and proceeds down a long lane of tall poplar trees. The **Argolic Gulf** makes its first appearance shortly after (on the right). A small shelter indicates the station for Tiryns. Homer's "wall girt Tiryns" stood by the sea during Mycenaean times and protected the sea approaches to Argos and Mycenae. Today, it sits on the Paliokastro hillock 1km back from the waters of the Argolic Gulf.

Tiryns

The **citadel** of Tiryns (daily 08.00 to 19.00; tel: 0752 22 657; admission 500, 300Dr) is over 3,000 years old, and contains massive stone walls that Pausanius claimed were "more amazing than the Pyramids". Some are estimated to weigh 14 tonnes. These walls are called Cyclopean because they are so large, it was believed that they could only have been built by the Cyclopean giants of mythology. Mythology and hyperbole aside, the size of the walls and the sophistication of the defences are a wonder. It is said that Hercules was born here and used Tiryns as the base for his labours. The site was explored by Schliemann and Dorpfeld in 1884–86 and major reconstruction of the walls took place in the early 1960s. Today part of the site is open for visitors. Tiryns is also the site of a penal farm/prison created by Kapodistrias in the mid-19th century. This, and the fact that the site is far less awe-inspiring than Mycenae, keeps away the hordes. It is a pleasant site.

Tiryns' walls can be seen from the train (left). Those not stopping should not be nonplussed because the site can easily be visited from Nafplion which is only four kilometres away.

Nafplion

The modern railway station (tel: 0752 26 400) is situated on the harbour near the passenger ship quays. The station is composed of two old red wooden passenger cars, now renovated and used as a ticket office and air-conditioned waiting room. The old tortuous entry through city streets is no longer used; but the old station, with antique railway cars and languishing steam locomotives in the yard tracks, has been restored as a chic music café which suits Nafplion's sophistication.

Rail passenger service was restored to Nafplion in the early 1990s. Today there are three daily through trains for Athens and two daily shuttles that connect at Argos. These shuttles are not shown in the handy pocket timetable issued by OSE but they are listed in the bigger system timetable. Unfortunately, rail connections from Nafplion to Patras are not good. As in France where all rail lines seem to merge in Paris, here rail schedules are geared to Athens-bound travellers. Passengers bound for Patras will have to change trains in Corinth and possibly wait as long as ninety minutes for a connection. There is some talk of operating a direct Patras–Nafplion service, at least in the busy summer tourist season, but for the moment this is just talk.

Nafplion (population 12,500) is the kind of Greek travel destination that makes one want to return repeatedly. It is an extremely appealing city with a long and rich history, and offers tourism-related facilities and services which make it an excellent base to explore the sights in the area: Mycenae, Argos and Tiryns are accessible on day trips with an evening's performance at the amphitheatre of Epidavros thrown in. A more relaxed visitor could use the city for several days of walking returning at night to the pleasures of arguably the most sophisticated of Peloponnesian cities.

Nafplion is situated on the sheltered side of the Argolic Gulf, protected by the twin fortresses of Its Kale and Palmidi. Two-storey buildings complete with iron laced balconies, Byzantine and Catholic churches, mosques, marble floored squares and Venetian and Turkish fountains create a beautiful city-scape and an ambience rarely equalled elsewhere in Greece. It is a human-scale city with no cars in its centre, and it has dramatic history to boot.

History

When Nafplion sided against Argos (625BC) and lost, the city was depopulated and the residents exiled to Methoni. It is again mentioned as a living city, in the 11th century, as a Venetian trading post. In 1540 it became the Turkish capital of the Morea. It was recaptured by the Venetians in 1686 and served as their capital until the Ottomans retook it in 1715 and promptly re-established it as their capital. After a one-year siege in 1821–22, it fell to Greek revolutionaries and became the first capital of the nascent Greek state in 1828. It became tragically the site of the assassination (1831) of first Prime Minister Ioannis Kapodistrias outside the church of St Spyridon by two members of the Maniat Mavromihalis clan. Bavarian born King Otto, placed on the throne of a specially created royal Greek family by the European powers, came ashore here in 1835. The capital was moved to Athens shortly thereafter, but the town continued to prosper as a trading and shipping centre for the Argolid. The nearly 7,000 British troops trying to flee the collapse of Greece on 26 April 1941 do not have such fond memories. Nazi dive-bombers and an unfortunate ship grounding marred the evacuation.

What to see

There are three forts: the Turkish **Its Kale** (inner castle) on the ancient acropolis over the headland; the massive Venetian built **Palamidi citadel** (Mon–Fri 08.00 to 18.45 and Sat–Sun 08.30 to 14.45, but later in the summer; 800, 600, 400Dr) imposingly placed nearly one thousand winding steps above the town it towers over; and the diminutive 15th-century **Bourtzi** on the islet offshore from the harbour are of prime interest. Excursion boats regularly sail out to the island, which has seen use as the lodging of the town's executioner, and as a hotel. It is doubtful that even the most enterprising traveller will do what the late actress and Minister of Culture Melina Mercouri claimed in her autobiography (*I was born Greek)* to have done: she consummated her first marriage on the islet.

The **Palamidi**, Nafplion's principal bastion, played a key role in the Greek War of Independence. The Greek leader Theodore Kolokotronis laid siege to the bastion for over a year before finally gaining control. After independence, the major rival rebellious (klepht) clans who provided the bulk of the armed manpower in the collective struggle against Ottoman hegemony, fell out. Each side occupied an opposing hilltop in Nafplion, just like in their Mani strongholds (see below), and proceeded to squabble while the townspeople watched their town degenerate under the thundering guns. Kolokotronis was even briefly jailed in the Palamidi.

Apart from the forts, Nafplion offers an award-winning **Museum of Folk Art** (1, Vass Alexandrou St; open Wed–Mon 09.00–14.30; tel: 0752 28 947, fax: 27 960; admission 300, 200Dr) containing delicately woven and embroidered local costumes using traditional textile techniques; and an interesting **Archaeological Museum** (Syntagmos Square in the old Venetian arsenal, open Tues–Sun 08.30–15.00; tel: 0752 27 502; admission 500, 400Dr) situated on the quaint square that served the city's rulers as a gathering-place of choice. This museum has a complete Mycenaean suit of armour and reconstructed frescos from Tiryns. An adjoining shop offers good quality handicrafts.

On the pleasant and pedestrian shopping street of Staikopoulo is the shop of Ioannis Kokkoris (Staikopoulou 40, tel: 0752 21 143 afternoons only) who is one of the foremost creators of the **Karegiosi shadow puppet figures** in Greece. Karegiosi are related to the famous Balinese shadow puppets.

Enter Ioannis' tiny shop and you will see him forming and cutting the magical figures that entertained Greeks until the advent of television almost destroyed the art form: it forced most itinerant Karegiosi theatre performers into retirement. They came out of retirement during the late 1960s and early 1970s, subtly criticising the then ruling dictators without incurring their wrath. Ioannis not only creates classical figures; he dabbles in inventive shapes and forms that pay homage to the medium. He is also one of Greece's foremost on-scene Karegiosi theatre players.

Where to stay

There is plenty of accommodation; but given the appeal of Nafplion, the better places are booked solid during the summer season and many weekends. The Lord Byron (2 Platonos Str. 21100 Nafplion tel: 0752 22 351, fax: 26 338) is an upscale place near the St Spyridon Church. The Pension Acronafplia (occupying various addresses in the square; tel: 0752 24 481 or mobile: 094 593 680) is also near the St Spyridon but is not so pricey. The King Otto (Farmakopoulou 2; tel: 0752 27 585) is a pleasant older hotel. The Youth Hostel (Argonafton 15) is in the new town; tel: 0752 27 754, IYHA card required. Nafplion does not have a local campsite, but a dozen or so are located on the southeast coast from Tolo (11km) to Iria (26km). The harbour sees the occasional cruise ship, and passenger ferries call during the season for Piraeus and ports south of Nafplion on the Peloponnese east coast.

Further afield
Around Nafplion are the beach resorts of Tolo (hourly buses from Nafplion) and the longer, less crowded beach of Kastraki where a long ancient wall is what remains of ancient Assine, destroyed by Argos in retaliation for having sided with Sparta. Further along this road are the villages of Drepano and Iria.

Epidavros
The main attraction besides those mentioned is the major archaeological site of Epidavros, approximately 35km to the east (site: daily 08.00–18.00, 17.00 in the winter. tel: 075 22 009; museum: Mon 12.00–18.00, Tues–Sun 07.30–18.00; tel: 0753 22 009; admission for both: 1,500, 1,100, 800Dr) with its evocative theatre (4th century BC) set in the forest. Built by Polykleitos as part of a much larger sanctuary, the 14,000-seat theatre has extraordinary acoustics; whispered voices from the beaten earth stage are easily heard high up among the 54 tiers of seats. These marvellous acoustics make the theatre an important venue for the annual Athens Festival productions of classical drama. These are staged on Friday and Saturday evenings from June until the last weekend in August.

The theatre is just a part of what was one of the most important sanctuaries in the ancient world, dedicated to the healing god, Asclepius, and a place of pilgrimage from the 6th century BC into Roman times. The **Asclepion Sanctuary** site is as large as Olympia or Delphi and holds great interest: all the buildings have been identified with various medical functions. The **museum** is important because the sanctuary was looted and destroyed by the Roman Consul Sulla in 86BC. Frequent buses run from Nafplion for evening performances, also direct charter buses and some hydrofoils from Athens make the trip.

NAFPLION/ARGOS TO MILI

The rail service from Nafplion consists of three daily through-trains to Athens. Passengers who want to travel to the south must change at Argos. Occasional local shuttle trains connect to southbound trains at Argos, but do not count on these.

Departure through the Argos yard tracks immediately leads into the flat, lush agricultural lands that have made the Argolid famous. This lower valley area was a marsh until the mid 20th century. Snakes have always played a part in the legends of this area. The bastion dominating Argos' Larissa citadel is still in view behind the train while the Palamidi fortress rises on the left off in the distance. The rail line skirts the west end of the Argolic Gulf, then heads toward a large stand of trees. Fans of vintage steam locomotives should be prepared for the extensive derelict brick buildings on the right as the train enters the Mili yard area. Over a dozen vintage steam locos are stored there, awaiting their fate. Some seem as if they could be coaxed easily into service while others are sadly beyond repair. At the time the locomotives were pulled out of service, the SPAP Railway Company could not afford to scrap them for junk metal. This was fortunate: OSE officials discovered they could be rebuilt and pressed into service for excursions. OSE possesses many dozens of locomotives stored throughout the Peloponnese and at Athens and Piraeus. At Mili, locomotives of two classes are stored: 140 and 141 built between 1914 and 1952.

Mili

Besides the railway interest, the ruins of an ancient city are situated under this modern crossroads village. Mili, located between Mount Pontinos and the sea, is the site of **Lerna** (daily except Mon, 08.30–15.00; admission 600Dr). Here the Lernaean mysteries in honour of Demeter were celebrated, and here Hercules slew the many-headed Hydra – the second of his labours. Local waters are still full of eels and snakes, both of which are considered delicacies in these parts.

The **archaeological site** is just 500m from the rail station, and it can be seen from the train: a high mound on the right in a grove of plane trees seen after crossing the road from Nafplion. Post Civil War excavations in the 1950s exposed Neolithic ruins of a house and a fortification wall that have been dated to 4,000BC. This pre-Greek site is one of the earliest discovered in the Peloponnese. A large building at the north end of the site, known as the House of Tiles, dates to 2,200BC and is thought to illustrate the earliest use of terracotta as a building material.

Certain sculptural and architectural likenesses to contemporary Anatolian design suggest Asiatic origins for the first inhabitants of Lerna but nothing substantial is known. Excavated finds, now in the Argos Museum, prove that the people of Lerna traded across the Aegean and up into the Balkan Peninsula.

The road divides at Mili. The coast road serves a variety of isolated little beach towns, from the low-lying Astros and Agios Andreas to the higher and more picturesque Paralia Tirou and Plaka. Set inland, **Leonidi** (population 6,000), at the terminus of a major Argos bus route, is the starting point for a spectacular road through the only pass in the impressive Mount Parnon range, climbing past the Monastery of Elonis to the high mountain village of Kosmas and ending in the attractive Byzantine centre of **Geraki**. Plaka, the port of Leonidi, is 4km distant and is a resting point for the road trip to **Monemvasia**. The inland road climbs past all the isolated mountain villages by way of a wide, paved road, carved out of the mountainside.

MILI TO TRIPOLIS

The railway, after Mili, continues beyond the villages of Andritsa through the red gorge of Kiveri before opening out into what looks like a dead-end canyon. It is, in fact, the valley of Achladokambos. The next 52 minutes of rail travel, far from the nearest road, give passengers the sight of the rugged high mountain terrain leading up to the province of Arcadia. Riders should look out of windows on the left after the train breaks into the lush valley. High above on the slopes of **Mount Parthenion** (1,215m) are a series of cement and concrete viaducts; the railway circumnavigates the mountain in a sweeping, climbing move that comes on so rapidly after the station stop of Achladokambos that dozers are caught off-guard.

Achladokambos, named for the wild pear that grew here, is an attractive village (population 844) dug into the side of the mountain 300m above the all-services railway station in the valley. Several railway sidings and a manual turntable attest to the importance of the railway here, before the road, above the village, was built. This village was on the frontier between coastal Argos and mountain-plain Tegea, an ally of Sparta. Clashes constantly occurred in the region. The site of one major battle, slightly east of Achladokambos, is **Hysiai**, where the Argives defeated the Spartans in 669–668BC.

After Achladokambos, the rail line starts to climb noticeably. Soon, it starts its ascent of the Arcadian Alps. On the initial steep gradient, the first signs of strain are audible increases in diesel engine noise. The rail line approaches the 69m-high, 250m-long, five-span concrete bridge built at 735m of altitude at the **Syrtis** curve. This is the highest railway bridge in Greece. When the original five-arch stone bridge was first completed in 1891, it captured Greek imagination. Wide-angle photographs splashed across double pages in the newspapers proudly announced what was at the time (several years before the completion of the Corinth Canal) the largest public works project in the modern history of the young republic.

The modern bridge was built in 1973–1974 as a replacement for the 1891 structure that was destroyed in 1944 by the retreating Nazis. For the thirty intervening years, trains went up the slope of the mountain with the locomotive behind the train to a switchback, where the loco once again found itself at the front for the stretch beyond the damaged bridge. Now, the switchback tracks (on the right) are full of unused goods wagons. Some observers claim that there are over 500 wagons of all sorts here. All the stored steam locomotives have been moved to lower ground.

Beyond this bridge, Achladokambos appears on the left side of the train. As the train passes slowly over the last four viaducts, always steadily climbing, the waters of the Argolic gulf come into view (left); and those with good eyes or binoculars should be able to see the Palamidi fort in the distance.

The railway then veers to the right through the extremely isolated villages of Eleochori, Partheni and Steno. **Steno** is on the high Plain of Tripolis. Early Bronze Age metallurgical kilns were found here. The ancient city of Tegea was situated nearby on the left. **Tegea** was a main city of Arcadia in classical Roman times and later (under the name of Nikli) in Byzantine times. A small museum (Tues–Sun. 08.30–15.00; admission 500Dr) adequately introduces the site. A short five-minute walk leads to the sanctuary **Temple of Athena Alea** (near the Church of Agios Nikolaos). It was one of the most highly regarded sanctuaries of the ancient world, where Spartan kings and errant priestesses took refuge. Near Steno the road rejoins the railway line. The train has entered the fabled province of mountain-ringed Arcadia. The ancients viewed Arcadia as the home of Pelasgos, the earliest man. The Arcadians are thought to be the earliest inhabitants of the region that has been romantically celebrated for its bucolic "spiritual landscape" by poets and early travellers for millennia.

Traces of modern road building are evident, albeit in their early stages. The rail line eventually levels out after Steno, skirts an industrial area and older houses then enters the extensive OSE Tripolis station complex. The rail station is about a ten-minute walk southeast of the centre. To get there, walk straight ahead along Lagopati and turn left on to Venizelo. There the major KTEL bus terminal for Arcadia is located. Taxis are in front of the Tripolis rail station; and nearby the railway station are located the bus shelters for the southern Peloponnese (Sparta, Mystra, Gythion, Monemvasia and the Mani). All of these destinations can be reached by first going through Kalamata by rail. This book will consider them from that perspective.

Tripolis

Tripolis (population 25,000) is a pleasant enough city, though often derided as being devoid of interest. Travellers often use it for bus connections to remote Arcadian villages, but they rarely slow down to enjoy an attractive modern city with small parks and café-lined terraces. But, for those interested in exploring Arcadia, which offers more than the simple comforts of small traditional mountain villages, Tripolis is worth a stop.

History

The city was inhabited from early times, after the separate Arcadian tribes first unified under Pelasgos. But the first reference to it is in 1467 when, as the capital of the Turkish Pashalic of the Peloponnese, it was named Droboliza. The heavily walled city was besieged by Kolokotronis early in the Greek War of Independence and surrendered in September 1821, after a six-month siege. Then, tragically, the Turkish population was massacred. Ottoman ally the Egyptian Ibrahim Pasha retaliated by completely destroying the city in the retreat of 1828. It revived after 1834.

What to see

Today, Tripolis hosts book fairs, and stage productions in its neo-classical 19th century theatre. Several outdoor cinemas near the Platia Areos are a relaxed summer's evening treat. The **Archaeological Museum** (8, Evangelistrias St, open Tues–Sun 08.30–15.00; admission 500, 400, 300Dr; tel: 071 242 148) is housed in a Ziller designed building used formerly as the Panarcadian Hospital. It contains a fine selection of inscriptions, pottery, reliefs and free-standing sculpture from various sites in Arcadia.

Where to stay

Accommodation includes: the Arcadia (Platia Kolokotronis, 071 223 465), the Artemis (Dimitrkopoulou 1, 071 225 221) as well as hotels encircling the large Platia Areos and a variety of rooms near the train station on Lambraki parallel with Lagopati.

Further afield

Bus connections are legion from Tripolis: the KTEL number six Arcadias goes from the bus station on Platia Kolokotroni to Alea, the site of Tegea, as well as other eastern Arcadian sites. The Mantinia region villages, west of Tripolis, can also be reached from the central Platia Kolokotroni, as can the traditional villages of Demitsana and Andritsena, though these also offer a more picturesque route through Megalopolis. Buses for the southern Peloponnese leave from their respective stops near the OSE station.

Mantinia

This is a loosely amalgamated series of villages to the north of Tripolis. The area was an important city-state that rivalled its major adversary Tegea. Some think the bitter rivalry was over a limited water supply for the high (629m) and arid inland Plain of Mantinia. The bus drops passengers near the front gate of the unattended archaeological site. It is hard to imagine this isolated area as the centre of a community that was known, respected and sought after as an ally by Athens, Corinth and Sparta. Traces of what were the city walls can be seen at various points on the site. They are considered among the best examples of Greek period fortifications and were probably built by the same architects and at the same time (370BC) as those of Messene. Up the same road 700m from the Archaeological Site on the left is a whimsical, eclectic modern church (1972): a Minoan-Classical-Egyptian-Byzantine mishmash that defies description. It is allegedly dedicated to "The Virgin, the Muses and Beethoven".

Visitors to Mantinia will see grape vines everywhere. There is an old winery on the right before the stop for the archaeological site, built by pioneer Greek winemaker Alexander Cambas late in the 19th Century. This winery recently changed proprietors and cannot be visited at present. This region is home to a particular local white grape variety – the Moschofiliro

– that bears some resemblance to the fragrant Muscat. It produces extremely attractive dry white wine and sweet or sparkling versions. There has been a remarkable revival of Moschofiliro-based wines in the last twenty years, notably by the Spiropoulos and Ioannis Tselepos. They both have new model wineries, tasting areas and shops up the same road as ancient Mantinia and the modern church offering a pleasant respite in an attractive setting. Telephone for a rendezvous with the Spiropoulos in Athens: 01 28 45 962-3, fax: 01 28 20 207; or directly to the winery: 0796 61 400 or fax: 0796 61 406. For Ioannis Tselepos, telephone/fax in Athens as well (01 80 30 310).

This area is approximately 15km from Tripolis and can be easily visited in half a day. Taxi fares with a midday return pick-up can be negotiated from the drivers congregating at the pleasant OSE café next to the station.

TRIPOLIS TO LEFTRON

South of Tripolis, there are four daily trains. One of these is a 03.27 express that is to be avoided if rest is the objective. The condition of the rail right-of-way south of Tripolis is spotty and not conducive to a smooth ride, let alone a night's kip. The scenery is splendid with small valleys, narrow, boulder-strewn river gorges and dramatic mountains. Excellent late 19th-century stone multi-arch railway bridges are prominent in this pastoral, extremely rural area.

Leaving the Tripolis station, the rail line skirts the city and turns west before smoothing out and curving to the south. It then starts climbing slightly to leave the Plain of Tripolis. Views back down towards the city can be had on the left side. The train shortly thereafter passes through cypress trees before arriving at the derelict station for Makri. Nearby are the signposted remains of **Pallantion**, the supposed mother city of Rome. According to legend, King Evander, the son of Hermes by an Arcadian nymph, founded from Pallantion a colony by the river Tiber, 60 years before the Trojan War. The name of the Palatine Hill in Rome is suggestive of Rome's Arcadian origins. With the building of Megalopolis, Pallantion faded away. After Makri, the railway climbs the Pass of Kaloyerikos (810m), curving over several interesting stone bridges, to settle into the plain of Assea. The railway line runs on a terrace just above the pass. This is the highest point (817m) on the Greek railways.

The high mountain range of **Taigettos** (2400m at Profitias Ilias) looms in front. It occupies the greater part of the middle prong of the Peloponnese, its crest dividing the provinces of Lakonia and Messinia. The name comes from a Doric word whose meaning is long lost. The mountain was sacred to the Olympian twins Apollo and Artemis. Artemis' followers were the wood nymphs called Nereides who tempted lone shepherds to follow them off cliffs with their suggestive dances. This mountain range, often hidden by snowy mist even in late June, offers some of the best wilderness and trekking in Greece. The line skirts the most difficult part of the range by heading west around Profitias Ilias (the Prophet Elijah).

The Assea station is several kilometres from the village, near the mountain springs that are the source of the river Alpheios. The acropolis of **ancient Asea** is on an isolated hill some 150m northeast of the station. This site was shown by excavations in 1936–38 to have been in continuous use from the Bronze Age to the Mycenaean era, and then to have been reoccupied in the Hellenistic period. A large stone water-tower attests to Assea's former role as a midpoint station where helper locomotives were added to assist southbound trains over the mountains. After Assea the railway winds its way through Rutsi to the Leftron junction for Megalopolis. Part of the attractive, rural railway is through tunnels and over stone viaducts in an idyllic setting; part is along a long ridge that runs north from Mount Tsempero (1,252m).

No passenger trains use the Megalopolis branch line at present though OSE shuttle buses transport passengers from Leftron. The massive State Power electric plant in the town is brought fuel by a nightly cylinder tank train from Elefsina. The rail line is in good condition and it is thought that the line will reopen for passenger service.

Megalopolis

In the large pleasantly wooded Plain of Megalopolis, is a small town (population 464): once a "Great City". It was both chief town of the surrounding area and capital of the federated Arcadian city-states.

Since no one could agree on a capital city when the Pan-Arcadian League was formed, a new city was built. It was sited by Epaminondas of Thebes on the banks of the Hellison where the modern town is, as part of a strategic barrier against Sparta. Among the buildings in Ancient Megalopolis (Tues–Sun 08.30 to 15.00; free) still standing is the theatre (4th century BC), the largest in ancient Greece. Megalopolis fared poorly and finally disappeared during the Slav invasions.

Buses from Megalopolis leave for Andritsena/Karitena twice a day; the alternative is to go by taxi. This region is among the wildest in Arcadia, with few roads and difficult access. Those who take the time will discover tidy vibrant villages, ebulliently rushing streams and secluded monasteries. There is medieval Karetina, the ancient stirring site of Gortys, the Louisios gorge and monastery of Prodromou, the metal-smithing village of Temnitsa and the quaint Dimitsana with its cobbled streets. Continuing on past Dimitsana towards equally quaint Andritsena, dirt roads give way to the main Tripolis–Pirgos road. Andritsena is a good base to visit the Temple of Apollo at Bassae, a Doric temple, as attractive as Athens' Temple of Ifastous in Thission.

LEFTRON TO KALAMATA

South of the Leftron Junction the rail line heads around the Taigettos Mountains. Through tunnel after tunnel and ever tighter curves the line harkens back to another age of transport when the iron horse dominated intercity transport in Greece. Dilapidated stone railway stations in the isolated villages of Xrani, Issari and Desylla recall that not only the railway, but villages in this area, are falling by the wayside as people desert the countryside for the cities. A sharp curve to the left, followed by a steady descent and views on the left of a green sea of olive trees, leads to brief stops at the larger villages of Diavolitsi and Kentriko. Then another sharp turn to the left and the rail line enters the Zevgolatio station trackage. It is now in the province of Messinia.

Zevgolatio, at the upper end of the Upper Messinian Plain, is the junction for Kyparissia, Pirgos and Patras on the Peloponnese west coast. Travellers are advised to continue into Kalamata as connections from Tripolis to the west coast are not good and Zevgolatio does not offer many possibilities except for the inveterate train-watcher. There is an agreeable café next to the station.

After Zevgolatio, the train charges down the centre of the extremely fertile and densely planted Messinian Plain. There is a brief stop in the busy market town of **Meligala** (population 1,600): an enormous clock tower is visible from the train. This area, the ancient **Steniclaros**, was the home of the Dorian dynasty of Kresphontes though the royal city has never been found.

Beyond Meligala, the rail line makes a beeline south for Kalamata. Just after Meligala in the broad valley (right) are the remains of ancient Messene (369BC).

Messene

Built after encouragement by Epaminondas, this fortified city was widely known for its military architecture. Many of the battlements, gates and towers still dominate the large site. This was the southernmost citadel of the chain, with Megalopolis and Argos, designed to undermine Spartan power and keep them at bay. The **Arcadia Gate**, through which passes the road from Mavromati at the north end of the site, the ruins of the **Sanctuary of Asclepius**, and the Doric **Temple of Artemis** are among the highlights.

Going to ancient Messene requires some planning. Taxis can be coaxed from Meligali to pass through the attractive village of Mavromati to the site. Both the site and the village are located on the lower slopes of Mount Ithomi (800m). The Zeus Pension (0724 51 025) in Mavromati has rooms for rent. A more adventurous entry to the site can be made by foot from the Valyri railway station. Here a path leads in less than two hours to the Monastery of Vourkano (383m) on the site. The Monastery, whose most recent buildings date from 1712, offers hospitality, but remember that first come first served is the rule. Given the remote nature of the area though, you are unlikely to encounter difficulty finding space at the monastery.

After Valyri come the tiny villages of Plati, Aris and Thouria. Near Thouria, east (left) of the village on the site of Paliokastro, are ruins from ancient Touria, inhabited from prehistoric times. Then comes Asprochroma station and the closed rail junction for the modern town of Messena (population 7,500). The branch line to the right has been closed for some time but could re-open. It passes directly in front of the recently rebuilt Kalamata Airport and, given the enthusiasm for the railways of Kalamata's current popular city administration, could be brought back on-line, as have the other short Peloponnese branches like Argos–Nafplion and Isthmia–Loutraki.

The line ends shortly thereafter at the attractive Kalamata rail station (tel: 0721 22 555).

KALAMATA

Kalamata (population 45,000) is situated on the Messinian Gulf, and is the leading commercial centre for the Southern Peloponnese. It is a bustling and attractive town getting on with its business after the devastating earthquake of early September 1986, which virtually levelled the town and forced half the population to flee.

Kalamata's city government is decidedly oriented towards rail transport with plans moving forward to equip the city with a modern light-rail tram network serving the city centre and the beach front.

The OSE rail station, surrounded by cafés and hotels, is conveniently located on Kefala Street, near its junction with the major avenue of Aristomenous at the large Platia Konstandinou Diadoknou. All necessary public services (police, post and OTE) are nearby. The tourist police (0721 23 187), down near the port, are helpful, as is the Municipal Tourist Office (0721 21 959) located on Makedonias Street..

The intercity KTEL bus terminal is not nearby. It is approximately one kilometre from the rail station, necessitating either a short cab ride or a long walk through Kalamata. To walk, take Railroad Street directly across from the station to its end at Nedonos on the Platia Konstandinou Diadoknou, then bear left on Nedonos and follow that along the river Nedon to the hectic bus terminal on the edge of town, under the gaze of the Frankish Castle.

The ebbing of the railway and of Kalamata's maritime exports is evident at the former maritime (Agios Demetris) station which is now a municipal park. This large multi-track terminal area near Kalamata's seaport (walk about ten minutes along the unused tracks from the Kalamata OSE station to the park) has become a pleasant outdoor museum-type repository for a great many old steam locomotives and passenger rolling stock. There is also a series of wooden cars from the Piraeus–Athens–Kiffissia ISAP line, as well as the railway right-of-way maintenance equipment for the abandoned Nafpaktos to Agrinion rail line in Western Greece. This park is an agreeable place to while away some time, located near the harbour district where are also many bars, cafés and hotels, all looking up to distant Mount Taigettos, which isolates the Mani, on its narrow peninsula, from the rest of Greece.

Those interested in obtaining further information on Kalamata's railway history, park or tramway plans can contact the Kalamata Association of Railway Friends, c/o Costas Triantafilos, PO. Box 68, 24100 Kalamata.

History

Kalamata occupies the site of the ancient Pharai founded by King Diocles. Pharai was subject to Agamemnon of Mycenae and participated in the Trojan War. In the 8th century BC, Pharai was annexed by Sparta, but regained its independence after the Battle of Leuctra (371BC). This name, Pharai, endured until the Byzantine era when it was supplanted by the present name, Kalamata. The precise origins of this name are unclear but could refer to a lost monastery, that of the Panagia of Kalamata, which possessed a miracle-producing icon.

By 1208, when Geoffrey Villehardouin acquired Messenia, the name Kalamata was well known. The hilltop castle, built in Byzantine times, was rebuilt by the Franks, and later by the Venetians who left their Lion of St Mark over the front gate. Additions were also made by the Ottomans. An amphitheatre at the base of the castle is the venue for a summer festival of dance and drama. A climb to the top offers exceptional views of Kalamata, the entire Messinian Plain and, of course, Mount Taigettos.

In the town itself are many churches from the Middle Ages: one, the Holy Apostles Church, is from the 12th century. A folk museum and a modern art gallery vie for attention, along with the Archaeological Museum housed in two old mansions belonging to the Benaki and Kyriakou families near the Agios Ioannis church. It is possible that this museum, seriously damaged during the earthquake, will reopen soon. The bulk of the remaining earthquake damage is visible in the residential neighbourhoods bounded by Aristomenous, Kolokotronis and Faron Streets. Here, the multi-storey concrete blocks erected quickly during the 1950s and 1960s did not withstand the shocks from the 1986 tremor, while the older buildings did.

Produce

Among the many fruits and vegetables that make up the renown of the rich Messinian Plain is the olive. Kalamata is blessed with a particularly succulent variety of table olive prized for its soft flesh. Kalamata olives are greatly desired around the world. As an example, France, itself an olive producing country, must import 93% of its yearly consumption of 29,000 tonnes of olives, much from Kalamata. Greece produces 70,000 tonnes but consumes 70% locally. With over 70 million olive trees devoted to table olives, Greece is ranked fifth in world-wide table-olive production.

Olive trees abound throughout the peninsula. Greece ranks third in the world behind Italy and Spain, producing 20% of the world's olive oil. Greek oil is particularly prized because consistently ideal growing-conditions give an extremely low quantity of oleic acid, making it particularly polyunsaturated. Italy and Spain, much more advanced than Greece in terms of bottling and marketing olive oil, try to incorporate as much of the better Greek oil into their oils as possible. The long, devastating early 1990s drought in Spain has put tremendous strain on Greek olive-oil reserves. Also, the world-wide interest in olive oil as the basis of a more healthy cuisine has further raised demand. Prices have risen dramatically and Greek homemakers, basing their cuisine on olive oil, have had to reduce dramatically the quantity they use. On the plus side, Greek oleo-culture has revived with farmers planting olive trees wherever there is space.

Where to stay

There is lots of good accommodation in Kalamata. Near the OSE rail station are: the Hotel George (0721 27 225) and the Hotel Vyzantion (0721 86 824); near the port are the Hotel Nevada (0721 82 429), the Hotel Plaza (0721 82 590) and the more upscale Pharea Palace (0721 94 421-24, fax: 93 969).

Further afield

Leaving Kalamata by rail, the traveller has two possibilities: to travel through Kyparissia (two daily trains), to Pyrgos (seven daily trains from Kyparissia), then to Patras; or to travel to Tripolis (four daily trains), then on to Argos and Corinth. Both of these routes will eventually feed back into Athens and Piraeus.

As previously stated, Kalamata represents an excellent base for the exploration of the southern Peloponnese. Car rental agencies abound and there are regular, multiple daily buses. The choice of destination, though, is more difficult, with much to choose from: west, between the Messinian Gulf and the Ionian Sea, is the region of **Pylos** with its immense Navarino Bay and the site of Nestor's Palace and the twin coastal citadel towns of **Methoni** and **Koroni** separated by the beach town of Finikoundas; south is **Areopolis** and the mysterious **Mani Peninsula**, culminating in the mythical entrance to the underworld at Cape Tenaro; east, in the province of Laconia, is **Sparta**, nearby **Mystra** and the other Byzantine sites of **Geraki** and noble **Monemvasia** leading down to the port of **Neapolis** on the Cape Malea Peninsula.

For those wishing to leave the railway for an extended period, **Gythion**, the small port south of Sparta, is a more attractive base for discovering Laconia. It is also gateway to the islands of Kythera and Crete.

BEYOND KALAMATA
West to Pylos, Methoni and Koroni

Fifty-one kilometres from Kalamata, delightful Pylos (population 3,000), a smaller version of Nafplion, sits on a slight promontory at the south end of a giant bay, formerly known as Navarino Bay. This was the site of the famous though seemingly inadvertent Battle of Navarino Bay on October 27, 1827, between the fleets of Britain, France and Russia and the combined Egyptian and Turkish flotillas. European philhellenism had led the Great Powers to try to end the long conflict politically (the Treaty of London, 6 July 1827). A 27-warship allied fleet was sent to Navarino to force the Egyptian Ibrahim Pasha to stop raiding Messinia from the Ottoman ships anchored in the deep, protected harbour. Visitors to Pylos will note that there is but one small, navigable, wide entrance to the large bay. Here, the allied vessels stationed themselves in front of the 87-ship Ottoman Navy. When the Allies took cannon fire during the night, they responded and destroyed the Ottoman fleet. The Ottomans lost 53 ships and 6,000 men (no ships lost by the Allies) and never significantly threatened the Peloponnese again. Greek Independence was assured.

Pylos

The modern town, known locally as Neokastro, dates from only 1828. It was built with arcaded streets around a large square (Platia Trion Navarkon) by the French General Maison after the landing of his 14,000-strong army. The French are also responsible for the coastal road down to the Venetian stronghold of Methoni. Several castles and forts provide historical interest. One, the 1572-built Neokastro (Tues–Sun. 08.00–15.00; free), was used as a prison until the 1970s. It was used mostly to keep feuding Mani clansmen apart. The battlements encircling the castle provide an excellent panorama of the area. Local travel agencies (try Sapienza Travel, 0723 23 207) organise tours around the area. There are no organised tourist information offices, but the local police (0723 22 316) are helpful. **Accommodation** is plentiful, but once again scarce during the summer. Try: the Hotel Navarino (on the waterfront, 0723 22 564) or the more pricey Karalis Beach Hotel (on the beach, 0723 23 021), and for organised camping Navarino Beach Camping (6km north of Pylos on Gialova Beach, 0723 22 761).

North, around the bay, is the archaeological site excavated in 1939 and worked continuously since 1952, attributed as the **Palace of Nestor**; "wise" King Nestor was the powerful contemporary of Agamemnon. Further around the bay on the protective outer island of Sfacteria occurred another battle (425BC), remarked upon by the historian Thucydides. An Athenian force laid siege to a Spartan contingent that promptly surrendered, greatly surprising the Athenians. Spartan soldiers from a young age vowed to never surrender. They were supposed to return either with their shield or on it.

North of Nestor's Palace it is possible to continue on to Kyparissia (six daily buses); but the trip south around the coast to the Venetian citadel of Methoni, one of Agamemnon's seven cities given to Achilles, is preferable.

Methoni
Methoni is a tiny seaside village, with a long, calm sand beach and a gigantic fortress (Mon–Sat 08.30–19.00, Sun 09.00–19.00; closes 15.00 during the winter; free). Considered a remarkable example of military architecture, the massive walls contained the entire village during Venetian times.

From Methoni several daily buses wind through the olive trees, mostly in constant view of the Methoni citadel, to the fishing/beach village of Finikoundas. This village bears a resemblance to Aegean island towns: an easy-going place with good, inexpensive seafood restaurants and an extremely long beach.

From here buses go to the other Venetian citadel town of Koroni. Unfortunately, there are no Methoni–Koroni through buses. Current schedules, though, fall perfectly in place for a long relaxed lunch and a swim in Finikoundas followed by a late afternoon arrival in Koroni.

Koroni
The Venetian Citadel of Koroni was long considered, with Methoni, "the Eyes of the Republic" on the long sea trade routes from the Orient to Venice. It is a beautiful village (population 1,400), with the city centre and built-up area climbing the promontory in a maze of stepped streets lined with stuccoed, pastel-painted houses. The village descends to the 2km-long, silvery, sand Zanga Beach, backed by fruit trees. The fort, most unmilitarily, contains the flower-bedecked Timiou Prodromou nunnery and the Panayia Elestrias church. Flourishing gardens and private homes garnish the citadel and create an atmosphere of calm and relaxation. An overnight stay here is recommended, with no shortage of **accommodation**. Try the Flisvos Hotel (0725 22 238) or the Auberge de la Plage (0725 22 401); for private rooms check in with the folks at the Symposium Restaurant (0725 22 385); and at the beginning of Zara Beach Andreas Koutoukos rents rooms over his taverna (0725 2 262). Campgrounds abound, with the Memi Beach (0725 22 130) and the Koroni (0725 22 119) being the best. Both are open from May to at least September.

Messinian "Outer" Mani
From Kalamata it is possible to begin an exploration of the Mani, long considered a most difficult, inaccessible region with the most ferocious residents battling it out from solid towers in blood feuds that lasted centuries. The road from Kalamata down to and beyond Stoupa along the inhospitable slopes of Mount Taigettos is a prizewinner for scenery, on vertiginous curves and heights. Pay particular attention to the area between Almyro and

Kambos, then the descent from Satropigi to Kardamili. Sit on the right side for the best views. Buses bound for Itilo and Areopolis pass through hamlets with quiet sandy beaches and the most profoundly blue water possible. With many organised and free campgrounds along the indented coast this area is an ideal getaway place.

Kardamili (population 350), another of the seven cities of Agamemnon offered to Achilles, is an enticing town though it tends to be overrun with tourists in the summer. Day-long hikes up the massive Viros Gorge on Mount Taigettos to tiny villages and an abandoned monastery are possible, but hikers should be well-equipped if planning long walks. Kardamili has a post office and a bank but no tourist office. Morgan Holidays (0721 73 220) answers queries about accommodation.

Further along the coast is the campground, Ta Delfina (0721 54 318), then the less-and-less isolated village of **Stoupa** with its several pristine beaches. It is said that Nikos Kazantzakis based the character of Alexis Zorba on a man working as a supervisor at a local mine near here. Today the village has somewhat of a bewildered air about it, as it is becoming an outpost of small group tourism. Many rooms for rent dot the village; it has no bank, police or tourist office.

South of Stoupa to Itilo and Areopolis, the countryside takes on more of the stark Inner Mani landscape: the village of **Langada** is typical with its plethora of menacing towers. This area has substantial segments of the Kalderimi, the built up cart-wide path complete with substantial stone arch bridges, that served as the main artery before asphalt came to the Mani. **Itilo**, the Mani's former 15th and 16th century capital, is next.

Itilo, where it is necessary to change buses for Areopolis or Gythion, has the substantially intact Turkish Castle of Kelefa. This dominating military feature was meant to keep the fierce Maniots out on their peninsula and away from the rich lowlands around Kalamata. It is a short walk through the impressive gorge from the bus stop.

The rest of the Mani will be discussed further on as a possible excursion from Gythion: see page 118.

Laconia

This province of Sparta, Mystra and Monemvasia contains extensive Classical and Byzantine ruins that are among the most evocative in the Peloponnese. But it contains no railway tracks. It is one of the few areas of Greece without them. Local wits like to say that is why Laconia has so many "manga", referring to the overdressed 1920s-era carefree men who lived fast and easy in Piraeus during the anarchic time when Greece was trying to assimilate over one million desperate refugees from the Smyrna debacle. According to an old song, the carefree "manga" were run over by trains. So no trains in Laconia means plenty of "manga".

Accessing Laconia from Kalamata means either a dramatic 60km passage over the spine of Taigettos via the 1524m Langada Pass, or a longer trip through the Outer Mani to Gythion and from there to Sparta. As remarked in the paragraphs describing the passage from Mili over Mount Parnon to the village of Kosmas, Laconia is a harsh area surrounded by mountains and with access to the sea limited to only a few areas. Its boundaries have not changed significantly since antiquity. It is no wonder that a people, the Spartans, who have given their name to a simple, unostentatious style of behaviour, should come from Laconia. Nor that the Byzantines, reeling from the shock of losing the Imperial city of Constantinople to the Ottomans, should seek refuge here.

Laconia has been inhabited since Neolithic times (6000–3000BC). The area seems always to have been densely peopled, with Mycenaean-era settlements being identified in many places. After the Dorian invasions (1100BC), their strongest settlement, Sparta, annexed all of Laconia. The Dorians, being numerically inferior to the pre-existing peoples developed a unique martial system of organisation to maintain their superiority over the conquered natives, the Helots, who remained a perpetually disaffected underclass. Barbarian invasions under Alaric in AD395 ravaged the area, which then saw a long period of peace under the Byzantines. The Turks marched against Laconia but never succeeded in fully conquering the area. Continual uprisings by truculent Maniots forced reprisals, and a perpetuation of the myth of Laconian harshness that has not dissipated to this day, despite the relative prosperity of the post Civil War era.

Sparta

The modern city (population 14,000) laid out at the base of Mount Taigettos, along the Evrotas River, only dates from 1834. It is an efficient city laid out on a grid plan with leafy, wide avenues, pedestrianised side streets and many cafés, and is a good example of how a small city can cope with urban growth.

Ancient Sparta, or Laikedaimon, occupied a large triangular area sprawling over six low hills on the right bank of the Evrotas. During its greatest period the city was without walls. The remains of the ancient city are few, not only because of earthquake damage and barbarian destruction, but because there simply wasn't much monumental building going on. Throughout much of its history Sparta was little more than a large armed camp. Lycurgos, architect of the Spartan constitution, stated that "men not walls make a city". A small archaeological museum (Dionyssiou-Dafnou St; open Tues–Sun 08.30–15.00; admission 500, 400, 300Dr; tel: 0731 28 575) contains some artefacts and the traces of the theatre on the ancient Acropolis which can be seen behind the municipal sports stadium. Most of the city's masonry was carted off: used to build fortifications when Spartan power declined and to build the now deserted Byzantine city of Mystra.

Mystra should be on any traveller's list of destinations. Sparta serves well as a base for the exploration of Mystra, and, more or less, cannot be avoided. The helpful EOT office (0731 24 852) and tourist police 0731 26 229) should help locate accommodation, but if you are staying in Gythion, Mystra can be visited adequately on a day trip. If continuing on to Monemvasia, early arrival in Sparta should allow for onward travel in the late afternoon. Confirm onward travel with KTEL. Mystra buses leave frequently from a café near the corner of Likourgou and Ayissilaou.

Mystra

This uninhabited, magnificently walled, pure medieval city spilling down from the slopes of Mount Taigettos once contained over 42,000 residents. Built by Guillaume de Villehardouin in 1249 to protect Franks and their subjects, it shortly thereafter became the Byzantine capital and seat of government when Emperor Michael VIII Palaeolous wrested the Morea back from the Franks. For the next 190 years Mystra prospered while the rest of Byzantium fell under the Ottoman onslaught. A school of humanist philosophy was founded by Gemistos Plethon (1355–1452), the rediscoverer of Plato, and the arts and architecture flourished. After Mystra fell to the Turks in 1460, Plethon's disciples fled to Rome and Florence, where they flourished and contributed to the Italian renaissance. Venetian control in 1687 meant a brief resurgence of interest in Mystra which became a centre of the silk trade. From then on it was in perpetual decline, being burned three times in less than 50 years: first by the Russians in 1770, then by the Albanians in 1780, and finally by Ibrahim Pasha in 1825. By the end of World War II, Mystra was a virtual ruin, though some people still resided in the lower city near the Metropolis or the Cathedral of Agios Dimitrios. A ferocious gun battle in October 1944 between various partisan groups forced the children to seek refuge in the 14th-century Pantanassa Convent. Battle scars can still be seen in the courtyard of the Metropolis. The last 30 families were relocated to the modern village next to the site in 1952. Many locals who work within the walls remember living in the ghostly old city with its empty stone streets still guarding memories of long-past grandeur.

Two ways exist to visit the site (open daily; 08.30–15.00; admission 1200, 900, 600Dr; tel: 0731 93 377): from the top gate near the entrance to the magnificent citadel (621m) that allows such dramatic views back into the Taigettos Mountains and over the Evrotas River valley plain; or from the lower gate, then walking up through the deserted streets of the lower and upper town to the citadel. The museum and refreshment stands are at the entrance to the lower gate as are the Metropolis (right on entering the Monemvasia Gate) and the Pantanassa Convent (straight on past the gate). Strictly speaking Mystra is not uninhabited, because the convent is still occupied. Nuns offer water to visitors: please respect them and be decently clothed when entering their domain.

Mystra is important for the insight it gives into life in a major Byzantine city, and for the intact frescos and intricately inlaid mosaics. Mansions, Turkish fountains and small churches are around every corner, reached around arched passageways. The Metropolis, built in 1309, is the oldest of Mystra's churches. It was here that the last Byzantine Emperor, Constantine IX Paleologus, was crowned in 1448 – the spot is commemorated with a marble slab that features the double-headed Byzantine eagle. The Pantanassa's 15th-century church is considered the best in Mystra, with colourful Byzantine frescos that have been compared to the rich painting of Gauguin. The chapel belonging to the Perivleptos Monastery contains an almost complete set of 14th-century frescos. The Vrontohion Monastery also has lively, colourful frescos.

From Sparta, the next major destination is the massive island fortress of Monemvasia. Between Sparta and the coast lies the intriguing village of Geraki (population 1,750). Little visited (there is no accommodation), Geraki, occupying the site of the ancient Geronthrai, merits a visit for its plethora of Byzantine chapels and its walled acropolis (591m). It was one of twelve Frankish fiefs of the Peloponnese. Today it has an upbeat air about it with a lively square and helpful locals. It should not be a problem locating the keys to the Frankish fortress (built in 1245 by Jean de Nivelet and ceded to the Byzantines in 1262).

Monemvasia

Monemvasia (meaning single entrance) is a large Gibraltar-type rock jutting out into the Aegean Sea. It was part of the mainland until an earthquake severed it in AD375. The Byzantines quickly took advantage of Monemvasia's impregnable position and it became a commercial centre to balance the spiritual centre at Mystra. It counted more than 60,000 residents in the Middle Ages when its wine, known as Malvasia or Malmsey, was prized in Europe. Now, despite a revival brought about by tourism, there are fewer than a dozen year-round residents. New Zealand veterans of World War II remember Monemvasia. During the spring 1941 retreat, 4,000 were evacuated from there. This is another of those mainland Greek places that reminds one of the islands with its steep streets and picturesque, semi-dilapidated houses hanging over precipitous cliffs. Quiet cobbled streets lead to mysterious Byzantine chapels, though few icons still survive. The citadel in the upper town with its Agia Sofia chapel is worth a visit. The whitewashed 16th-century Panagia Chrysaphitissa overlooks the sea, and the Cathedral of Elkomenos Christos (Christ in Chains), built in 1294 by the Byzantine emperor Andronicus II Comnenus, dominates the lower town.

There are no banks in the town, but Gefyra over the causeway on the mainland has full tourist service through Malvasia Travel (0732 61 432). Two inns open year-round can be found on Monemvasia: the Ardamis (0732 61 886; fax: 071 233 533) and the Vizantino (0732 61 254; fax: 61 562). At Gefyra is Camping Paradise (3km south: 0732 61 123), the simple Akrogia

(0732 61 360) and the Filoxenia (0732 61 716). There are others, plus many rooms for rent along the waterfront.

South of Monemvasia is a little-visited region leading down to Neapolis, the southernmost town of mainland Greece. This sometimes stark region has been well evoked by an American woman, Thordis Simonsen, in *The Dancing Girl*, who reminiscences of her life in the village of Elika. The burgeoning resort town of Neapolis offers the possibility of taking a caique to Elafonissi 400m offshore, or small ferries to Kythera, Antikythera and Crete. Especially noteworthy sand beaches can be found on Elafonissi.

Gythion and the Mani

If time is limited, Gythion (population 5,000) is a good base for its closeness to Sparta/Mystra, Monemvasia and the Mani. It offers reasonably priced hotels, restaurants and night life along the port-side promenade and it is a port for Crete. Banks, tourist information centres and travel agents abound. There is no sense of pressure to find a place quickly because of the variety of accommodation. Try the several campgrounds on the beach towards Areopolis: Meltemi (0733 22 844), Gythion Beach (0733 23 441), Mani Beach (0733 23 450); attractive rooms are offered by the Koutsouris Family (0733 22 321) and the Kalathis (0733 22 504); more upscale is the Hotel Gythion (0733 23 452).

As the seaport and naval arsenal of Sparta, Gythion claims a long past. Ancient inhabitants believed Hercules and Apollo jointly founded the town. Chroniclers talk of Minoan colonists and dark-skinned Phoenician traders in magenta dye. Paris and Helen spent their first night together on the offshore islet of Kranae, now known as Marathonissi, after her abduction from Menelaus' palace at Sparta.

Most modern visitors will use Gythion to set out for the Inner Mani. Though not as well served as Sparta, the Mani does see regular bus services.

Areopolis, with its giant statue of Petrobey Mavromikhalis in the main platia, is the first stop. Areopolis means town of Ares (god of war), because it was from here that Mavromikhalis united the feuding Maniot clans into one of the most effective Greek combat forces during the Greek War of Independence.

It is often necessary to change buses here for other destinations in the Mani. The 30km-long area from Areopolis to Cape Matapan is called the **Kakovouna** (bad mountain).It is a stark, treeless region where existence means being imaginative and wary. Olive trees are crammed into minuscule hand-tilled terraces, created from the rocky ground. **Cape Matapan** was the home of an important Spartan shrine and their main oracle resided nearby. This lends credence to the theory that this stark region of the Mani was the last refuge of the Spartans, escaping the decay of their territory during the Slav invasions. During the summer it is a hot, dry area. Respite from the sun is available in the many attractive Byzantine chapels that dot the region.

Some 8km south of Areopolis is the hamlet of **Pirgos Dirou**, where there are a series of well-documented and visited caves (June–Sept 08.00–18.00; Oct–May 08.00–15.00; 1,800Dr). A small museum (Tues–Sun 08.30–15.00; 400Dr) contains Neolithic finds. South of here comes a narrow 17km plain with a large concentration of barrel-vaulted churches, although practically devoid of population. Further south, the villages of **Kitta** and **Nomia** boast many of the tower houses used in the constant clan warfare. Kitta is reputed to be the site of the last major outbreak in 1870. Following are **Boularii** with its many fresco-adorned Byzantine churches. The small coastal town of **Gerolimenas** has adequate tourist services. Buses continue down the road to Alika where the road forks east to Layia in the mountains, and straight on through Vathia to **Porto Kayio** on the coast, or to the trail for the **Cape Matapan** lighthouse.

Vathia was chronicled by the early 19th century explorer Colonel Leake who was warned to bypass the village because of an ongoing feud that had already lasted 40 years. Exceptional views can be had back across the Mani from this high road, dramatically cut out of the mountain. Cape Matapan is the second most southerly point on the European mainland.

The eastern fork of the road circles back along the barren coast to Areopolis. Public transport is sparse in this moonscape-like region. Good clothes, footwear, water and a map are needed here. It is a two-hour walk along the road to Layia where a daily bus returns to Areopolis.

Where to stay

Accommodation is available in the Inner Mani, often in converted old tower houses purposely transformed into inns by private owners or EOT. In Areopolis try the following which are open year round: Londas (0733 51 360; fax: 0733 51 012) or Pyrgos Kapetanakoy (0733 51 233; fax: 0733 51 401); in Gerolimenas the following which are currently open only from April to September: Arhondiko (0733 54 285; fax: 0733 54 285); Stavri (0733 56 297; fax: 0733 56 297); in Vathia open from April to September is: Vathia Village (0733 55 244; fax: 0733 55 292).

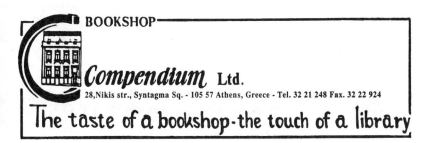

Part Four

CENTRAL GREECE

Here, on the east coast of mainland Greece, bounded on the west by the high, austere crags of the Pindos Mountains, is the legendary province of Boeotia. Its capital is ancient seven-gated Thebes, known locally as Thiva; exotic Levadia continues the Sacred Way west to Delphi. The Brallos mountain passage via the three rail bridges which include the famous Gorgopotamos of World War II fame over and around Mount Orthrys introduce rail riders to the region of Thessaly and its vast Plain of Thessaly – the fertile breadbasket of Greece.

The rich earth of Thessaly that has sustained Greeks since the beginning of time stretches some 250km from Volos on the coast, west to Kalambaka in the foothills of Epirus. This region was also known for its fine cattle and excellent horses. Thessalian horses provided the cavalry mounts used by Greeks up until Alexander's conquests in Asia. Here in Thessaly, a widespread Neolithic culture was followed by the arrival (about 2,500BC) of people speaking a form of Greek. These newcomers were the first Greek speaking people to arrive in the Balkans. According to mythology, it was in Thessaly that Helen (after whom the Greeks are named Hellenes) gave birth to the three branches of the Greek people: Dorus, Xuthus and Aeolus.

Further north beyond Larissa is Apollo's sacred Vale of Tempi that separates Thessaly from Macedonia. Beyond is fabled Mount Olympus and the marshes around the Thermaic Gulf leading into the thriving metropolis of Thessaloniki.

Historically, this area has been the meeting point of various land-based cultures, mostly intent on the conquest of the south. Its soil is marked with innumerable monuments to ancient clashes. The railway line skirts the centre of the plains to hug the contour along mountain terraces. The Greek state railway meets the Turkish-built railway at the purpose-built Platy junction north of the Vale of Tempi. The Thessaly Railway pushed west from Volos right up to the foothills of the Pindos mountains but stopped, thwarted by lack of funds and World War I.

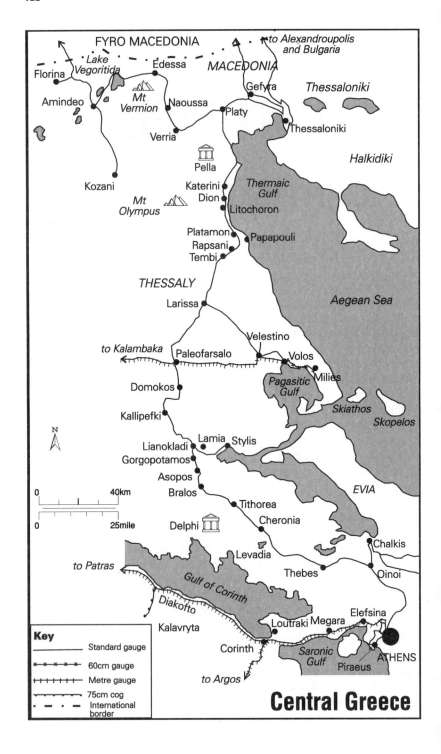

Central Greece

Chapter Ten

Athens–Thessaloniki

INTRODUCTION

This is the international standard gauge north/south Greek main rail line. It links the two largest cities in Greece, Athens and Thessaloniki, with 520km of railway, and it passes through some exceptionally scenic areas.

The line has become something of a showcase with new tunnels and fast 200km/hour stretches of new, ultra-smooth double track. For the summer 1996 schedule, OSE initiated non-stop Athens–Thessaloniki–Athens IC trains 50/51 named Hermes: the fastest trains ever to operate in Greece. They cover the 520 kilometres in 5 hours 50 minutes. By 1997–1998, schedules of many IC trains should be about the same, because new stretches of right-of-way will come on line by the summer of 1997. As of the 2 June 1996 timetable, 328km of railway line were already double tracked. After all the tunnels and new rights-of-way are in place, electrification (25KV, 50HZ over 1,260km) of the entire line will follow. At that time, somewhere in 2001, the non-stop Athens–Thessaloniki trip should be reduced to only three-and-a-half hours.

Ten trains per day cover the entire line: five IC and five expresses. Two of the expresses are overnight trains: number 504 only carries passengers in couchettes or sleeping cars. Two local trains leave the main line at Lianokladi for Lamia, and Stylis to the east. Two daily IC trains leave the main line at Larissa for Volos while two other locals only go as far as Larissa. One IC (60) leaves the main line at Platy, just south of Thessaloniki, for Kozani to the west.

The main-line expresses are presently powered by massive ex-German Bundesbahn diesel locomotives. These came on line in 1989 and are temporary replacements until the new locomotives ordered from ADTrans (formerly ABB but now merged with AEG to form ADTrans) are delivered sometime in early 1997. These powerful two-engine diesel locomotives are designed to be easily convertible to electric service. Their normal operating speeds will then increase from 120 to 160km/hour.

From the midpoint junction station of Paleofarsalo on the Thessalian Plain south of Larissa, it is possible to transfer from the main line to the old metre gauge Thessaly Railway linking Paleofarsalo with Kalambaka (Meteora), and Epirus by road to the west, or Volos by rail to the east. Massive rebuilding of the Paleofarsalo–Kalambaka segment of this line is currently under way. By 1998, this segment of the Thessaly Railway will be of the international standard gauge, with a direct Athens–Paleofarsala–Kalambaka service.

As far as scenery goes, this is an extremely beautiful railway line that skirts the Agrafa mountains, thunders through the Thessalian Plain, then tiptoes through the legendary Vale of Tempi before running past Mount Olympus and along the Thermaic Gulf into Thessaloniki. There are excellent views from both sides of the train.

It is also a relatively young railway line with the through Athens–Thessaloniki service only begun in the 1920s. It used to connect Greece with Europe until summer 1996 when the international service was restricted to Thessaloniki. Time-keeping in the Balkans has deteriorated to the point where OSE cannot count on international trains arriving in Thessaloniki without severe delays. Greeks bound on long-distance trips south of Thessaloniki could not depend on these schedules for reliable travel, and abandoned these trains. OSE then decided to terminate them in Thessaloniki.

The first part of this route, from Piraeus/Athens to Oinoi, was discussed in *Chapter Four*.

OINOI TO THEBES

Just beyond the Chalkis turn-off is a large blue-and-white billboard-size sign (right) that announces that the following segment of track was rebuilt with EU funds. The sign is easy to miss; but, significantly from here, the train begins to pick up speed dramatically while the ride smoothes out noticeably. Motor vehicles on the parallel National Athens–Lamia toll-road seem to be standing still as the train roars through the great green valley that made the ancient city of Thebes self-sufficient.

The various peaks of the Mount Parnassos range begin to make their appearance on the left. Hidden deep in this range is the ancient and most revered sanctuary of all, **Delphi**. Local trains call briefly at the village halts of Tanagra, Eleon and Ypaton before arriving at Thebes station. **Ancient Tanagra** occupies an almost circular hill on the right of the railway, rising from the north bank of the Asopos River. It was the scene of a Spartan victory over the Athenians in 457BC and allegedly the birthplace of the poetess Corinna, who beat Pindar in a musical contest. Terracotta figurines discovered in the necropolis, and other associated artefacts, are in the Thebes museum.

Thebes

All trains, northbound ICs 40 and 54 as well as southbound ICs 41 and 53, call here. Thebes is a modern town (population 21,000) about 3km towards the west (left) of the rail station. Called Thiva today, the modern town is built on the ancient acropolis over the Classical city.

History

Legendary Thebes was the birthplace of Dionysos and Hercules, and in the known historical period of Pindar, Epimanondas and Pelopidas. The "seven-gated city" plays a significant part in Greek myth, literature and history. Here is where the adult Oedipus entered the city of Thebes, after unknowingly killing his father who was the city's ruler. Oedipus entered after successfully answering the Sphinx's riddle. The Sphinx, vexed at being outwitted by Oedipus, killed herself. Grateful Thebans made Oedipus king and allowed him to marry the queen – his natural mother. When enlightened by an oracle, the queen killed herself. Oedipus, traumatised, gouged out his eyes and wandered the countryside as a blind beggar.

This city also claims the invention of the Greek alphabet. Thebes was the dominant city of Boeotia, traditionally Athens' foe, and for a short while in the 4th century BC was the leader of all Greece. Alexander the Great sacked and completely destroyed Thebes in 336BC for rebelling against Macedonian control. Thebes was rebuilt but declined again in 86BC when it sided against the Romans. It regained something of its old stature in the Middle Ages, as the political seat of the Byzantine rulers of Greece and as an important economic centre with control of silk manufacture. It was from Thebes that silk culture was introduced to Italy. After Sicily gained control of silk manufacture, Thebes declined again. The Turks then made neighbour Levadia the administrative centre.

What to see

A visit to the fine five-room **archaeological museum** (Keramopoulou Sq; open Tues–Sun 8.30–15.00; admission 500, 400Dr; tel: 0262 23 559) within the courtyard of the 13th century Frankish castle should precede any search for ancient ruins. The modern city centre is built directly on the ancient acropolis, or Kadmeia, which makes digging for the ancient city extremely difficult. The classical topography is becoming more and more difficult to ascertain as modern sprawl obliterates reference points. Outlines of the **theatre** and **Agora** are visible from the railway-station entrance to the city. The **Fountain of Oedipus**, where he wiped off his father's blood, is located in a small pleasant park on the Chalkis road outside the Proetidian Gate. Other remnants of the past are scattered about and are more or less easily recognisable.

Wine drinkers should try to visit the local wine co-operative. It has made a name for itself producing interesting wines from local varieties. The up-to-date Thebes Wine Co-op can be visited for tours and tastings. Telephone 0262 28 714 or fax 28 144 for details.

Where to stay

Those interested in an extended stay have a choice of three similar basic hotels: the Meletiou (0262 27 333); the Neobe (0262 27 949) and the Tsapara (0262 23 522), but this hotel is not central. It is in Aliartos, 10km north on the railway line.

Further afield

An excursion 18km to the hamlet of Levktra leads to the battlesite where Epaminondas defeated the Spartans in 371BC. This finally ended the legend of Spartan invincibility, and made Thebes the top Greek city-state.

THEBES TO LEVADIA

The railway north to Levadia continues through the Teneric Plain; to the left can be spied the little villages hidden high in the hills that are represented by the tiny tree-shaded stone stations: Sfinx, Aliartos (on the right), Petra, Ypsilantis, Alalkomene and Rachi. The area around the village of Sfinx, situated on the low rise of Mount Fagas, the ancient Sphingion, was the reputed haunt of the Sphinx of the Oedipal myth.

The entire area left of the rail line is an extremely primitive area that is, in essence, the back country above the northeastern end of the Gulf of Corinth. Much of it is inaccessible by car. One area deep in these mountains is the **Valley of the Muses**, in the upper reaches of the Permessos River. Here the Musean Games were held every four years, and music and poetry contests; winners received a wreath of myrtle. In addition there were games in honour of love, called the erotica, including athletic contests and musical competitions. The area developed into a sanctuary and was adorned with statues of the muses, of Dionysus and of the great lyric poets. The sanctuary was despoiled by Byzantine Emperor Constantine the Great. Be warned that this area has no modern tourist services.

To the immediate right of the railway is the drained plain of what was once the biggest lake in ancient Greece, the reed-filled **Lake Copais**. A reedy swamp most of the year, it dries during the summer months. The reeds growing around its banks were the raw materials of the Greek flute. The natural outlets were swallow-holes called *katavothrae*. Prehistoric ancients, probably the Minyans whose origins are disputed, channelled rainy season waters into these *katavothrae* and reclaimed the lake. But their dykes and canals were blocked and destroyed by earthquakes. Engineers employed by Alexander the Great tried to drain the lake with tunnels but the reclamation was not finally completed until 1931. The land was then cultivated with cereal and cotton. In 1311, the Catalan Grand Company which controlled the area of Levadia annihilated the Frankish Knights that controlled Athens, and much of central Greece, by tricking them into this swampy area near Orchomenos.

Aliartos was one of the several fortified places that controlled the only natural highway through Central Greece – the road from Thebes to Central Greece. Medieval and classical fortifications can be seen in the town.

Levadia

All trains including IC call here. Intriguing Levadia (population 19,000) is hidden almost 7km above and to the west (left) from the railway. This pleasant and untouristy city is built on both high banks of the mythically renowned Herkina River which runs out of the gorge from its mountain spring sources. The prosperous modern town makes textiles and is a pleasant stopping-point before proceeding west to Delphi, or on a slight detour east to Orchomenos or the Citadel of Gla.

History

The town is renowned for the **Oracle of Trophonios** and the Catalan stronghold above the Herkina. The Oracle of Trophonios was renowned from at least the 6th century BC, possibly because it was the only one in central Boeotia, and was consulted until at least the time of Pausanias – the 2nd century AD Roman traveller and explorer who seems to have gone everywhere. The Turkish governor used to rest near the entrance to the sacred caves. These entrances have been tentatively identified near the summit of the medieval fortress.

Levadia was of some strategic importance, and played a meaningful role during the Turkish era. At Independence in 1835, it was the second city of the Greek mainland.

Where to stay

Two comfortable hotels are available here: the Levadia (0261 23 611-7) and the Philippos (0261 24 931-3); as well as two simpler inns: Hotel Erkyna (0261 28 227) and the Hotel Elikon (0261 23 911).

Further afield

East of Levadia (ten minutes by local bus) is modern **Orhomenos** (population 5,600), with its ancient city, inhabited from Neolithic to Hellenistic times by the Minyans – a people from the Thessalian seaboard or from North Africa. Remains include the **Treasury of the Minyans** (open Tues–Sat: 08.30–15.00, Sun: 10.00–14.00; free) with an intricately carved stone ceiling in its inner chamber and two **Byzantine chapels**: 4th and 9th century. The 9th century Church of the Dormition is built entirely of blocks from the classical theatre and column segments from the temple.

Twenty minutes further east by local bus near the village of Kastro is the massive **Mycenaean Citadel of Gla** (free), with walls much larger than those at Mycenae or Tiryns, which may have been a defensive fort or the palace of an unknown Mycenaean noble. Other than the fact that it stood on an island, little is known. Rarely visited, with gates and walls 5m high it is an evocative place.

Another road east from Levadia leads through heavily cultivated land to Atalanti. Here is situated one of Greece's best known and most progressive wine-making installations, the **Ktima Hatzmichali**. Visitors are welcome to taste and chat with the well informed staff. Check with the Athens office for details (tel: 01 80 76 714 or fax: 80 76 704).

West of Levadia begins the dramatic road over, but mostly around, **Mount Parnassos** and its lesser peaks. It continues to Delphi and beyond, to the Corinthian Gulf. About halfway to Delphi is a triple road junction identified as the Oedipus crossroads where Oedipus murdered his father, King Laertus of Thebes, and his two attendants, not knowing who they were.

From this crossroads it is possible to visit the Byzantine Monastery complex at **Ossios Loukas** via Distomo, another town like Kalavrita that suffered massacres at the hands of Nazi soldiers in reprisals for guerrilla attacks. Ossios Loukas contains two main domed churches: the smaller 10th century Theotokos and the 11th century Katholikon as well as vividly frescoed crypts. Both contain stunning mosaics from the last great Byzantine flourish before the decline. Ossios Loukas is thus a precursor to Mystra in the Peloponnese. Though some monks still live here, it is essentially maintained as a museum (open daily: 08.00–17.30; admission 800, 600, 400Dr; tel: 0267 22 797).

Back along the main road towards Delphi is **Arhova**, a rapidly developing winter sports resort deep in the Mount Parnassos mountain range. If you are bound for Delphi, Arhova makes a delightful halt with more authentic and well-priced hotels and accommodation. Try the Appollon (0267 31 427) towards Levadia or the Pension Nostos (0267 31 385) towards Delphi.

Beyond Arhova is the ancient sanctuary of **Delphi**.

Delphi

Though it may no longer be the navel of the earth, as the Greeks believed for over 1,000 years, Delphi still has a spiritual presence. This is as much as anything due to its evocative location, on the dramatic high southern slope of Mount Parnassos, above a vast plantation of olive trees; and overlooking the Gulf of Corinth and beyond to the mountainous crags of the Peloponnese.

History

Here was located a prophetic Oracle who acted as a spiritual centre for the otherwise fiercely independent Greek city-states. As such, it was an essential cornerstone of the ancient Greek civilisation. All Greeks made pilgrimages here, along the Sacred Way, to consult a mystic Pythian priestess who would impart cryptic and often equivocal answers to those fulfilling the prerequisites of animal sacrifice and ritual cleansing. These answers would be interpreted by an attendant priest waiting besides the Oracle, a village woman over 50 years old, who traditionally sat on a tripod over a deep open rock chasm.

The responses and their interpretation often led to war, devastation, great wealth or personal well-being. The Oracle was respected partly because it was the "most truthful" according to Strabo, but also because the Delphic priests were extremely well-organised, with a network of informers throughout the Greek world. "My lad, you are invincible," said the Oracle to Alexander the Great. The reverence and respect of the various city-states was reflected in offerings of temples, monuments, statues and fountains.

Mythology tells us that the first oracles established in this area before the Mycenaean era were dedicated to the Mother Earth – Geia – and Poseidon. Geia's son, the serpent Python, resided in a cave and communicated through a priestess. Apollo arrived from Crete in the form of a dolphin, hence the name Delphi, slew Python and established his cult.

The Oracle's fortunes rose and fell with those of its benefactor states. Philip of Macedon used political intrigues initiated here to subject the southern Greek states after the Battle of Charoneia in 338BC. The Romans had no belief in the Oracles: Sulla plundered the site and Nero made off with over 500 bronze statues. The advent of Christianity made the Oracle defunct.

The sanctuary site was lost until late in the 17th century and intermittently explored until the late 19th century when the French School of Archaeology, competing against the Germans and Americans, leased the land, displaced the villagers living in the ruins and began serious excavations and reconstruction. A 2km-long temporary railway was built to haul away the enormous quantities of earth and debris with locomotives and rolling stock purchased from the recently completed Corinth Canal project. Excavations continued in the late 1930s and early in the 1990s.

What to see

Visitors to the site should start off at the **archaeological museum** (open Mon: 11.00–17.30, Tues–Fri: 07.30–18.30, Sat–Sun: 08.30–15.00; admission 1,200, 900, 600Dr; tel: 0265 82 312, fax: 0265 82 966) before visiting the site (open Mon–Fri: 07.30–18.30, Sat–Sun: 08.30–1500; admission 1,200, 900, 600Dr; tel/fax same as above).

The museum contains many life-size bronze statues like the Charioteer and the Twins of Argos, as well as an ancient copy of the Omphalos. According to legend, Zeus released two eagles at the outer limits of the universe. Their converging flights determined the exact location of the earth's centre – a point marked and symbolised by the sacred stone known as the Omphalos. The site is near the museum east of the tourist village. Not to be missed on the three-part site divided by the Arhova road are first: the various offerings and treasuries from the city-states of Thebes, Sikyonia and the Arcadians among others, leading up the Sacred Way to the **Sanctuary of Geia** and the Doric **Temple of Apollo**, where the Oracle is believed to have presided. Behind the Temple is the 4th century BC 5,000-capacity **theatre** and, further up the slope (rarely visited by tourists because of its height), the 6,500-capacity **stadium** said to be the best preserved in Greece. Beyond the stadium, a path leads up the slope to give a grand view of the entire sanctuary site. The **Castalian Fountain** at the spring (east on the Arhova road, on the left around a sharp curve) where pilgrims to the Oracle cleansed themselves shouldn't be missed; neither should the **Marmaria** (across the road from the spring) containing the Sanctuary of Athena and the graceful circular Tholos rotunda.

Where to stay
The village of Delphi is completely oriented to serve visitors to the sanctuary. The municipal tourist office (open: Mon–Fri: 08.30–14.30; tel: 0265 82 900, at Paulou & Fredrikis 12, 33054 Delphi) is friendly and helpful for all related services. There are three campsites, the Apollo (0265 82 762) and the Delphi (0265 82 363) open all year round, and the Chrysso (0265 82 050) open during the tourist season; lodgings include the YHA Hostel (0265 82 268), the Hotel Athena (0265 33 054), the Hotel Parnassos (0265 82 321) and the upscale Hotel Vouzas (0265 82 232).

Suggested itinerary
An excellent itinerary that encompasses a train trip from Athens to Levadia, a bus through Delphi to Nafpaktos then a ferry to Rio and a train back to Athens can be comfortably done in three to four days. This allows short visits to Levadia, Delphi, Nafpaktos and possibly Corinth during the summer when more intercity buses operate.

LEVADIA TO CHERONIA

The railway beyond Levadia begins the ascent up the eastern tentacles of Mount Parnassos leading into the fertile Plain of Thessaly. This area, as far as Larissa, is studded with historically significant sites and some of the most dramatic railway lines in Greece. This segment of railway was built between 1902 and 1909 by the French Société Batignolles de Paris. The construction of this line over the formidable obstacles of Mounts Iti and Othrys, and across ill-drained plains, was hailed as one of the most notable pieces of railway engineering in Europe.

Cheronia

This station (local trains only) is the first after Levadia at the entrance to the defile of Kerata. Formerly known as Kapraina, the village recently adopted the ancient name. It was on a battlefield here (left of the railway) that Philip of Macedon at the head of a 50,000-man army (30,000 infantry and 20,000 cavalry commanded by his son Alexander) soundly defeated an army led by the orator Demosthenes and composed of Athenians and Thebans. After initial advantages gained by the Athenians, the Macedonian cavalry turned the Athenian flank, overwhelmed the Theban Sacred Band who fought to the last man, and were victorious.

This decisive Macedonian victory (338BC) opened Philip's way to the south and led directly to Macedonian hegemony over all Greeks.

The Macedonian dead were buried in a great Tumulus (left of the railway), the Athenian corpses were burned with the ashes sent to Athens, and the Theban members of the Sacred Band were buried in a common tomb – the Polyandiron – guarded by a tall blue-grey Boeotian marble lion seated on its haunches. The eight-metre-high statue was found in 1818, almost completely buried. Greek military forces led by the self-serving Odysseus Androutsos during the War of Independence smashed the statue in the mistaken belief that it contained treasure; and the Greek Archaeological Society restored it and replaced it on its plinth in 1902–04. This lion is not visible from the railway An archaeological museum (tel: 0261 95 270; temporarily closed for renovation) near the tomb contains artefacts from both tombs and Mycenaean remains from Orchomenos, including a fragment of fresco from the palace.

CHERONIA TO BRALLOS

Beyond Cheronia are three small stations – Davlia, Parorion and Kifissos – serving their respective villages hidden in the low hills on the left. From the Davlia station it is possible to backtrack to Agios Vlasios, a name referring to St Blaise, above which (on the left) stand walls and ruins of the ancient city of Panopeos, the reputed home of Epeios, the builder of the Trojan Horse. The village of Davlia is 7.7km from the station and from here the ruins of ancient Daulis can be visited. The railway curves up and over the Pass of Belessi, known in ancient times as the Pass of Parapotami. Philip came through this pass on his way to Cheronia. Before the Macedonian era, this was the traditional northern boundary of Greek territory.

On the left in front of the train is the long Kalidromon mountain range. The next stop, **Tithorea**, should be of interest to those wishing to hike on **Mount Parnassos**.

Parnassos has two main peaks: a higher summit called Lyakoura ("Wolf Mountain"; 2,475m) and the slightly lower Gerontovrachos ("Old Man's

Rock"; 2,435m). For the Greeks, Parnassos was sacred to Dionysos. Latin poets, including Ovid, considered it the home of Apollo and the Muses. Though no longer a mountain wilderness, with ski resorts at Fterolakkas near Kalivia accessible from Arkhova, it still offers stunning views and lovely flora and fauna. The Hellenic Alpine Club has a 28-bed refuge on the mountain at Katafiyion Sarantari at 1,890 metres.

From the Tithorea station, hikers need to go to Ano Tithoria about 4km away to the left. This small village (population 1,005), anciently called Valitsa, still has ruins of the massive (3m thick) walls near the central platia. A cave above the town was the lair of the bandit captain Odysseus Androutsos during the War of Independence. The trail, which should take about seven hours for the ascent and six for the descent via Delphi, begins behind several park benches overlooking the deep Valitsa ravine southeast of the village. Though water is available at the Tsares spring (four hours into the hike) it is the only major source on the route. Hikers are advised to take maps or a good guide book, wear solid footwear and bring plenty of water.

Hikers can cross Lyakoura to Delphi along stretches of an ancient path called the "Kaki Skala" or evil staircase. This trip will take about 16 hours or two full days of walking. On the downhill slope is the Corycian cave sacred to Pan and the nymphs in ancient times. Rites were held here in November when Dionysos ruled, and ancient inscriptions can be seen inside the long cave. It is better to not enter without artificial light as the cave is a veritable labyrinth.

After Tithoria the rail line traverses a defile between Parnassos and Kalidromon. The next stop is the small town of **Amfiklia** (population 3,145) but the biggest settlement in the Nome of W Lokris. The town, also called Dadi, is built on terraces like its ancient counterpart to the west. The acropolis is marked by a Frankish tower. Great vistas down to the plain around Lamia can be seen on the right. Mountain and railway photographers are advised to prepare their cameras for the increasingly grand scenery. Amfiklia is also a long stop for northbound trains because the country beyond is savagely mountainous and thus, only single track. It is doubtful that it will ever be double tracked, so it will always remain a bottleneck, with trains within the 42km Amfiklia to Lianokladi district often having to wait for track time.

The next stop in the mountainous country is **Lilea**. Here an intact citadel sits on a precipitous edge of a remote slope of Mount Parnassos. Tall classical and Frankish walls and towers stand to great heights: one particularly large tower is over 13m tall and 7.5m in circumference.

Brallos, the important road junction connecting Lamia through Amfissa with the Rion ferry to Patras, is next. The station platform is extremely short here, and those in the last coach are advised to move forward to alight or risk a steep drop to the ground. A British Military Cemetery with the graves of 95 British soldiers from the First World War is located in the nearby village of Gravia.

Brallos to Thermopylae by road

A sealed secondary road in good condition leads down to the legendary Pass of Thermopylae between the steep northern slope of Mount Kalydromiou and the sea. This narrow five kilometre long pass will long be remembered for the devotion of Leonidas and his 300 Spartans during the Persian invasions of 480BC. All but two perished against an army of 200,000 Persians led by Xerxes.

Visitors today can visit the burial mound, where the valiant Spartans held back attacks under impossible odds from their front and rear. Modern Thermopylae with its hot springs and baths has a memorial erected in 1955 to Leonidas and the Three Hundred, with stirring scenes from the battle. The Asclepios Hotel (0235 93 303) is open from June to October.

BRALLOS TO LIANOKLADI

The railway now starts its slow, arduous climb clinging to the mountain wall over the **Pass of Fournataki,** the col connecting Mount Iti on the west (left) and Mount Kalidromon. Stunning views are to be had from the right side of the train. The tiny station of Eleftherochori is the starting point for short walks up to the mountain refuge on Mount Kalidromon. (Lianokladon further north is the starting point for organised walks up Mount Iti; the Hellenic Alpine Club in Lamia will provide details and keys. See the section on Lamia below.)

The tiny unmanned shelters at Asopos, Trachis and Arpini are request stops for locals and visitors in the middle of the sinuous passage through this col. The rail line crosses over long viaducts high over mountain rivers, the Papadias and the Tosopou, winding their way to the sea. These are separated by two long tunnels, between which a long iron viaduct crosses the Asopos River. Further ahead, another long photogenic viaduct crosses the Gorgopotamas River. This was the viaduct blown up in November 1942, by a combined force of British commandos parachuted in, and rebel Greek guerrilla bands operating in the area.

The success of the Gorgopotomas operation – known officially as the Harling Mission – was due as much to luck as to good planning. Nazi armies had conquered most of Continental Europe, were threatening Moscow, and were on the move against hard-pressed British forces in North Africa. The British High Command in Cairo felt that if the Greek railways were cut for six months, the Nazis would have to fly their supplies to North Africa and would thus be vulnerable to effective allied air attack. Though Crete was in Nazi hands, the Cretan Sea between the island and North Africa was not, and the air belonged to Allied air forces.

The plan was to air drop teams of highly trained soldiers into the area, who would link up with Greek resistance fighters and destroy the three bridges. The plan depended on reasonable autumn weather, and the goodwill of the various Greek resistance groups on the ground. Neither was assured.

Though ideological antipathies had not created the total schism that would eventually result in a tragic and murderous civil war, relations between left and right were shaky. Three squads of four men commanded by CM Woodhouse were to parachute out of three bombers on the full-moon night of 28 September 1942. Only two did so, with the other squads being forced back Cairo, returning to Greece a month later. The three British squads linked up when the late arrivals were met on the ground by partisans of the leftist EAM-ELAS band led by Aris Velouchiotis, who arranged a meeting with an EDES unit led by Napoleon Zervas. These two leaders would square off in vicious fighting during the Civil War.

In late November, with tensions between the two Greek bands palpable but under control, a large force of nearly 160 men and approximately 20 heavily loaded mules set out on their mission, clambering over Mount Iti in steady drizzling rain and making camp in the snow. The force was divided into seven groups whose missions were to attack both ends of the bridge, neutralise the guards, and prevent the arrival of reinforcements from Lamia while explosives experts dynamited the metal railway supports. On the night of 25 November 1942, the single-track bridge was attacked and destroyed. Nazi supply lines were disrupted and the Gorgopotomas bridge was out of commission for six months. This was the first successful allied action in Continental Greece and the first and only time rival Greek resistance groups worked together in a common cause.

The Gorgopotomas bridge was again blown up by retreating Nazis in 1944, only to be rebuilt by US Army Engineers in 1948. Hikers interested in this campaign can follow the still-existing trails and visit the cave near the village of Stromni on Mount Giona (2,510m) which became the Harling Mission's permanent base and headquarters. A commemorative plaque was placed on this cave on the 50th anniversary of the attack in 1992. The area where the rebels operated and the attack was planned is called the Agrafa – "the Unwritten Places" (see the Thessaly section in *Chapter Eleven*).

Shortly after passing over the Gorgopotamos, the rail line reaches the Lianokladi junction station for Lamia and Stylis. Mainline trains halt here for several minutes before continuing – almost as if they are catching their breath after the long ascent from Brallos.

The interesting 23km rail line east to Lamia and Stylis reopened for rail passenger service in 1991. It is still served by local trains (but with two daily second-class-only local trains from and to Athens); regular buses for Lamia meet all trains. Also, the main road west through Ipati for Karpenissa passes by the station. Mount Giona trailheads begin in Ipata. Hikers planning on walking on Mount Giona should leave the main-line train here. Ipata-bound buses can be found on exiting the OSE station (right out of the station door to the crossing guard's booth – this is an official KTEL bus stop).

Lianokladi to Lamia and Stylis

The Stylis line winds 6km along a hillside to Lamia providing excellent views of Mount Iti, and at one point a glimpse of the Gorgopotomas viaduct (right).

Lamia

Though not an important tourist destination Lamia (population 44,000) is a lively market town and the chief town of the Nome of Fthiotis. It is sited below two wooded hills, with a Catalan castle (1319–93) dominating one of them with great views across the Plain of Lamia. The recently completed (1994) and well-regarded **archaeological museum** (open: Tues–Sun, 08.30–15.00; admission free; tel: 0231 29 992) is in the castle; it contains a wide assortment of prehistoric finds from Neolithic to Mycenaean times as well as pottery, sculpture and small finds of the Classical, Hellenistic and Macedonian periods.

Historically Lamia is remembered for the Lamian War (323–322BC) during which the Athenians tried to free themselves from Macedonian rule. A stronghold in the Middle Ages, it was called Gipton by the Franks and El Cito by the Catalans, hence the Turkish name Zitouni.

The town is based around three main squares: Platia Laou, Platia Eleftherias and Platia Parhou. The fountain in the shaded Platia Laou gushes with water from the Gorgopotamos, while the city and Nome administration buildings, the cathedral and several hotels are grouped around the central Platia Eleftherias. Platia Laou is the main shopping area with banks and a lively Saturday market.

The Hellenic Alpine Club in Lamia (Ipsilandou 20; 0231 26 786) should be on any trekker's list of important addresses: it provides information and the keys to high mountain refuges on the local peaks.

Accommodation is varied and plentiful: two budget places on Platia Laou are the Emborikon (0231 22 654) and the Neon Astron (0231 26 245); more upscale are the Appollonion (0231 22 669, fax: 44 993) and the Samaras (0231 28 971, fax: 42 704).

Beyond Lamia on the rail line are the village stops of Roditsa and Megali Vrissi (site of a prehistoric mound that may be Homeric), before reaching the coast at the fishing and beach village of Ag. Marina. The end of the rail line is at Stylis, the port of Lamia and once one of the Aegean's major ports.

Stylis

Stylis (population 5,000) may be the site of the ancient Thessalian Phaleron. Stylis' past glory is represented by the opera house. It is where Maria Callas' grandfather outsang a visiting Italian star and started the dynasty. Seasonal hydrofoils serve the Sporades from here. Schedules and tickets are available from Zontanos Bros. (Falarou 2; 0238 22 820). **Accommodation** includes Camping Parras (0238 22 221) and the Skyland Hotel (0238 22 798). The north/south toll motorway passes through here to Volos, but it avoids the beaches and the small port of Glifa, the ancient city of Androna, which has car-ferry service to Agiokambos on Evia.

Two daily trains link Stylis, through Lianokladi, with Athens in 3 hours and 40 minutes. The re-opening of this line in the early 1990s has been another great success. The attractive Stylis stone station merits a good look.

The region beyond Stylis is known as Magnesia, and has attractive beaches fronting a large fertile agricultural area that is the beginning of the Thessalian Plain. In antiquity this area was marshy and people stayed well away from it.

From Lianokladi to Ipatis, Karpenissa and Agrinion by bus

The main reason for undertaking a major bus trip in this direction is to access the **Agrafa Mountains** through Ipatis and Karpenissa.

From the Lianokladi rail station the road gradually rises through the broad green Sperkeios Valley with the huge bulks of Mount Iti (2,152m), Mount Giona and Vardoussia looming off to the left.

Ipatis, attractively situated on the north slope of Mount Iti, is the ancient city of Hypata or Neo-Patras of the Franks and Catalans (whose castle site provides excellent views). It served as the capital of the Athenians, rebelling against Macedonia during the Lamian War, and the battlefield where John Doukas defeated the Byzantine Michael VII Palaiologos in 1275. The town was taken by the Turks in 1318 and became the seat of a pasha (regional governor).

The verdant, heavily forested Mount Iti is the focal point for the **Iti National Park**, established in 1966. This is the mythical site where Hercules built his own funeral pyre and died with his spirit ascending to Mount Olympus. Trails up the mountain to the Trapeza Refuge (at 1850m) begin from Ipatis. Check with the Lamia branch of the Hellenic Alpine Club for space availability. Other accommodation also exists at Ipatis: the Hotels Panhellinion (0231 59 640) and Panorama (0231 59 222).

Karpenissa (population 5,500) is the chief and only sizeable place in the Nome of Evritania: by population the smallest Nome in mainland Greece. The setting is magnificent, tucked in at the base of the Timfritos peaks and at the head of the small, mountain-ringed Karpenissiotis valley. The town itself suffered greatly during World War II and the Civil War when it was razed by Nazis and strafed by the US Air Force.

Trekking, lake and canoe kayaking, white-water rafting, mountaineering, canyoning and all winter ski sports are available from here. Check with the local Alpine club office (0237 23 051) or Trekking Hellas (0237 25 940) for details. Some attractive mountain villages, such as Korishades, Mikro Horio and Megali Horio, are near here and worth exploring. **Accommodation** is plentiful and should pose little problem except on weekends and during the peak season months of July–August. Try the Hotel Panhellion (0237 22 330), Galini (0237 22 914), Elvetia (0237 22 465), Anessis (0237 22 840) or the upper scale Mount Blanc (0237 22 322).

A high paved road from here descends to the pleasant and prospering city of **Agrinion**, the city of Messalongi on the Corinthian Gulf and the Ionian Sea coast.

LIANOKLADI TO THESSALONIKI

Continuing north along the railway line from Lianokladi is more dramatic mountain scenery. The 126km stretch from Lianokladi to Larissa takes the railway out of the mountains and into the large Plain of Thessaly. Leaving the Lianokladi station there are good views to the west (left) up the Sperkeios Valley. From here, the rail line climbs steeply for nearly 36km up Mount Othrys. It passes the small stations of Lygaria, Stryfaka, Karia, Kallipefki and Aggie, winding through a succession of bridges and 27 short tunnels. The railway reaches the summit (585m) to the east (right) of Mount Moklouka (892m), then descends sharply, crossing the west end of the drained Lake Xynias. There are good views on both sides, as bridges and tunnels come into view high in the distance and are then reached several minutes later.

Beyond Aggie, the rail line closely follows the river Sofaditikos through a gap in the hills. The wide broad Plain of Thessaly suddenly appears far below (left) for the first time just beyond Therme. The rail line follows the ridge line past the station of Kypheria, with the town now below in the plain. Beyond Thavmakos the castle of Domokos can be seen (left).

Domokos (population 1,939) is the first large village in the 66km since Lianokladi. It is rather picturesquely situated on a rocky hill (520m) with lengths of classical walls near the centre of the village. Domokos acquired its name, which means astonishment in ancient Greek, because of the view of the vast plain of Thessaly which suddenly becomes visible to travellers climbing over rugged hills into the village.

Train speeds noticeably increase on the flat plain surface, past the crossroads junction of **Neo Monastiri**: trains positively race into the rail junction of Paleofarsalo. For the immediate future, rail travellers must change here to the metre gauge Thessaly Railway for Karditsa, Trikkala and Kalambaka to the west, or Velestino and Volos to the east. The large new rail station under construction south (left) of the present facility is evidence of the large-scale infrastructure work continuing at a steady pace to convert the 80km Paleofarsalo–Kalambaka rail segment to standard gauge. Details of Thessaly and the Thessaly Railway will be discussed in the following chapter.

From Paleofarsalo to Larissa (46km), trains race along on a new high-speed double-track alignment that is to the east of the old main-line track. The trains speed past cars on the parallel highway. High-tension electric power lines march across the wheat field towards the Mount Olympus chain, vaguely visible in front of the train on the left.

Entrance to **Larissa**, the largest city in the plain of Thessaly, is through the rail yards (right) with the bulk of the low-rise city visible to the left. Larissa is also a junction station with a 61km standard gauge branch east to Volos leaving the main line just north of the busy, though plain, 1960s passenger station. Two daily IC trains from Athens and one IC train from Thessaloniki share this branch line with a procession of 14 daily locals to Volos. This route segment will be discussed in the following Thessaly Railway Chapter.

Northbound from Larissa, the rail line passes a series of sugar refineries, then leaves Larissa rapidly behind and heads directly for the escarpment of the **Mount Olympus** range. The great volcanic (extinct) cone of **Mount Ossa** (1,978m – also known as Kissavos), isolated as it is, is visible on the right beyond a series of stony foothills.

In their war with the Gods, Giants are reputed to have piled the mountainous Pelion Peninsula (see Volos) on Ossa to reach the heights of Olympus. The western slopes of Ossa provided marble for the buildings of ancient Rome. Hiking expeditions from the town of Ajia (accessible from Larissa by bus) are available to the summit of Ossa. From Ossa there are far-reaching views to Mount Athos and, in extremely fine weather, the Asia Minor coast of Turkey.

The 88km, fast-running double-track main line from Domokos ends at the village of Evangelismos (right) near the entrance to the legendary Vale of Tembi. Near here is the small textile-producing town of Ambelaki located (at 600m) on Mount Kissavos in the foothills of Mount Ossa. The rail line crosses over the Pinios River (left) on a 120m bridge.

Beyond Evangelismos is the deep green **Vale of Tembi**, cut by the passage of Thessaly's principal river, the fast-running Pinios, on its winding course from the Pindos to the Aegean Sea between Mounts Olympus and Ossa. Called Lykostoma (Wolf's Mouth) during the Middle Ages, this glen, 10km long and 50m wide, is the result of a seismic convulsion, which according to myth was caused by a thunderbolt from Poseidon. It allowed the Larissa lake to drain, thus creating the Thessalian Plain. In antiquity it was sacred to Apollo who, after killing the Python at Delphi, came here to cleanse himself. It is one of the easiest land approaches from Macedonia to the south. Both Xerxes and Philip of Macedon used it to move their armies towards southern Greece.

The railway now shares the narrow Vale with the motorway, but a new rail tunnel, currently under construction, will pass under it. The future of this picturesque rail segment through the Tembi, as Greeks refer to it, is in doubt. It could revert to a nature trail or be used for steam train excursions. Fragrant odours of laurel and thyme invade the train; canoeing and hiking possibilities are recommended here; and it is a perfect spot for railway photographers.

Four kilometres past Evangelismos, already deep into the Tembi, is the small station of the same name. The fast-running Pinios rushes past. This is the station for the previously mentioned village of Ambelaki.

Already known for its cottons and silks in the 1600s, **Ambelaki**, meaning little vineyard, acquired during the 18th-century Turkish era a great deal of political autonomy and economic prosperity. Democratic elections, free assemblies and extensive textile exports were supported by branch offices as far away as London. In 1780, it became the centre of a "joint partnership" of spinners and dyers reputed to be the world's first industrial co-operative. The noble experiment ended in the early 19th century when Ali Pasha, from Ioannina, destroyed the town in 1811 and the Viennese bank holding Ambelaki's wealth collapsed a decade later. Over 36 grand mansions still stand from the glorious era, with those of Georges Schwartz (open Tues–Sun; 09.30–15.30; free), the co-operative's last president, and his brother Dimitrios, of particular interest. Their rococo painted interiors have been meticulously restored. (*Schwartz*, by the way, is the Germanic translation of *mavros*: "black" in English.)

Though little wine is made from Ambelaki's vineyards, the nearby village of Demetra is home to one of the dynamic young vintners of northern Greece. Asterios Lellis bottles fine red and white wines. His new winery can be visited by appointment (tel/fax: 041 50 32 471; address: PO Box 1674, 41002 Larissa).

The village of Ambelaki is reached by walking up a signposted cobbled path (one hour) from the Tembi rail station (or by bus from Larissa, then a walk down to Tembi). It has become somewhat of a resort: rooms available at the Ennea Mousses Inn (0495 93 405).

Beyond Tembi station are the **Spring of Venus** and the ruins of the **Kastro Tis Oraias** (the Castle of the Beautiful Maiden) on the right, one of four Frankish defensive forts found in the Tembi. The rail line passes under a 700m gallery, to arrive at the stop of Agia Pareskevi. A graceful pedestrian-only suspension bridge crosses the river to a chapel and grotto. First glimpses of the waters of the Thermaic Gulf are seen on the right in front of the train.

The Pinios curves to the right and is lost among fish hatcheries as the rail line heads straight for the noted wine town of **Rapsani** in the northern Ossa foothills east of Mount Olympus. A wine-making co-operative and the town are visible on the left: there are vineyards throughout the area. A full red wine that needs some ageing, from a selection of local grape varieties, is the speciality of this region. Warm sea breezes and cold wet mountain winds temper grape production, and the idea of quality varying with vintage years is more important here than in more southerly sunny Greek regions. The co-operative (open Mon–Fri: 09.00–14.00) is available for tastings and visits.

The Hellenic State Railway line ends just beyond Rapsani near the small stone Papapouli station. Further north were the railway lines of the Ottoman-sponsored railways. The two railway systems were not to be connected for over 30 years – until Macedonia passed into Greek control in 1916.

The massive **Crusader fort** (built 1204-1222) above Platamon (left) marks the beginning of Macedonia. Sights and possibilities on this route will be detailed in the following Macedonia section (*Chapter Twelve*), but are outlined here.

The **Platamon** OSE station is in the midst of inns and pensions just above a long sandy beach (right). A succession of beach resorts and campsites is available north of the station while unspoilt beaches can be found to the south. Both Platamon and the next village **Skotina** (also with a station) have a selection of year-round and seasonal accommodations. Try the Maxim (0352 41 305); and the Artemis (0352 41 406) in Platamon or the Orfeas (0352 91 344, fax: 91 433) in Skotina.

The next two stops, Leptokarya and Plaka, are notable because the railway once again enters a new section of double track where speeds pick up noticeably to Katerini 48km away. The large stone Leptokarya station is being rebuilt. Next to it is a towering old chestnut tree with branches so large they easily dominate the station area. The sea is a short, pleasant walk from the station. The rail line itself is never far from the waters of the Thermaic Gulf, although the new alignment is about 100m above the old.

Rising abruptly on the left are a series of high, normally snow-capped, mountains. This succession of rugged heavily forested mountain peaks leading back through the Mavrolongos Gorge is the legendary Mount Olympus range. Its highest peak, Mount Mytikas at 2,917m, is the second highest peak in the Balkans between Austria and Turkey.

Litochoro and **Dion** are the next two stops. Litochoro is the recommended stop for treks up Mount Olympus. It is served as a request stop by the following express trains: 500/501, 602, 602/507, 502/503, 604/605. Litochoro is better-treated in the section on travel from Thessaloniki. But, a word of advice to those in a hurry and wanting to use the overnight trains to save time. A sleeping place should be used on the overnight train if an early start is being considered. The Litochoro station is at sea level and the climb to the 2,917m summit, though not requiring sherpas and Himalayan type organisation, is strenuous. Sitting in a straight-backed seat all night then charging up a mountain is not conducive to enjoying the experience or appreciating the wondrous views.

Dion, in the Olympus foothills, was the Macedonians' sacred city. It is only served by local trains. After the request stop of Mavronero, the rail line crosses the river of the same name and enters the city of **Katerini** (population 43,000). Katerini is a more convenient stop for Dion as all trains stop here: IC, express and locals. The station café is particularly lively.

From Katerini, the rail line continues on a fast, flat course curving slightly to the east around marshes and salt flats. This area has become a centre for aquaculture and further north continues to provide the salt that was one of the pillars of ancient Macedonia's wealth. The rail line crosses the Aliakmon River, Greece's longest, on a 450m low steel girder bridge. The river is close to its mouth here.

The important rail junction station of **Platy** is next. This is also where the Hellenic State Railway joined the Ottoman *Chemin de Fer Oriental* after Macedonia became part of modern Greece in 1916. Passengers change here for stations to the west including Veria, Edessa, Amindeo, Florina and Kozani.

Connecting passengers to the west should be aware that Platy is an extremely small station with few services. If a connection is not timely and a wait of several hours is necessary (highly unlikely), then it is recommended that they continue 37km to Thessaloniki. Or, if travel is to the Florina branch but only a Kozani train is arriving (or vice-versa), then board that train and change elsewhere. Both Florina and Kozani trains use the same line for 124km before branching off.

Beyond Platy, the rail line continues along the flat marshy plain on a new fast alignment into the important **Thessaloniki** terminal. If travel is for points beyond Thessaloniki, passengers should proceed with care because Thessaloniki's stub-end terminal is a large multi-platform edifice that bears more resemblance to Central European main-line stations than to the normal one-platform, two-track station that is the rule in Greece.

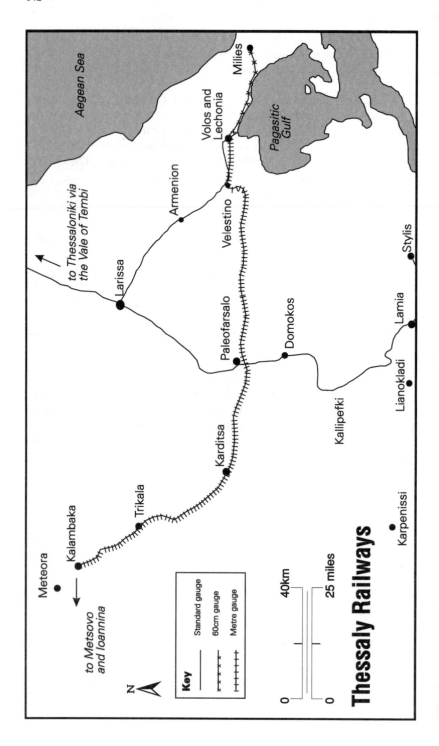

Thessaly Railways

Aegean Sea

Pagasitic Gulf

to Thessaloniki via the Vale of Tembi

to Metsovo and Ioannina

Meteora

Kalambaka

Trikala

Karditsa

Larissa

Armenion

Velestino

Volos and Lechonia

Milies

Paleofarsalo

Domokos

Kallipefki

Stylis

Lamia

Lianokladi

Karpenissi

N

Key

Standard gauge

60cm gauge

Metre gauge

40km

0

25 miles

0

Chapter Eleven

The Thessaly Railway: Volos, Kalambaka, Pelion

INTRODUCTION

This unusual 251km metre gauge railway features a meandering 164km main line from the seaport city of Volos on the Pagasitic Gulf west through the heart of the Thessalian Plain to the foothills of the Mountains of Epirus in Kalambaka – where exotic Byzantine monasteries nestle on the pinnacles of Meteora. The railway also includes an exciting 26km long, 60cm gauge line from Volos east to Milies in the mountainous Pelion Peninsula. The popular Pelion branch was abruptly closed in 1971; but segments of it were reopened to much acclaim in 1996. It is the only regularly operating steam-powered railway in Greece today. If the 61km line (converted to standard gauge in 1960) from Larissa to Volos is added to the network, the Volos station joins France's La Tour de Carol and Austria's Jenbach in the small select club of European railway stations still served by tracks of three different gauges.

As well as linking the sea with the mountains and providing transport for the produce of the Thessalian Plain, this line permits access through Karditsa into the wild high country of central Greece known as the Agrafa, and through Kalambaka to the mountainous Pindos area. These are lightly populated areas, where deep snows and long winters are the rule. As such they offer excellent adventure travel possibilities including hiking, rock climbing, canoeing and white-water rafting. The standard-gauge rail line to Larissa links Volos directly with the major metropolises of Athens and Thessaloniki.

There are four daily through Volos–Kalambaka–Volos services on the metre gauge line and these pass through Paleofarsalo where they connect to north/south main-line trains. Six additional trains serve the Paleofarsalo–Kalambaka segment. The line uses sets of rail diesel cars. There are no food and beverage services on any of these trains. The rebuilding of the Paleofarsalo–Kalambaka segment into a standard gauge railway should be completed by sometime in early 1998, by which time Volos will be linked to Kalambaka through Larissa using the standard gauge line throughout.

Given the extremely fast track between Larissa and Paleofarsalo and the new fast track between Paleofarsalo and Kalambaka, travel time on the new route should be considerably faster than at present. Kalambaka will also offer direct through service to Athens and Thessaloniki. The future of the 63km metre gauge line from Velestino (west of Volos) to Paleofarsalo is in doubt.

VOLOS

Volos (population 102,000) is considered by some to be best avoided because it is Greece's fastest growing industrial centre but that opinion is not entirely shared. Many Athenians find Volos attractive, with its lively seafront area, the Argonafton, its access to fine beaches along the Pagasitic Gulf, its vibrant villages in the high Pelion Mountains, its fast hydrofoils to the islands of the Sporades and its long historical past.

The two-storey Volos railway station with its distinctive roof and plentiful service to all Greek points is a highlight of Greek rail travel. Volos also has something of a reputation for being a rail travel nirvana with its three gauges, (often all on the same right-of-way with four rails paralleling each other) and its extensive street and seaside operations. OSE personnel at Volos have recently converted the loft area below the station's gingerbread-style roof into a museum to house artefacts from the area's rich railway past. The museum can be visited by contacting the office of OSE regional Chief Engineer Ioannis Antonidis (tel: 0421 23 424, Mon–Fri: 08.30–15.00). It is not well known that cars of the Greek royal train, in excellent condition, are stored in Volos, and can be visited with some persuasion of local officials. Local rail aficionados have formed an association to preserve and promote rail passenger service in Volos. They can be reached by contacting Mrs Melitsa Karathanos (Iasonas Street 118, 38221 Volos).

History

Historically, Volos is the site of ancient Iolkos, home to Jason and the Argonauts, the famous travellers who set off in search of the Golden Fleece. A bronze statue of the Argo is on display in the Argonafton area along the seafront. Prehistoric vestiges from Mycenaean times, evidence of Helladic and medieval settlements and ruins of the Ottoman fortifications are dispersed throughout the city. Archaeologically, the most important part of Volos is between the railway station and the football stadium, an area known as Palia. Here a large 9m tall mound contains the remains of a classical temple that could be related to ancient Iolkos.

What to see

The seven-room **Archaeological Museum** on the other side of the city centre from the railway station is well respected and worth visiting (1

Athanaski St; open Tues–Sun. 08.30–15.00; admission 500, 400, 300Dr; tel: 0421 25 285). The upper city, **Ano Volos**, is the picturesque medieval town with many old houses climbing the steep (793m) hillside. One such house has frescos (1912) painted by Theophilos (1873-1934), the renowned naïve painter from Lesbos who lived and worked in Volos. A small museum (open Tues–Sun 08.00–15.00; admission free; tel: 0421 49 109) relating to his Volos period can be visited in Ano Volos.

A fine summer outdoor cinema, the Exoraistiki, is at one corner of Platia Giorgiou near the archaeological museum and the major café-laden seafront park where young people gather for coffee and pizza after dark. This area was part of the old Volos port area, where tracks of the three railways converged to exchange goods bound for ships in the harbour. Rail enthusiasts should note the abundance of railway tracks (with the hand levers for the manually operated switch points still in place) in the Dimitriados Street side of the Platia Yiorgou. Buried in the dirt but still visible are a series of tracks, all with four parallel rails: double the usual number.

Not surprisingly, the port is the major attraction of Volos: much of Thessaly's bounty passes through the Volos docks. In the mid 20th century it rivalled Piraeus and was destined to be Greece's pre-eminent port until severely damaged by a succession of earthquakes in 1954 and 1955. The recent start of a regular road and rail ferry service from Europe to the Near East through Syria has revived the port, and the passenger port area has become a lively centre of night-life, as well as providing regular passenger service to the Sporades, Limnos and Thassos. Note the large-scale oil paintings depicting the tiny train to Pelion in the café on the Argonafton.

Where to stay

Accommodation should not be a problem, with many hotels available throughout the city centre: the Avra (Solonou 3; 0421 25 370) and the Kypseli (Agios Nikolaos 1; 0421 24 420) are older but clean; upscale properties include the Hotel Aegli (Argonafton 24; tel: 0421 24471, fax: 33006) and the Park (Dimitriados & Deligiorgiou 2; 0421 36 511, fax: 28 645).

Further afield

From a traveller's perspective Volos is extremely important with its regular ferry and hydrofoil service as well as its immediate access to the nearby Pelion Peninsula. The EOT office (tel: 0421 23 500, 36 233, 37 417, fax: 24 750) on the central Riga Ferraiou Square between the railway station and the city centre is very helpful, as are the the tourist police (tel: 0421 27 094).

It has three distinct railways: the 60cm Pelion line, the metre gauge ex-Thessaly Railways to Kalambaka and the standard gauge line to Larissa.

THE LARISSA LINE

The Larissa Line, a 60km standard gauge rail line, is served by all the IC trains to Volos and the regular 14 daily diesel rail car shuttles. This section will look at the Larissa line from Larissa to Volos as that is the point from which most rail travellers begin their trips to Volos.

Larissa

Larissa (population 120,000) is by far the largest city in central Thessaly. It is an important road and rail junction, as well as being the seat of government and religious administrations. It is a much-maligned city and difficult to avoid for travellers from every direction.

History

Recent excavations have unveiled traces of pre-Hellenic settlements. It is known that Accilleios, Bishop and patron saint of Larissa, was present at the religious Council of Nicea (325); otherwise traces of Larissa's ancient past are few and difficult to place in context. The 3rd century BC Greek theatre, a 2nd century AD Roman theatre, Byzantine castle and small mosque with minaret are the major destinations for sightseers. The single room Archaeological Museum (31 August Street 2; open Tues–Sun: 08.30–15.00; admission free; tel: 041 288 515) contains Thessalian finds from the Larissa district and is worth visiting.

What to see

At the city's centre is the lively, spacious Platia Sapka. Shaded by spreading lime and orange trees, the majority of the city's cafés, patisseries and cinemas are either on this square or nearby. The busy city has been modernising at a furious pace, but vestiges of its medieval past can be found, most evidently on Venizelos Street. The Alkazar Park, across the Pinios River from the centre and near the Kozani KTEL terminal, offers a pleasant respite for road-weary travellers, but it is on the opposite side of the city from the OSE rail terminal and the central bus station. These are both situated on the same square in the southern section of Larissa. Detailed city maps are available at the full service kiosk in the OSE rail station. There are left-luggage facilities and a small restaurant at the rail station which is in the throes of expansion to include longer platforms and an underpass between platforms.

Where to stay

Several older hotels can be found close to the rail terminal: the Diethnes (041 234 210); Neon (041 236 268) or the Pantheon (041 236 726). Newer hotels include the Astoria (041 252 941, fax: 229 097) and the Metropole (041 229 911, fax: 255 242). Other lodgings can be found by checking with EOT (041 250 919).

LARISSA TO VOLOS

Leaving Larissa for Volos, the rail line quits the main line just before it passes under the road. After the obligatory passage through a sloppy industrial zone, the line begins to offer views of Mount Ossa on the left and long vistas across the wide Plain of Thessaly on the right. It descends on a gentle gradient passing through such villages as Chalki, Melia, Kypseli, Armenio, Stefanovikio and Rizomylos, before arriving at the rail junction station of Velestino.

Armenio is the approximate site of Homer's Armenion. Huge Mycenaean walls on the promontory of Petra near Stefanovikio (left) denote the site of ancient **Kerkinion**. To the left near Rizomylos was the large (24km by 8km by 4–6m deep) marshy **Lake Karla**. It was drained in the early 1960s, when the rail line was widened to standard gauge. Several archaeological sites around its former shore attest to its former size and its role as natural drainage for rivers on the eastern edge of the Plain of Thessaly. Its waters are now used for irrigation, for various crops and experimental agriculture.

Velestino (population 3,900) occupies the site of the significant ancient town of **Pherai**. The leaders of Pherai had pretensions to rule ancient Greece in the 4th century BC. These were put down by Philip of Macedon. Ruins of the extensive ancient site have recently been uncovered. In the modern town centre is one of the two ancient fountains named Hyperaia. Velestino is also known as the birthplace of a hot-blooded poet Rigas Feraios (1757–98) who was executed in Belgrade by the Turks for fomenting a local uprising against their hegemony. In the centre of the pleasant town is a well respected Museum of Agricultural Implements (open Tues–Sun: 09.00–14.30; free).

Rail enthusiasts will note the arrival of the metre gauge tracks on the right. From here to Volos the rail line is composed of three rails to accommodate trains of the two gauges. Intrepid rail riders can organise a triangular half-day rail journey from Larissa to Velestino, and from there to Paleofarsalo for a change back to Larissa. This is also possible from Volos. Such a ride would permit a visit to an extremely rural part of Thessaly and be undertaken on trains operating over two different gauges.

From Velestino trains originating in Larissa continue to Volos over the defile of Pilav-Tepe (137m), named after a conical Hellenic tomb (right). The bulk of the mountainous Pelion Peninsula looms out of the distance (left) with Volos at its base. The rail line heads directly for the Pelion after the Lafomio stop with Volos on the Pagasitic Gulf clearly visible below (right).

Entrance to Volos is through an emerging industrial area. The Volos OSE repair and maintenance shops sprawl over a large area, and many old steam locomotives can be seen on the right as trains enter the passenger station area.

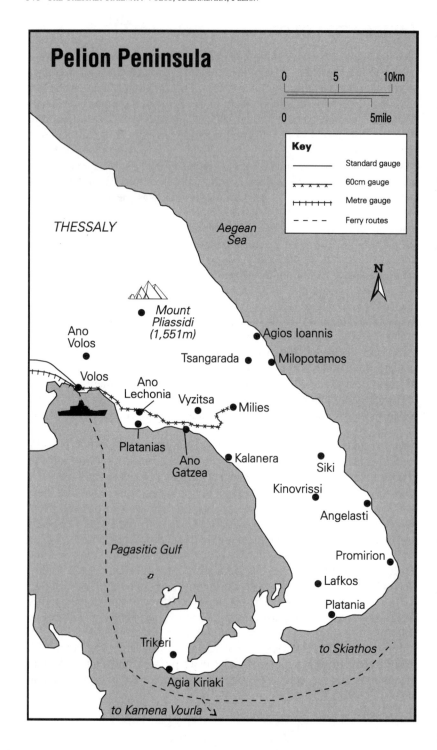

THE TINY TRAIN TO PELION

This 29km, 60cm line is arguably Greece's major historical railway jewel. And the fact that is has joyously reopened, 25 years after it was unceremoniously closed in July 1971 during the dark years of the 1960s dictatorship, is another sign of Greece's railway revival. The positive side of the line's closure is that none of the original equipment was changed before the line ceased operations. All the locomotives and rolling stock from its 1903 debut are still on the property, and have been or are being restored for service over the beautiful Pagasitic Gulf railway line.

The Pelion Peninsula is one of Greece's most enchanting places. Home to the half-man, half-horse centaurs, and a centre of Greek civilisation throughout the long night of Turkish occupation, the Pelion resisted entrance to the modern world late into the 20th century. The rail line pushed into the wild mountainous interior in the early 20th century, but paved roads following the railway line didn't appear until well into the 1970s.

In mythology, Pelion was home to Chiron, the wisest of the Centaurs, who taught Achilles the art of music and looked after Jason as a youth. The trees of Pelion supplied timber for the Argo. The ancients also looked to Pelion for its healing, medicinal herbs and plants like meadow saffron, henbane, hemlock, bittersweet and nightshade.

Pelion is a roughly talon-shaped mountainous peninsula, 60km long, curving east and south from Volos, with Mount Pliassidi (1,651m) forming its western border. Desolate it is not, with many sweet-water springs naturally irrigating the heavily forested and cultivated slopes. The peninsula can be divided into three sections: the relatively inaccessible east coast, the more docile west coast with its beach developments, and the inland area north of Volos. The sea is visible from most parts of Pelion.

The climate is cool and refreshing with summer temperatures often $10°$ degrees below those in the lower country. Rushing brooks tumble through gorges; the atmosphere is conducive to idle relaxation. A series of ancient cobbled and well-maintained footpaths make hiking or just strolling a delight, as do the profuse vegetation and fragrance of eucalyptus and jasmine. Several villages featuring half-timbered houses and large squares shaded by massive old plane trees, including the delightful Makrinitza and Vizitsa, have been declared traditional settlements. Others, like the railway terminal of Milies, are more modern but still have charm.

The tiny train from Volos remains the best way to enter this wonderland. At present, the 60cm wide, single-track rail line begins in **Ano Lechonia**, 10km from its Volos OSE rail station. The first 10km are still closed to rail traffic because the railway is in the middle of the road, requiring trains to operate in the street and often running the wrong way on two long stretches of highway. Until the issue of re-routing trackage (through downtown Volos and the village of Agria) is resolved, the rail line will begin at Ano Lechonia

(KTEL bus from Iasonas Street near the Hotel Agra).

The Pelion line was the brainchild of a Constantinople-based Greek banker named Mavrokordatos, who saw the economic potential of a railway to the peninsula as a way more easily to transport its abundant produce to market and export through Volos. Before the railway, goods and passenger transport was by donkey along the ancient *kalderimi* footpaths. It is also believed that the wealthy banker was influenced by Pelion's history and cultural contributions to Greece.

Italian civil engineer Evaristo de Kiriko, father of the noted Modernist painter Gregorio (who was in fact born in Volos), travelled the region on horseback during the early 1890s looking for the least difficult passage through the rugged terrain. The French construction firm then built the line in three phases: the first comprising Volos to Ano Lechonia, hugging the coast around difficult roadless mountains to Ano Lechonia (1892–1896); the second (1896–1903) consisting of tunnelling, bridging and laying track through the mountains above the coast from Ano Lechonia through Ano Gatzea and Ogla (for Kala Nera) to Milies; the third phase (1904) entailing running steam-powered trains up through the mountains to Milies. All the stone-arched viaducts and tunnel facades were finished by local craftsmen who realised they were helping to open their isolated enclave to the outside world. The line was supposed to continue on to Tsangarada but, due to the perennial financial difficulties that always seemed to plague railway schemes in Greece, ended at Milies.

Today many Greeks remember the "tiny train" from school outings and family visits to the villages of their parents. When the line reopened for service on 24 May 1995 (Sat–Sun; dep. 11.00 from Ano Lechonia and return at 16.00 from Milies; single/one way ticket 600Dr, return 1,000Dr), trains filled immediately (without publicity) with local residents wishing to revisit their youth, when they depended on the tiny train and rode it from their isolated villages to schools in bigger villages down the rail line.

This rail line is strongly recommended for its grand vistas down to the Pagasitic Gulf and across to the tail end of Pelion, its many attractive multi-arched stone bridges, tunnels and galleries, and the atmosphere it engenders among its passengers. Firemen are known to descend from the locomotive to gather boughs of fragrant wildflowers to distribute to passengers, while locals and foreigners strike up warm, lively conversations in the time-honoured railway tradition.

At present three vintage open-windowed central-corridor wooden coaches, all with open platforms on both ends, are hauled by a chuffing and snorting little steam locomotive that seems to have a personality all its own. Two of the three 1903 Belgian-built locomotives are completely restored: Milia and Pylion. Four original coaches, called winter carriages, are available, as well as two completely open "summer" carriages with bench seating only. OSE is investing substantial funds to rebuild the stone station buildings and rail facilities at Ano Lechonia, Gatzea and Milies to their original condition. The tracks and right-of-way structures were so well built originally that little was needed to put them back in condition. Stone masons are restoring tunnel facades and constructing a picnic area near the bubbling brook at the entrance (left) to the Milies station.

The **Ano Gatzea** station and buildings, including a late 19th century herbal pharmacy, overlooking the blue waters of the Pagasitic Gulf, are being restored. This is a required watering stop for the locomotives. Refreshments are available at the small café under the plane tree. A trail leads down from the station to the beach at Kato Gatzea where two campsites are located: the Hellas (0421 22 267) and the Marina (0421 22 277).

Rail photographers should not miss the wide five-arched curved stone bridge on the first major curve after Ano Lechonia or the Taxiarchos steel bridge just before the last major turn into Milies. The curved Taxiarchos bridge is special because the single track is laid directly on the bridge surface without an embankment. It looks like a model-railway set piece expanded to full scale. A covered picnic area is located at the south end of the Taxiarchos bridge where trails head off to the north away from the railway. Do not forget to watch railway staff push and tug to turn the tiny locomotive on the manual turntable before the equally tiny engine house at Milies.

Future plans for this line call for a daily service on the Ano Lechonia-Milies segment and, when the Volos street running segment is transferred off Dimitiradis Avenue to the port facing Argonaut Promenade, multi-daily service along the coast to Agria using purpose-built diesel locomotives which are on order. The entire 29km line will reopen to service when the road from Agria to Ano Lechonia is replaced by another one further inland.

Milies

Milies is a tiny village, founded in the 16th century, that profited from its semi-autonomy during the Turkish era to develop as an important agricultural centre packing the local olive oil, fruits, nuts and silk products down to the plain. It equally profited from the railway, as the substantial railway terminal buildings attest. The old eight-room station guesthouse has recently been restored by a local, Stathis Gouliotis (Palios Stathmos, 37010 Milies-Pylion; tel: 0423 86 425; closed only in November). This inn and restaurant are highly recommended. Stathis likes trains and is co-author of several books on the Pelion line. As such, he is a fount of knowledge and only too eager to discuss this particular railway.

During the 18th century, Greek schools founded in Milies helped to establish the intellectual and cultural climate conducive to the various independence struggles of the following century. Revolutionary patriot Andonios Gazi (1761–1828) who raised the Thessaly revolt in 1821 was born in Milies. The Milies Folk Museum (Tues–Sun; 10.00–14.00; free; tel: 0423 86 602) in the village centre offers a display of local crafts. Other accommodation in Milies is available through the affable Mihalis Pappas (0423 86 207).

Beyond Milies by road

From Milies, a cobblestone trail winds through the wooded hills west past slate-roofed houses to **Vyzitsa**, just 2km away. Rooms are available in the Kontos Mansion (0423 86 793) or the appealing Karagiannopoulos Mansion (0423 86 373), with its stained-glass windows and carved-wood ceilings. Another major trail leads, in four hours, to the large sprawling village of **Tsangarada** tucked into plane and oak forests. Four separate communities make up Tsangarada. Most activities centre around the 1,500–year-old plane tree in Platia Pareskevi. Rooms are available here at Pension Konaki (0426 49 481) and Pension Paradissos (0426 49 551). The smart Thymeli Inn in a restored two-storey stone building dating from 1857 (tel/fax: 0426 49 595) is a treat.

From Tsangarada, strollers can continue down to the east coast at **Milopotamos** and its sheltered beach, or can circle back to the picturesque so-called "Balcony of Pelion" village of **Makrynitsa**. It was founded in the 13th century by Byzantine refugees fleeing the sacking of Constantinople by renegade crusaders. It contains half a dozen notable churches and several dozen large mansions. Traditional houses are built on terraces with one floor at the rear and three in front. Some have been restored and are available for rent: the Arhondiko Repana (0421 99 548) and the Arhondiko Karamarli (0421 99 570, fax: 99 779). Makrynitsa's charm is enhanced by the lack of cars, which are banned from the centre of the village.

From Makrynitsa, **Ano Volos** is not far. A long (eight-hour return) wilderness walk is possible north from Makrynitsa to the almost forgotten, half ruined Survias Monastery. Trekkers will be rewarded with a church containing vivid 16th century Byzantine frescos.

South from Milies, it is necessary to descend to Kala Nera and proceed along the west coast road to the large country town of **Argalasti**, then either through the picturesque fishing villages-cum-resorts of **Horta** and **Milina**, or directly overland to **Platania**. Small boats or hydrofoils from Volos and the Sporadic Islands call here. Accommodation is available near the harbour at the Kyma (0423 71 263) or Platania (0423 71 250) and several other small hotels and pensions. The coast beyond the port of Milina, though equipped with an unsealed road to Trikeri and the fishing port of Agia Kiriaki, still feels remote, as if it is from another era. The fact that there are few roads, fewer beaches, and that the region was used as a place of exile for political prisoners after the 1946-49 Civil War keeps most locals away.

The delightful little railway well complements the idyllic Pelion. The only regret is that it does not play a primary role in transportation in this verdant area. It is hoped that the current revival will lead to greater interest being placed on preserving the area's delicate ecological balance.

THE KALAMBAKA LINE

This 164km metre gauge railway leads all the way back through the Plain of Thessaly to the foothills of the Pindos Mountains. It was responsible for the early 20th century agricultural development of the area and still serves the small villages and towns along its route, as well as providing travellers with an easy access to the Agrafa villages and the northern Pindos mountains. As stated above, the 80km segment from Paleofarsalo Junction to Kalambaka is being rebuilt to modern main-line standard gauge capacity. As such, it will allow for through Athens/Thessaloniki–Kalambaka service. Volos will still have main-line service through Larissa, but the nature of the line will change. This rail line, much like the Peloponnese west coast line, is characterised by its easy-going nature where human contact counts as much as the scenery.

Visionaries at OSE would like to see an extension of the new rail line from Kalambaka to the west-coast Epirot port of Igoumenitsa via high mountain Metsovo and Ioannina. Others are interested in completing the "ghost line" from Kalambaka to Kozani. This line was surveyed in the 1930s with some bridges, tunnels and even stations being built before the idea was dropped. The standardisation of this line, planned to open in 1998, will speed schedules to Kalambaka and permit long-range rail planning for onward expansion realistically to proceed.

VOLOS TO KARDITSA

After leaving Volos, this line follows the rail route of the standard gauge line to Velestino before veering sharply to the left, heading south to cross between two low passes round the east and south of Mount Khalkodonion. This area is famous for a number of ancient battles. The first in 364BC pitted Alexander of Pherai against the combined forces of Thessalians and Thebans. Alexander won and the Theban general Pelopidas was killed. The second battle in 197BC irreparably weakened the power of Macedonia. Romans led by Flamininus completely stopped Philip V of Macedon, the issue being decided by a charge by elephants. The battle at Pydna 29 years later ended Macedonian rule, establishing the Romans as rulers of Greece.

The village stop of **Aerino** is 5km to the north of the ruins of Phthiotic Thebes. The site is ringed by classical walls with 40 towers. Remains include a temple of Athena, a theatre and a stoa. Finds are on display at the Volos Archaeological Museum.

Beyond Aerino, trains trundle through the Plain of Thessaly, where much evidence of the successful use of irrigation can be seen. Stops include Chalkodonio, Rigeo, Dasolfo, Sitohoro and Farsalo. The largish town of Farsalo (population 8,000) is off in the distance (left) in the foothills of Mount Othrys. A tree-clad hill in front of the train near Farsalo, Fetihi-Djami, has been occupied since Neolithic times.

The Battle of Pharsalus (9 August 48BC), fought on the plain near where the railway line now runs at Evidrio, decided the fate of the Roman world. Pompey and Caesar battled with infantry and cavalry; the result was a decisive win by Caesar.

The rail line continues on past Enotiki, dips under the National Road and the main-line standard gauge railway, then curves off its main route to the left to allow trains to call at the Paleofarsalo station. This 63km segment could possibly be abandoned when the Paleofarsalo–Kalambaka line rebuilding is finished. Some would like to maintain it to run regular steam excursions. It is doubtful though that OSE will keep it, as it will be the only metre gauge rail segment left in Central Greece.

Departing Paleofarsalo, trains rejoin the main Thessaly Railways metre gauge line and proceed along many irrigated fields to Karditsa. Between Paleofarsalo and Trikala there are some 80 bridges across the numerous water courses, which seam the surface of the plain, the largest being those across the Pamisos, Pinios, Koumerkis and Agia Moni Rivers. In season, fresh earth odours pervade the trains and passengers can be overheard discussing the progress of the cotton, tobacco and soya crops.

Karditsa

Karditsa (population 35,000) is often described as an uninteresting town with few ancient associations. Many storks make their nests on tops of telephone poles and it has a pleasant park. General Nicolaos Plastiras (1883– 1953), a leader of the 1922 revolt, was born here. Karditsa is a market town where produce from the Plain of Thessaly meets that from the Agrafa region to the south. It allows visitors from the west bound for the wild Agrafa region to access it without going around to Karpenissa.

Accommodation in Karditsa is plentiful enough: the Afroditi (0441 55 860) and the Xenonas Kastanias (0441 94 155) being two more modern hotels. Check with the Tourist Development Enterprise of Karditsa (0441 42 449; fax: 27 824) for other places.

The Agrafa

The Agrafa means "Unwritten Places", and owes its name to the fact that it was never put on the Ottoman tax rolls during their control of the low countries. But, its reputation of being beyond control could date further back to early Christian struggles to create a theological ideology.

Though bulldozers are fast carving roads into the remote area, there are regions requiring beasts of burden or sheer foot power to access hidden villages where no more than a handful of residents – mostly summer only – maintain the traditional homesteads for their relatives who have left the harsh mountains for the city.

The mountains have always been bastions for Greeks seeking to avoid interference from outsiders. Be it on the many islands, where the main towns are often hidden behind hills out of view of the sea, to Pelion or the Agrafa, the mountains have been refuges where Greeks could live their lives and preserve what they could of their customs and traditions. At one point the little valleys of the Agrafa produced almost as much olive oil and wheat as the entire Peloponnese Peninsula. But when peace came and brought a relative degree of prosperity, people fled the harsh reality of mountain life to live in warm houses with electricity and indoor plumbing.

Seeing themselves as protectors of Christianity, Agrafa warriors considered it their duty to prey on Turks and anyone doing their bidding which from the 16th to the 18th centuries meant just about any strangers who came near. This fierce tribal tradition helped greatly during all of Greece's modern struggles, from the War of Independence through World War II. Later, mountain men took sides in the tragic episode of the civil war.

Adventure travel was an incomprehensible idea to a generation who had only recently escaped the area and had few notions of the outside world. Westerners trudging through with backpacks and heavy boots were synonymous with invading armies. Those ideas have changed and locals, those few who are left, now view this sort of outside interest more sympathetically.

Travellers to this area should be well-equipped and ready to experience a part of Greece not on most tourist itineraries. Maps have been made available recently and adventure travel guides and organised group trips have begun to encroach on this area. Individual trekkers will do well to know some Greek or run the risk of enduring hardships or being totally put off by the hardy and wary locals: "...in the mountains you can't visit on your own terms. You can't be a tourist with a schedule..." is how Tim Salmon puts it in his fine book *The Unwritten Places*.

Karditsa is a jumping-off point for this region, but as such has fewer services than Karpenissia. As it is, most visitors will combine trips to the Agrafa with others to Meteora where the trekking companies have offices.

Most trips begin behind the man-made hydroelectric Lake of Megdova reservoir behind the Tavropos barrage and continue up and over the peaks of Mount Bolero (2,032m), Mount Plaka (2,013m) and Mount Flindzai (2,018m). Through the high mountain valleys, trekkers will find overgrown cobblestone paths following the terrain along riverbeds and high terraces to little villages where only a handful of houses are occupied or even habitable. At times bulldozers have stripped away the paths that took generations to lay, leaving only an ugly gash. Those willing to invest the time and effort will be rewarded by spectacular views and chance encounters with locals markedly different to those in the lowlands.

KARDITSA TO TRIKALA

After departing Karditsa, trains snake around the north side of a rocky hill, called the beacon, or *fanari* in Greek. Here clearly visible from the train (on the left) is a large Byzantine fortress dominating the summit of the hill. It was important in the 13th–14th centuries and is far from being inconspicuous with its 14m tall walls and six towers. This structure incorporates ancient masonry from "rugged Ithome" of the Iliad, one of the towns incorporated in the fortified rectangle protecting the Plain of Thessaly from marauders coming from the Agrafa and Pindos areas. Brief halts are made at both Fanari and Fanari Chorio (population 850) before the train continues on through Magoula, Kalivia and Drosero to Trikala.

Trikala

This is the third largest (population 47,000) town in Thessaly, and is comfortably located at the north end of the Thessalian Plain on both banks of the Lethaios, west of its confluence with the Pinios. Trikala is the ancient Trikke of Homer, one of the four cities (with Ithomi) forming the defensive perimeter around this end of Thessaly. It is also the reputed birthplace of Asklepios. The plain around ancient Trikke produced the best of the renowned Thessalian horses, whose descendants are still raised here. The name Trikala first appeared in the twelfth century. The Turks made it their principal Thessalian town, and it became the base of the left wing during the early days of the Greek Civil War.

The city is a pleasant enough place with the Byzantine fortress, built on Hellenistic foundations and adopted by the Ottomans, and their Kursum Jami mosque (1550) being highlights. Both are currently closed, but slated to be repaired and reopened soon. At the base of the fortress is the quiet old Turko-Greek quarter of Varousa where the majority of the old churches are located. The Greek Archaeological Service believes it has found the Sanctuary of Asklepios. A Folk Museum and Art Gallery in the centre is worth visiting.

Where to stay

Accommodation should not be difficult to obtain here, as Trikala is not on many travellers' agendas: the Hotel Palladion (Vyronos 4; tel: 0432 28 091) and the Hotel Dina (Asklepiou and Karanasiou 38; tel: 0432 27 147, fax: 29 490) are economical, while the Hotel Divani (Platia Kitrilaki; tel: 0432 27 286) is more expensive.

Further afield

South of Trikala, 19km across the railway tracks, is the village of **Pili** which is known for its 13th-century church of Porta Panagia, situated at the beginning of the attractive Stena tis Portas gorge where the Portaikos

River spills out of the Pindos Mountains. A pair of mosaic icons and Byzantine frescos create the awe anticipated by its builder Ioannis Doukas. Further up the gorge is a splendid arched medieval bridge of which the Pindos has many. Above on the outcroppings is the **Monastery of Dousiko** (1515) known locally as Ai Vessaris. Splendid views of Thessaly and an exceptional cycle of frescos (1550–1558) by the Mount Athos painter Tzortzis are found within, but the small community of monks is temperamental and doesn't like its privacy disturbed. Women are not allowed.

TRIKALA TO KALAMBAKA (METEORA)

Leaving Trikala by rail, trains head in a northwesterly direction across the rapidly narrowing valley of the Pinios River through the flag-stop shelters of Kefalovrisso, Vasiliki (here is located a fifteenth century cemetery and church to St George), and Theopetra, on to line's end at Kalambaka. For most, arrival at Kalambaka means a soaring look up behind the station and beyond to the oddly shaped "rocks in the air" as Meteora is translated.

Kalambaka

Kalambaka (population 6,200) is a pleasant enough resort town spreading comfortably on the verdant slopes at the base of the towering basalt Meteora pinnacles, near where the Pinios River emerges from the Pindos Mountain gorges.

In antiquity the settlement here was called **Aiginion**, and was stated to be impregnable. Caesar joined Domitius here before marching on Pompey at Pharsalus. The cathedral bears a 12th-century inscription to its founder Manuel I Comneos. But the rest of the town dates to after the end of World War II, and the town's destruction is another example of Nazi atrocities against civilians. The main reasons to come here are to visit the striking Byzantine monasteries perched on their rocks, and to take the bus towards Epiros. Near Kalambaka, 20 minutes by foot, is the more charming Kastraki, situated directly under the Meteora which tower above.

Where to stay

Accommodation is not a problem. Most visitors stay one night then leave. Camping is possible at Theopetra (0432 81 405) or Philoxenia (0432 24 446) both on the east-side of Kalambaka and Meteora Garden (0432 22 727) on the west-side towards Ioannina. Rooms are available through the Totis family (0432 22 251) or Eleni Karogorou (0432 22 162). With over a dozen hotels in town choices are varied: the Astoria (0432 22 213) is in sight of the rail station; the Odyssion (0432 22 320) and the Meteora (0432 22 367) are in the centre; towards the path to the Agia Triada Monastery is Koka Roka Rooms (0432 24 554).

In Kastraki there are two campgrounds: Vrahos (0432 22 293) with its own rock climbing school (Climb a Rock, fax: 0432 23 134), and Boufidis/ The Cave on the far side of the village below two monasteries rearing over it. Kastraki seems to have more potential for private rooms and there are enough to go around even in the most crowded tourist months.

The Meteora
These formidable basalt pinnacles and cones were formed by the actions of the great inland sea that covered the area 30 million years ago. That much is certain. How and why monasteries were built there remains as swathed in myth and mystery as the high peaks of the Pindos rising behind them are swathed in cloud.

History
Earliest evidence shows that hermits took up residence during the 10th century in the many caves that notch the rocks. With Byzantium wavering, they were joined in the 14th century by monks seeking refuge. In 1336, two monks from Mount Athos, Gregorios and Athanasios, visited. Gregorios returned to Athos but ordered his companion Athanasios to build a monastery on the rocks, which he did. How Athanasios got to the top no-one knows. Some believe he was flown up on the back of an eagle. Others, more convincingly, suggest that local villagers helped him climb the craggy peaks. The growing community was aided by John Paleologos, a Byzantine nobleman, who refused the throne of Serbia to become the monk Ioasaph (1371). The community reached 24 monasteries by the time of Ottoman Emperor Suleyman the Magnificent (1520–66). They all became wealthy and well endowed with gold icons, mosaics and frescos. Decline set in with the modern age and by the 1950s only a half dozen or so were occupied and functioning as monastic institutions. Several others have been converted into museums. But they all provide insights into the difficult lives and times of all those who turned their backs on conventional life to devote themselves to piety and worship.

The monasteries
Each monastery has essentially the same layout. They are built around a central courtyard surrounded by chapels, a refectory and monks' cells. In the centre is the main church called the Katholikon. The first monasteries were reached by removable rope ladders, then these were replaced by nets until the 1920s when steps were cut out of the rocks. Today the monasteries are linked by asphalt roads. Walking along the remaining paths, as did the first visitors, is still the most evocative way to visit this surreal area. A full day should suffice to see the area but a fuller appreciation calls for a minimum of two days.

With six monasteries to visit, its best to divide them into two groups. Do not forget that dress codes are enforced: below-the-knee skirts for women and long trousers for men. Shoulders should be covered. There is an admission charge to most monasteries (500–700Dr, less for students of theology).

The six monasteries are **Agios Nikolaos** (daily, summer 09.00–18.00; winter 09.00–13.00 and 15.00–17.00) which contains excellent 16th century frescos in its katholikon (or main church building) by the Cretan painter Theophanes. The **Great Meteora** (Wed–Mon, 09.00–13.00 and 15.20–18.00), founded by Athanasios, is the largest and grandest of all, with a majestic Katholikon and arcaded buildings, cellars and appropriately smoke-blackened kitchens around it. **Balaam** (Sat–Thurs, 09.00–13.00 and 15.20–18.00), considered the most beautiful, was founded in 1517 by two brothers from Ioannina who reoccupied the site of a 14th century monastery. It still retains its 1536 ascent tower complete with a rickety pulley and platform. **Roussanou** (daily, summer 09.00–18.00; winter 09.00–13.00 and 15.30–18.00) is a tiny, compact convent, probably built in 1288 and rebuilt in 1545, perched on a narrow-topped pinnacle and approached over another rock. **Agias Triados** (daily 09.00–18.00) is approached by a 130-step climb through a tunnel in the rock. **Agios Stefanos** (Tues–Sun, 09.00–13.00 and 15.20-18.00) is another active convent. It is the furthest along from Kastraki, but can be reached by a well-signposted path from Kalambaka in about 30 minutes' steady walking. Other buildings like the Agia Moni monastery near Agios Nikolaos (closed by an 1858 earthquake) and the chapel-hermitage of Doupiani (the first communal church in the area) near Kastraki add to the romantic ambience of the region.

Further afield

No **railway tracks** can be found beyond Kalambaka. The right-of-way for the proposed Kalambaka–Grevena–Siatista–Kozani can be easily traced and tunnels, bridges and stations are in place, though in a woeful state after 60 years of neglect. This was designed to be an easier-to-build metre gauge rail system up through the lower Pindos Mountains. Much talk and many studies take place and great support is always expressed when the subject of this line comes up. Nothing is certain; but given OSE's new-found railway-building energy and new rail-building equipment, it is possible that this logical extension could be completed.

An impetus is the Albanian desire for a southern railway link to their system, giving Albania its only direct access to a major port – Thessaloniki. It would be necessary to lay 110 kilometres of track from Florina to the Albanian railway terminal west of the Prespa Lakes. Such a link-up would provide OSE with direct standard gauge access to an Adriatic Sea port through Durres. Thus, this new routing would permit an increase in traffic to the northwest without risk of congesting the existing north/south main line. Whether this transpires is anybody's guess.

Travel beyond Kalambaka **by road** is possible and highly recommended. The high Pindos Mountains of Epirus, with their traditional villages and peoples, make for intriguing travel. The forbidding Katara Pass is one of only two all-year all-weather routes over the Pindos. Metsovo, Ioannina and the hidden Zagoria villages on the other side of the Katara offer many possibilities for those who want to get off the proverbial beaten track. This route also leads to the Adriatic seaport of Igoumenitsa with connections to Corfu, the other Ionian Isles and Italy.

For those not wishing to go so far afield, Kalambaka is also a jumping-off point into the wilds of Agrafa, though perhaps not as accessible as either Karditsa or Karpenissi.

Part Five

NORTHERN GREECE: MACEDONIA AND THRACE

Most of this area is far from the Greek tourist trail and feels little like those typical blue-and-white postcard images of sunny Aegean islands. Here the predominant colours are the greens and browns of the dense forests and rich deep earth.

Colours are not the only things that are different here.

Northern Greece consists of two distinct provinces: **Macedonia** in the west and **Thrace** in the east. These two provinces are rarely visited by Sun–worshippers drawn to the islands, nor by romantic visitors to the old stones of the Peloponnese. Discerning travellers will find much, however, to keep them occupied in this area.

Macedonia is by far the largest province, extending from the upper foothills of the Pindos mountains south through the peaks of Mount Olympus to the Aegean Sea coast, then around the Thermaic Gulf through the three-tentacled Halkidiki peninsula and east to the Nestos River. The northern boundaries consist of the borders of Albania, the Former Yugoslav Republic of Macedonia (FYRO Macedonia) and Bulgaria. These three countries are among the most volatile places in the Balkans. Their instability contributes to a real sense of unease felt along certain segments of the northern borders. Thessaloniki is by far the major city in the province, but not the only important urban centre. Veria, Edessa, Florina and Kozani, all on rail lines to the west; and Kavala, not on any rail line to the east; are lively, vibrant and growing cities. But Macedonia has more than cities. It has important natural wildlife reserves where wolves and bears roam, and some of the most enticing landscape in Europe.

Thrace stretches east beyond the Nestos River to the Evros River border with Turkey. It is long but narrow, bounded by the Sea of Thrace and the high Rhodope Mountains that constitute the Bulgarian border. This province is never more than 75–90km wide. In reality, it should be called Western Thrace to distinguish it from the larger eastern segment extending from the Evros to the Dardenelles at Istanbul. Eastern Thrace is now part of Turkey and permits that essentially Asian country to call itself European. Thrace also counts striking physical geography from the Nestos River Gorge to large, untouched forests and lowland marshes. Modern Thrace is Greece's melting pot, with Orthodox Christian Greeks sharing the province with Muslim Bulgars, Turks and Gypsies.

The ancient people of Thrace are a mystery. Though considered to be of Indo-European stock, they assimilated poorly and refused to co-exist with outsiders. They contributed much of the foot soldiery for Alexander's Asian campaigns but otherwise did not greatly distinguish themselves. The Macedonian people are more a subject of controversy and are at the basis of the current debate over whether Macedonia, in the larger sense, is even Greek.

The ancient historian Herodotus states that the Macedonians were a Doric tribe who dwelt in the Pindos, where it was called Makedon, and then extended steadily to the east of the mountains and much farther beyond to Corinth, Sparta and other areas of the Peloponnese.

The way of life consisted primarily of transhumant pasturage in the upland valleys and plains around the major rivers and high mountains of the area. The creation of permanent settlements and steady contact with other areas after the 7th century BC brought the Macedonians in closer contact with their cousins to the south. Because of their location on the northern fringes of the Greek world, the Macedonians also had the first contacts with foreigners coming from the north. Macedonians guarded the gates to the city so to speak. This contact meant that invaders and more benign foreigners were always in the midst of Greek peoples. Today's mixed settlements in the area, which have given rise to the French term Macedonian for a mixed salad, comes from this intermingling. Travellers attuned to languages would do well to listen closely, for a wide variety of tongues are spoken in this area. The Thessaloniki rail station café is a good place to hear the different languages.

Two distinct peoples who populate Macedonia and Thrace and proudly guard their roots should be cited: the **Vlachs** and the **Sarakatsani**.

The **Vlachs** speak a language based on Latin, but all their own. They could be of ancient Greek stock and they could have been chosen by the Romans to protect the Pindos mountain passes, but little is known because their language is oral leaving little trace. They base their lives on tending large flocks of sheep and goats, pasturing them in the lowlands during winter then herding them to mountain pastures in summer. This transhumance was done on foot, but now the annual migrations are done by truck/lorry.

The **Sarakatsani** speak Greek and, though also a shepherd clan, were more nomadic than the Vlachs. They claim to be able to trace their roots back to antiquity and still have certain rites and ceremonies that are proper only to them. Modern times and rigid Balkan borders have forced these people to settle, but they can sometimes be seen attired in their traditional clothing in rail stations of the north.

Other minorities include Albanians, Serbs, Bulgars, Gypsies and Turks. The region truly is a melting-pot of peoples and cultures – more so than the rest of Greece. For more in-depth observations of these peoples in the early 20th century, refer to Patrick Leigh Fermor's *Roumeli: Travels in Northern Greece*. The railways through Macedonia and Thrace offer the opportunity to meet these people, who do not often go south.

After a brief look at the city of Thessaloniki and the area around the Halkidiki Peninsula, this section will proceed by describing the rail lines: south to Mount Olympus and the sacred Macedonian city of Dion; then west along the route through Veria, Naoussa and Edessa to Amindeo and the junction for Florina and Kozani; the international routes possible from Thessaloniki; then east through Eastern Macedonia and Thrace to Alexandroupolis and north along the Evros River border to the end of the modern Greek world at Dikea/Ormenio.

SAMPLE FARES: NORTH OF ATHENS

TICKET FARES TO THE NORTH OF ATHENS

1. class

FROM \ TO	CHALKIS	THIVA	LEVADIA	BRALOS	LIANOKLADI	P/FARSALOS	KARDITSA	TRIKALA	KALAMBAKA	LARISSA	VOLOS	KATERINI	PLATI	VERIA	NAOUSSA	EDESSA	KOZANI	FLORINA	THESSALONIKI	KILKIS	SERRES	DRAMA	XANTHI	KOMOTINI	ALEX/POLIS	SOUFLI	DIDIMOTICHON	N. ORESTIAS	ORMENIO
ATHINA	–	1270	1590	2080	2430	3330	3500	3990	4050	3990	4250	4640	5060	4590	4590	4900	6550	5580	5900	6960	840	8820	9330	10070	10740	11040		6120	7060
CHALKIS		720	1180	1660	1950	2860	5230	3410	3940	3320	3610	4150	4630	4330	4390	4390	4600	6310	5050	5060	6310	6960	7870	8380	9120	9790	10090	10290	10510
THIVA			520	1320	1460	2340	2660	3010	3230	2790	3370	3990	4150	3990	3990	4260	5800	4640	5060	6310	6770	7880	8390	9130	9600	10100	10300	10520	
LEVADIA				840	1170	1850	2180	2430	2790	2340	3010	3330	3990	3690	3690	3990	5250	4050	4610	5760	6360	7290	7800	8540	9210	9510	9710	9930	
BRALOS					520	1330	1650	1910	2110	1750	2430	2790	3230	3260	3260	3550	4850	3500	3990	5210	5090	6740	7250	7990	8660	8960	9160	9380	
LIANOKLADI						1170	1370	1650	1850	1520	2110	2430	3010	3100	3100	3150	4330	3890	4850	5700	6550	6960	7820	8490	8790	8990	8310		
P/FARSALOS							480	770	1080	640	1330	1590	2010	2430	2550	2550	2760	3660	2430	2890	4050	4850	5670	6180	6920	7570	7890	8090	8310
KARDITSA								480	750	980	1260	1850	2340	2790	2800	2800	2990	3230	4430	5060	6120	6550	7170	8070	8370	8570	8790		
TRIKALA									350	1330	1910	2180	2660	2910	2910	2910	3260	4250	3120	3410	4640	5580	6360	6770	7360	8360	8660	8860	9080
KALAMBAKA										1520	2110	2430	3010	3100	3100	3410	4430	3330	3990	4850	5700	6550	6960	8000	8670	8970	9170	9390	
LARISSA											840	1230	1590	1910	2010	2260	2390	3240	1950	2430	3660	4410	5190	5700	6360	7110	7360	7610	7830
VOLOS												1740	2230	2560	2710	2850	3880	2660	3120	4250	5060	5900	6360	6960	7820	8120	8320	8240	
KATERINI													690	1060	1250	1460	1840	2340	1190	1520	2790	3410	4430	4850	5680	6310	6550	6770	7070
PLATI														480	560	900	1350	1650	520	1060	2230	2980	3760	4270	5010	5680	5980	6180	6400
VERIA															160	560	1140	1400	900	1260	2460	3010	3620	3970	4250	4770	4910	5390	5670
NAOUSSA																480	1100	1290	1080	1350	2580	3010	3620	3970	4250	4770	4910	5390	5670
EDESSA																	870	1080	1260	3620	2590	3010	3620	3970	4250	4770	4910	5390	5670
KOZANI																		860	1660	1950	2690	3150	3830	4090	4510	4910	5390	5520	5940
FLORINA																			2060	2460	3690	4290	5270	5660	6060	6810	7010	7700	8090
THESSALONIKI																				560	1710	2460	3240	3750	4490	5160	5460	5660	5880
KILKIS																					1290	1950	2990	3690	4100	4680	5160	5270	5660
SERRES																						900	1760	2250	2990	3690	3840	4100	4490
DRAMA																							1220	1560	2250	2990	3150	3690	3840
XANTHI																								6030	1290	1950	2250	2580	3080
KOMOTINI																									900	1560	1760	2160	2580
ALEX/POLIS																										900	1230	1470	1860
SOUFLI																											480	770	1230
DIDIMOTICHON																												480	900
N. ORESTIAS																													590

Prices do not include supplements for special services
(Intercity, sleepers, couchettes, etc.).
These supplements are listed in following pages.

TICKET FARES TO THE NORTH OF ATHENS

2. class

FROM \ TO	CHALKIS	THIVA	LEVADIA	BRALOS	LIANOKLADI	P/FARSALOS	KARDITSA	TRIKALA	KALAMBAKA	LARISSA	VOLOS	KATERINI	PLATI	VERIA	NAOUSSA	EDESSA	KOZANI	FLORINA	THESSALONIKI	KILKIS	SERRES	DRAMA	XANTHI	KOMOTINI	ALEX/POLIS	SOUFLI	DIDIMOTICHON	N. ORESTIAS	ORMENIO
ATHINA	600	850	1060	1390	1620	2220	2340	2660	2700	2660	2830	3090	3370	3060	3060	3260	4370	3720	3940	4640	5360	5880	6220	6710	7160	7360		4080	4240
CHALKIS		550	850	1180	1370	1980	2150	2270	2660	2220	2470	2770	3150	2970	2970	2970	3110	4210	3370	3370	4210	4640	5310	5650	6140	6590	6790	6920	7070
THIVA			350	880	980	1560	1780	2000	2150	1860	2250	2660	2770	2660	2660	2840	3870	3090	3370	4210	4510	5250	5690	6530	6730	6860	7010		
LEVADIA				560	780	1240	1450	1620	1860	1560	2000	2220	2660	2460	2460	2640	3500	2700	3070	3840	4240	4860	5200	5690	6140	6340	6470	6620	
BRALOS					350	890	1100	1270	1410	1170	1620	1860	2150	2180	2180	2370	3230	2340	2660	3480	3940	4600	4840	5330	5780	5980	6110	6260	
LIANOKLADI						780	910	1100	1240	1010	1410	1620	2000	2080	2080	2680	2270	2950	2220	2590	3230	3800	4370	4640	5210	5660	5860	5990	6140
P/FARSALOS							320	510	720	430	890	1060	1340	1620	1700	1700	1800	2440	1930	2700	3230	3780	4120	4610	5060	5390	5400	5540	
KARDITSA								320	500	650	840	1240	1560	1860	1870	1870	1990	2660	1860	2150	2950	3370	4080	4370	4780	5380	5580	5710	5860
TRIKALA									230	890	1270	1450	1780	1950	1950	2180	2830	2080	2270	3090	3720	4040	4510	4970	5570	5770	5900	6050	
KALAMBAKA										1010	1410	1620	2000	2080	2080	2080	2270	2950	2220	2660	3230	3800	4370	4640	5330	5780	5980	6110	6260
LARISSA											560	810	1060	1270	1340	1510	1590	2160	1300	1620	2440	3460	3800	4240	4740	4910	5070	5220	
VOLOS												1180	1480	1710	1780	1800	1890	2580	1780	2080	2830	3370	3940	4240	4640	5220	5420	5550	5700
KATERINI													460	710	830	980	1230	1560	790	1010	1870	2270	2950	3230	3780	4210	4370	4510	4710
PLATI														320	370	600	900	1100	350	710	1480	1990	2510	2850	3340	3790	3990	4120	4270
VERIA															105	370	760	930	600	840	1080	1730	2010	2410	2640	2830	3180	3270	3600	3780
NAOUSSA																320	730	860	720	900	1720	2010	2410	2640	2830	3180	3270	3600	3780
EDESSA																	580	720	840	1080	1730	2010	2410	2640	2830	3180	3270	3600	3780
KOZANI																		570	1110	1300	1800	2100	2550	2730	3010	3270	3600	3680	3960
FLORINA																			1370	1640	2460	2860	3510	3770	4040	4670	5130	5390	
THESSALONIKI																				370	1140	1640	2160	2500	2990	3440	3640	3770	3920
KILKIS																					860	1300	1990	2460	2730	3120	3440	3510	3770
SERRES																						600	1170	1500	1990	2460	2560	2730	2990
DRAMA																							810	1040	1500	1990	2100	2460	2560
XANTHI																								420	860	1300	1500	1720	2050
KOMOTINI																									600	1040	1170	1440	3720
ALEX/POLIS																										600	820	980	1240
SOUFLI																											320	510	820
DIDIMOTICHON																												320	600
N. ORESTIAS																													390

Prices do not include supplements for special services
(Intercity, sleepers, couchettes, etc.).
These supplements are listed in following pages.

Extract from OSE Timetable 1996-97

Chapter Twelve

Thessaloniki–Platamon

Thessaloniki–Platy–Katerini–Dion–Litochoro–Platamon

THESSALONIKI

Thessaloniki (population 750,000) is the second city of Greece but the first city of the North. Here are located all the government ministries for northern Greece as well as numerous Roman and Byzantine archaeological finds, not to mention the many treasures from the recently excavated Macedonian tombs of Alexander's father King Philip of Macedon. There is plenty to do and see in Thessaloniki. In fact, locals like to boast about their city, claiming it never fell to such ignominious depths as Athens. It was the first city of the Macedonians and the Romans in the east as well as the second city of the Byzantine and Ottoman empires. Today, with its vibrant port, well equipped railway facilities and large yearly trade fair, it is the first city of the Balkans.

It is the Cultural Capital of Europe for 1997. This honour bestowed on the city has resulted in a whirlwind of activity including restoration and renovation of many of its monuments and sights. Travellers to Thessaloniki often remark on having the sensation of being in more of a European/Balkan city. The railway station certainly contributes to that feeling.

The railway terminal

This colossal marble-faced edifice is the largest train station in the Balkans. Travellers coming here from other points in Greece, including Athens, will have the impression of arriving someplace. That was the impression the builders wanted to make. The station was commissioned in the 1930s by the Dictator Ioannis Metaxas who, like his Italian counterpart Benito Mussolini, wanted a large and modern rail station that would reflect the former glory of ancient Greece. Unfortunately, reality in the form of World War II and the Civil War thwarted the plans and delayed completion until 1954 of a simpler, though still very big, station. It is the first and still the only major Greek railway station with electric catenary (1995) and was awarded in the summer of 1996 a multi-billion drachma grant, as part of the Cultural Capital of Europe general city-wide clean-up. It provides all rail services and has in-house post and telecommunications offices and its own chapel (Agios Dimitrios dedicated in 1994). Many metropolitan bus lines have their terminus in front of the station as do many of the KTEL companies. The police station outside the main doors of the terminal (left side) is helpful for directions and information.

Even though already 42 years old, this station is still often referred to as the "new" railway station to distinguish it from the long demolished 1894 station designed by Pietro Arinconi. The much-regretted old station was situated west of the current station in what is now yard trackage. An extremely active local association of railway friends led by Dimitris Pappadimitriou (Viziis Visantos 4, 40 Ekklisies, 54636 Thessaloniki, tel: 031 209 926) is working to create a railway museum that will prevent the further loss of Thessaloniki's railway heritage as well as striving for improvements to the northern Greek rail network.

History

Thessaloniki was founded in 316BC when the Macedonian general Kassandros regrouped the inhabitants of 26 townships into the present location on the Thermaic Gulf. The name means "victory in Thessaly". The Romans immediately saw the city's strategic value on the Gulf and on their new east/west road – the Via Egnatia – and named it as the capital of their Province of Macedonia (168BC). The city's fortunes stumbled with the barbarian raids of the 4th century AD but it survived and flourished under the Byzantines who made it their second city. Its site and location made it an inevitable target for all who passed through. Its strong walls saved it on numerous occasions. The Normans were among the first to sack it (1185) and the Marquis Boniface de Montferrat made it the centre of his feudal kingdom in 1205. In 1246 it passed back into the hands of the Byzantines. The Turks captured Thessaloniki, virtually razing it, in 1430. They kept it until 1913.

During their reign, the city once again prospered. This was in great part due to its large Jewish population. Over 20,000 people, banished from Spain by the 1492 Edict of the Alhambra, joined the existing Bavarian Jews to eventually create a largely autonomous community that thrived until the Nazi era of the mid 20th century. This community did so well for itself and lived in such harmony with the other communities of Thessaloniki, that Zionist leaders of the 1920s and 1930s considered it a model for the Jewish homeland planned for Palestine. Today few Jews live in the city and their language, Ladino, a form of Castilian written in Hebrew characters, has largely disappeared.

The city's physical face is still greatly determined by its site at the base of the Thermaic Gulf. The centre is in an elongated grid form with its neighbourhoods rising irregularly in the form of an amphitheatre up the low hills around Mount Hortiatis and sprawling beyond the thick Byzantine walls (8km long of which about 4km survive). The imposing 10th-century sea-facing walls were knocked down in the mid 19th century, probably contributing to the extensive damage done by the fire of August 1917. The 1923 refugee situation exacerbated the difficulties. Rebuilding followed a general plan drafted in 1925–1930 but was disrupted in 1978 by a severe earthquake that damaged many of the Byzantine churches and Turkish buildings. These are only now being rebuilt as part of the 1997 celebrations.

What to see

The city centre is modern, attractive and busy with many squares, pedestrian promenades and sidewalk cafés. Traffic, unfortunately, is heavy, with delays and blockages the norm. A multi-station underground metro is in the last stages of planning but will not be a reality for at least seven years. Walking is recommended and in the compact city centre is often faster than a city bus. The evening stroll along the seaside is a highlight especially on clear evenings, when the many snow-capped peaks of Mount Olympus are highlighted before the setting sun. The old Kastra neighbourhood above the centre and below the ramparts often impresses visitors with its village-like atmosphere. A tour of the old walls is possible and recommended.

Within the city, visitors should first visit the exceptional seven-room **Archaeological Museum** with its finds from the Vergina tombs (M. Andronikou St 6 on Hanth Sq; open: Mon 10.30–17.00, Tues–Fri 08.30–17.00, Sat–Sun 08.30–17.00; admission 1,500, 1,100, 800Dr; tel: 031 830 538). Near the archaeological museum across the park, on the sea side, is the **White Tower** (open Mon 12.30–17.00, Tues–Fri 08.00–17.00, Sat–Sun 08.30–15.00; admission 800, 600, 400Dr; tel: 031 267 832). This 15th century tower is the symbol for the city and often used to introduce it on news broadcasts. Formerly a Turkish prison, it has been restored and houses Byzantine frescos and icons, as well as providing great panoramic views of the city. The excellent **Folklore Museum** (Vass. Olga St 66, Open Fri–Wed 09.30–14.00, admission 200, 100Dr; tel: 031 830 591, fax: 844 848) provides insights into everyday life through exhibits and photos. It is housed in a 19th-century mansion typical of Thessaloniki and is being renovated as part of the 1997 Cultural Capital activities. The Folklore Museum is a fifteen-minute walk from the Archaeological Museum along busy Vass. Sofia Avenue. Vass. Sofia was the preferred address for wealthy Ottoman politicos and business people of all types during the prosperous days of the 19th century. It still counts numerous finely crafted multi-storey mansions, many of which are being restored for 1997. The stroll to the Folklore Museum is recommended for those interested in seeing these buildings (some are to be used during the 1997 festivities).

Other important sites from Thessaloniki's Roman and Byzantine past include the large fenced-in **Roman Agora** in the upper part of Platia Dikastirion; the **Complex of Galerius**, near the eastern limit of the city centre, which includes a triumphal arch (built AD303) and an unusual 3rd-century **Rotunda** (with a 24.15m diameter dome) that is a current centre of some controversy because it was consecrated as the Church of St George then became a mosque (with its minaret still in place) in the Turkish era. It is being renovated by the Ministry of Antiquities but the Orthodox church claims it was never de-consecrated and wants it back as it is the oldest church in the city. The most impressive church is the 5th-century **Agios Dimitirios Church** on Agnotou Stratiottou above the Roman agora with its somewhat damaged though still exquisite 8th-century mosaics. Dimitrios was born in Thessaloniki and is considered the city's patron saint. The church is the largest in Greece. The 4th- or 6th-century (the date is disputed) domed basilica of Agia Sofia nearby on Vass Sofia resembles its magnificent namesake in Istanbul.

The above-mentioned churches along with the early (4th to 5th century) timber roofed, three-aisle Hellenistic styled Aheiropeitos Church between the Agora and the Rotonda north of Vass. Sofia make a grouping that comprises some of the earliest Christian churches in existence. The little 5th-century Church of Ossios David with fine frescos is in the Kastra area, and at least a half dozen other early churches dot the city.

Thessaloniki's Moslem past is represented by a great number of roofed markets, mosques and domed Turkish baths, many of which were built by the Byzantines but adapted for Muslim purposes. Though damaged by fires, earthquakes and neglect, they merit a visit. Many are being restored for 1997. The 15th-century **Bezesteni Market** at the intersection of Egnatia and Venizelou streets was considered by contemporary traders to have been the most beautiful market in the Balkans. The **Alkazar Mosque** (circa 1468) near the Bezesteni Market, the **Alatza Imaret Mosque**, and the series of bath houses called **Hammams**, some like the 1430 Hammam Bey and the more recent Pasha Hammam still in use, give an idea of Thessaloniki's cosmopolitan past. Mustafa Kemal, later to become Attaturk, was born in Thessaloniki (1881). His house is a museum called Attaturk's House (Apostolou Pavlou; daily; 14.00–18.00; free after interview with Turkish consulate nearby at Agiou Dimitriou).

Those interested in more information on these and other monuments are directed to the well-illustrated 140-page book entitled simply *Monuments of Thessaloniki* by Apostolos Papagiannopoulos. This book (2,080Dr) with handy map is available at the Molcho bookshop on Tsimiski 10 in central Thessaloniki.

Visitors interested in events planned for the 1997 Cultural Capital of Europe Festivities should contact the Organisation for the Cultural Capital of Europe – Thessaloniki 1997, Vasilissos Olgas Ave 105, 54643 Thessaloniki; tel: 031 867 860, fax: 867 870.

Where to stay

Accommodation is not a problem with a vast number of hotels of all categories in almost every part of the city. Near the railway station, try the Hotel Averoff (Leontos Sofou 24; tel: 031 53 8498); the Hotel Acropol (Tandalidou 4; tel: 031 53 6170) and the more upscale Hotel Capsis (Monastiriou 18; tel: 031 52 1321, fax: 510 555). Closer to the centre are: the Hotel Bill (Syngrou 29; tel: 031 537 666), the Orestias Kastorias (Agnostou Stratiotou 14; tel: 031 276 517) and the very upscale Electra (Aristotelous Sq 9A; tel: 031 232 221, fax: 235 947). In the eastern section are the IYH Youth Hostel (Svolou 44; tel: 031 225 946), the YWCA (Agias Sofias 11; tel: 031 276 144), the ABC Hotel (Angeliki 41; tel: 031 265 421) and the Hotel Metropolitan (Vass. Olgas 65; tel: 031 824 221).

Campsites can be found at a distance east around the coast: the Akti Thermaikon (tel: 0392 51 352) at Agia Triada beach (27km); or at Ormos Epanomis (tel: 0392 41 378) 6km further on. Trekkers interested in exploring the Mount Olympus area should contact the Thessaloniki offices of one of the two Greek mountaineering clubs that have refuges on the mountain: either EOS (tel: 031 278 288) or SEO (tel: 031 224 719). The Trekking Hellas Company office in Thessaloniki can also provide information on trekking possibilities. Two good camping supply stores can help round out supplies: Petridis at Vasiliou Irakliou 43 and World Jamboree at Ionnos Deliou 6.

Further afield

Day-trippers from the city should contemplate going to **Panorama** (11km) or on to **Hortiatis** (11km further on) in a refreshing region known as Hilia Dendra (Thousand Trees). The bus ride out to Hortiatis midway up the slopes of Mount Hortiatis (1,201m) passes traces of the ancient aqueduct (right) that brought drinking water to the city.

Longer trips are possible by bus or car east to the **Halkidiki Peninsula**. There is no railway here but traces can be seen, notably near Lagina northeast of Thessaloniki, of a 60cm gauge military railway built by the Allies during the First World War (open 1916, closed 1956) to the small fishing port of Stavros on the Strymonikos Bay several kilometres west of Amphipolis. Railway activists would like to revive this line, albeit at a wider gauge, and build a connection east to the abandoned line at Amphipolis. More ambitious types would like to see it extended around the marshy coast to Kavala. OSE is at present surveying a rail line to Kavala, but from the east, to connect to the main line at Xanthi.

Halkidiki peninsula and Mount Athos

This large agricultural and mineral-rich area southeast of Thessaloniki has been dubbed Greece's Riviera. It is also the site of the last vestige of the Byzantine Empire at the mystical semi-autonomous Mount Athos peninsula.

The Halkidiki peninsula

The name Halkidiki originates with the colonisers who were from the ancient city-state of Chalkis on the island of Evia. The Halkidiki can be divided into the beach resort slivers of Kassandra and Sithonia where campsites and hotels line the silvery sand beaches, and the monastic republic of Mount Athos. Both Kassandra and Sithonia are popular with residents of Thessaloniki, but pine-covered Sithonia offers better possibilities of finding isolated beaches further from the madding crowd than Kassandra.

Wine aficionados touring the Halkidiki should contemplate visiting the state-of-the-art Tsantalis winery at Agios Pavlos on the main east-coast road to the Kassandra peninsula, just north of the turn-off for Eliohora. The Tsandalis family is one of Greece's better known vintners since the 1950s. They specialise in wines from Macedonia and Northern Greece. For visits and tastings telephone 0399 61 394, fax: 61 466.

Sithonia is also the location of the Domaine Carras wine-growing area. This new wine-growing area, Playes Meliton, with its yacht harbour located south of Neos Marmaras on the west coast of Sithonia, has distinguished itself as the largest (450ha) appellation vineyard area under one owner in Europe; and has proven since its first vintage in 1971 that quality French grape varieties can comfortably coexist with quality Greek varieties. Those who want to visit and taste the quality dry white, rosé and red wines as well as the fine locally produced olive oil should telephone 031 268 626 or fax 031 237 110. Campsites and hotels abound on these two peninsulas.

Mount Athos

The Mount Athos situation is an entirely different matter. This area, off limits to females since the 11th century, is a monastic retreat and walkers' delight, as few roads disturb the eerie calm and tranquillity of the region. The total lack of industry has turned the peninsula into somewhat of a nature preserve with reports of wild boar and some wolves living in the region. Thessaloniki is a good base from which to organise a visit.

Hermits first came to the area in the early days of the Byzantine Empire. Emperor Basil I proclaimed an edict (in 885) recognising Athos as the sole preserve of monks, who then formed communities and began to build monasteries. The first is considered to be the great Lavra (983). The monastic state was recognised by the various Byzantine emperors then, after some difficulties with Vlach shepherdesses, Constantine IX issued a bull in the late 11th century that remains in force today, banning women. The monasteries became internationalised during the 12th century with monks from Romania, Russia and Serbia. By the early 15th century there were over forty monasteries (reputedly with up to a thousand monks in each), but Orthodox monastic life declined during Turkish rule: only twenty communities with their cloister-like dependencies and solitary hermits exist today. There are about 1,700 monks now on Athos, living individually in caves, or on isolated cliffs, or in one of the twenty monasteries. The Theocratic Athonite community has a hierarchy, with the Great Lavra considered first and Kastamonitou last. It is governed from Karyes by the Holy Superintendency, which comprises one member from each monastic community elected for one year.

Clocks are set to Byzantine time and the day begins at sunrise. It is important to remember this when requesting access for the evening. The calendar is the Byzantine Julian which is 13 days behind ours; which is relevant because the day shown on the entry permit relates to this calendar. Visitors, besides their permits, should be equipped for walking and for finding their way. A good map and electric torch are essential.

After obtaining authorisation to visit (see below), visitors are brought by caique from Ouranopolis down the coast to Daphni, or more rarely to the various monastic docks further south and around the coast. It is not possible to enter Athos from the village of Ierissos on the north coast of the peninsula. Ierissos is known because of a canal dug near here at Provlaka, the narrowest point on the peninsula, by Xerxes in 480BC, as an attempt to avoid circumnavigating the peninsula. His predecessor Mardonius lost 300 ships and 20,000 men trying to round the promontory in 491BC. Little trace remains of Xerxes' efforts.

The sights on the Athos peninsula include the attractive pastoral countryside and the mystic Mount Athos (2,039m). Visits should be based on either the southern or the northern groups of monasteries.

In the southeast, starting at ghostly Karyes (inland from Daphni), and heading south around the peninsula are: the cloister-like **Agiou Andreou**, **Koutloumousio**, **Filotheou** and **Karakalou** near the hamlet of Karies; the vast late 10th-century **Iviron monastery** with its miraculous Portaitissa icon and the mosaic (1053) in the katholikon, the largest on the mountain; further south (and accessible by caique or trail from Ivirion) the **Great Lavra monastery**, the only monastery on the mountain not to be damaged by fire, containing no less than 15 chapels and excellent frescos (1535) by the Cretan Theophanes; the dependencies of **Prodromou** and the hermitage-cave of Saint Athanasios in the south; the dependencies of **Agias Triadas** and especially **Agias Annas** near the southwest coast (prepare for the four-hour ascent of Mount Athos); the **monastery of Agios Pavlos** towards the north, painted by Edward Lear in the 1850s; and beyond it the hanging monasteries of **Dionisiou** with its 16th-century frescos by Tzortzis and Theophanes, Osiou Grigoriou; and, before walking to Daphni, what is perhaps the most visually striking monastery on Mount Athos: **Simopetra**.

In the northwest, accessible from Daphni, are the Russian monastery of **Agios Pendelimon** with its onion domes and great bell considered the second largest in the world; the 18th-century **Xeropotoamou**; the Greek coastal monasteries of **Xenofondos** and **Doiariou** with its exceptionally lofty katholikon; lowly **Konstamonitou** deep in a valley; the furthest-inland monastery of **Zografou**; the Serbian monastery of **Hilandariou**; the Orthodox fundamentalist **Esfigmenou** built directly on the water; the coastal **Vatopediou**, larger than the Great Lavra and seeming like a town with its plaza and cells for over 300; the coast-hugging **Pandocratoros**, and **Stavronitika**, the best example of the Athonite coastal fortress-monasteries and therefore the most crowded. The above-mentioned Tsantalis family received permission in 1973 to replant vineyards in this area, near Agios Pandelimon, and have succeeded in creating a fine bottled white wine called Agioritikos (from Agios Oros).

Authorisation to visit Mount Athos is obtainable in Thessaloniki or in Athens. Potential visitors first require a letter of recommendation from their consulates (many in Thessaloniki) or their embassies (Athens only). Then this should be taken in Thessaloniki to the Ministry of Macedonia and Thrace (Directorate of Political Affairs – Room 222, Platia Diakistiriou, 54123 Thessaloniki; Mon–Fri 11.00–13.45), or in Athens to the Ministry of Foreign Affairs (Akadamias 3, 5th floor; Mon, Wed, Fri 11.00–13.00). The letter is exchanged for authorisation called a *diamonitirion*. This is a four-day permit to stay in the monasteries. An extension may be possible, but only one night is allowed in each monastery. The process must be finished in the same city where it began and a specific date of entry must be given. Only an extremely limited number of foreign visitors is allowed and during the summer tourist season, as there are a very great number of requests, flexibility in timing is the key.

The tiny port of Ouranopolis with its 13th-century Byzantine tower (recently restored and converted into a small museum housing finds from the Halkidiki) does have some rooms for rent, shops and tourist services, but visitors to Athos are advised to stock up in Thessaloniki and make arrangements to take the appropriate KTEL bus so as to arrive early enough in Ouranopolis for the caique to Daphni, and the appropriate connections beyond.

THESSALONIKI TO PLATAMON

This is the northern segment of the longitudinal north/south Greek standard gauge main rail line. As such it is mostly double track, and counts a great number of daily trains with the Alexandroupolis-bound trains leaving the main line 12km from Thessaloniki just before Sindos (no stop), then international expresses leaving 9km further south at Axios, then the west bound IC, expresses and locals for Florina and Kozani branching off 15km further down the line at Platy. In all, 13 daily trains ply the rails all the way between Thessaloniki and Platamon. This 118km route offers possibilities for those interested in archaeology or just relaxation.

Rail fans should note the extensive rail traffic (both goods and passenger) and the on-going rail infrastructure work. The main-line electrification project costing 45 billion drachma will begin from this end of the railway. Riders along this route should be aware that not all trains make all stops along this segment. IC trains (except the non-stop Hermes-IC 51/50) only call at Platy and Katerini. Expresses add Platamon to this list. Locals call at the little stations by request only. Enough trains serve this route to be able to ride down to Platamon, for example, in the early morning then return to Thessaloniki in the early evening.

The major geographical features on this route include the coast (left) and the peaks of Mount Olympus (right). Historically, this route includes the sacred Macedonian sanctuary at Dion, the mythically important Mount Olympus and the salt marshes around the mount of the Aliakmon River whose impact on the ancient Macedonian economy should not be ignored.

Leaving Thessaloniki, riders will note the great many steam locomotives, many marked for the US Army, stored on the left. Two of these large machines are being restored to cover service requirements for the new daily train on the Drama–Xanthi–Drama route through the Nestos River Gorge (see below – *Chapter Fifteen*).

The branch to **Serres** and **Alexandroupolis** veers off to the right near Diavata (right – no stop), where a memorial to French dead from World War I is located. The rail line crosses a 170m iron bridge over the Gallikos. Gold in small quantities is extracted from its sandy banks. The first possible station stop is Sindos where important archaic and classical cemeteries were found during construction in 1980. The rather interesting finds can be seen at the Thessaloniki Archaeological Museum.

Beyond Sindos, after a long, flat plain comes the 14-span, 620m girder bridge built by British sappers in 1945 over the Axios River. This area was once a lagoon into which flowed both the Axios and Aliakmon Rivers. As late as classical times it was navigable for nearly 38km to Pella. The Axios River is the largest in Macedonia. Its sources are deep in former Yugoslavia and it only flows for 80km in Greece. Greek Prime Minister Eleftherios Venizelos was responsible for flood and reclamation works in 1925: before this, the area was a dangerous malarial marsh. The Axios station stop is followed by another bridge 152m long, with the Yugoslavia branch heading off to the right. Near here the 1912 agreement surrendering Thessaloniki to Greece was signed. The rail line continues its broad sweeping curve to the left. Next comes the stop at the appropriately named Adendron (no trees). To the right is the region of **Pella**, the home of the Macedonian royal family and the birthplace of Alexander the Great. The archaeological site is about 16km from the rail station at Adendron.

The Pella region was first inhabited (over 16 settlements have been discovered) during the Neolithic era by colonists from Crete. Makedon tribesmen pushed them out and Pella eventually became the capital of Macedonia and, after Philip united the Greeks in 336BC, the first capital of Greece. At one time a canal connected Pella with the Thracian Gulf.

Ongoing excavations at the 3.8km site have uncovered statues, reliefs and exquisite mosaics that are visible on the site (open Mon–Fri 08.00–15.00; admission 500, 400, 300Dr; tel: 0382 31 160) and at the small museum (open Mon 12.30–15.00, Tues–Fri 08.00–15.00, Sat–Sun 08.30–15.00; admission 500, 400, 300Dr; tel: same as the site). Visitors by train will have to take a taxi from Adendron; or from Platy because so few trains call at Adendron.

The rail line crosses the artificial Loudias River, created as part of the 1925 drainage project, then proceeds through the rail junction at Platy. Beyond Platy are a series of small villages, then a 450m bridge over the **Aliakmon River** before the station stop at Aliakmon. The Aliakmon is the longest river in Greece, rising in the Pindos Mountains on the Albanian frontier, then flowing 175km into the Thracian Gulf. The upper segment is through gentle valleys, the middle is characterised by narrow gorges and the mouth has been dammed near Verria (1973).

Continuing south are the little villages of Egiaion-Kolindros, Nea Agathoupolis and Methoni. All of these were founded by Greek refugees from Anatolia after 1923. **Kolindros** (population 3,900) is known for its long-surviving custom on January 8 (St Domenica Day), first reported by ancient playwright Aristophanes, when women take control of the village, ejecting men from the cafés. Ancient **Methoni** was often used by the Athenians as a base against the Macedonians, and Philip II reportedly lost an eye to an Athenian arrow besieging it. There is a small hotel here, the Arion (0353 41 2214).

The first sandy beaches are visible on the left at the Makrygialos station. Hotels, campgrounds, cafés and restaurants mark this village, which is the first beach resort accessible by train from Thessaloniki. Of the many hotels, there are the Achillion (0353 41 210) and the seasonal Panorama (tel/fax: 0351 41 269). Lofty Mount Olympus dominates the skyline (right-forward). Three kilometres south between the Pydna and Aliki local request stops is the site of the **Battle of Pydna** (168BC) where the Romans utterly defeated Perseus, the last Macedonian king, and conquered Macedonia.

Aliki (left), surrounded by the Touzla Marsh, contains the largest salt mines in Greece. These have been worked since antiquity. The Touzla Marsh is the site of the ancient harbour of Pydna. Ruins at the village of Kitros, possibly Roman, are visible on the left, as is a large mound relating to Pydna.

Discoveries of potential archaeological sites in this area have hindered the double tracking of the railway. This region, on higher ground than its surroundings during antiquity, was heavily populated during ancient Greek and Roman times with country villas of the wealthy scattered about. The hard-pressed Greek Archaeological Service finds it difficult to keep up with the sheer number of recent discoveries. During the current railway construction boom, OSE has had to change routings slightly in several locations to avoid such small digs. But this means delays and difficulties in keeping up with construction schedules. This situation with archaeological digs is not limited to the railway. Some villagers whose public works projects have been seriously delayed, like a celebrated case in the remote White Mountains villages behind Chania in Crete where an irrigation canal was delayed, have taken to destroying open digs so their pressing projects can continue.

The relatively wide and dry coastal plain here is called the **Pieria**, the mythically attributed birthplace of the Muses.

The large market town of **Katerini** (population 48,000), with Mount Olympus towering behind it, is the next important rail station: all trains call here. Katerini is known as a Uniate centre with one of the two Uniate churches to be found in Greece. As only a handful of local trains stop at Dion, Katerini should be the stop for the ancient site and museum of Dion. But Dion is the main reason to come to Katerini and, as such, a visit there could be combined with time at the beach. Several hotels are available in the centre: the Acropole (0351 61 425) and the Stella (0351 61 612) are open year round. The tourist police (0351 23 440) can advise as to others in the centre or at the beach.

Dion (open daily 08.00–17.00; admission 800, 600, 400Dr; tel: 0351 53 206) was the site of the most important Macedonian sanctuary with both Philip and Alexander offering their thanks to the gods – after the capture of Olynthos in the Halkidiki for Philip and before his departure against the Persians for Alexander. It could be here that Alexander, at age 12, received and tamed his legendary horse Bucephalus. The little settlement stands in the northern foothills of Mount Olympus and completely dominates access from Macedonia to Thessaly. Archelaus (413–399BC) built a temple to Zeus, a stadium for festival games held there until 100BC and an amphitheatre for which Euripides wrote plays. The walls surrounding the site in a relatively square plan are attributed to Cassander. The Macedonians concentrated their armies here before heading to war. After the Battle of Pydna, the Romans established a colony here and the town was well enough esteemed to have a bishop in 346AD. Alarac sacked the settlement which faded into oblivion until 1928–31 when digs began.

The majority of the finds date to the Roman and Byzantine eras, but the sanctuaries fundamental to the Macedonians – to Zeus, Demeter, Artemis, Asclepios, the Muses and the Egyptian gods Isis and Seraipis – are located here as well. For visitors, the most comprehensible finds in the more recently excavated areas are the mosaics, temples and vast public baths. Macedonian cemeteries located to the north and west of the city centre have yielded gold rings, bracelets, wreaths, sculpted funerary stelae and statues. These and other finds from the various sites around Pieria (Pydna among others) are displayed in the fine new museum (open Mon 12.30–17.00, Tues–Fri 08.00–17.00, Sat–Sun 08.30–15.00; admission 800, 600, 400Dr; tel: 0351

53 206). A booklet and map of the site are also available at the museum. In Dion there is the Hotel Dion (0351 53 682); and two all-year campgrounds are available on the beach at Variko (5km): the Niteas (0352 61 290) and the Stani (0352 61 277).

For those preferring to go direct to Dion, the shelter is served as a request stop by an early morning and late evening locals. The next important stop south (although a request stop, but for seven daily trains) is at Litochoro. This is the stop for hikers and campers bound for the Mount Olympus range looming up (right) directly over the station. The station is close to the coast about 7km from the village at the mouth of the Mavrolongos Gorge, but only a two-minute walk from the road where all buses to the village of Litochoro pass. Campsites along the shore and only minutes from the station include: Minerva (0352 22 1778), Olymbos Beach (0352 22 112), and Olymbios Zeus (0352 22 115).

Mount Olympus is a chain of mountains with the peak, Mount Mytikas, at 2,917m. The range is so large it has its own microclimate (it is said that it receives 12 times the thunder and lightning bursts found anywhere else in Greece) and has its own micro flora and fauna. There are some 1,700 species of plants, some of which are found only there. The heavily wooded slopes are covered with a variety of trees. It's no wonder the Greeks chose this imposing mountain to be the home of their gods.

A local man, Christos Kakalos, and two Swiss mountaineers were credited with being the first mortals to scale Mount Mytikas in 1913. The range became Greece's first National Park in 1927.

Trekking on the mountain has become quite popular and Litochoro has also rediscovered its vocation as a health spa of sorts. This means it's best to be organised before coming to the area and/or to reserve space on the mountain refuges. Trekking Information is available through EOS (Mon–Fri 09.00–13.00 & 18.00–20.30, Sat 09.00–13.00; tel: 0352 81 944) or SEO – the Association of Hellenic Climbers – (daily 18.00–22.00; tel: 0352 82 300). Both offer insights and brief pamphlets on possible routes up. EOS has three refuges on the mountain and SEO one. The EOS refuge at Spilios Agapitos (2,100m) is manned and reservations are strongly advised during the summer (open mid May–mid Oct; tel: 0352 81 800). The SEO manned refuge at Yiosos Apostolidis (2,700m) is open from July to Sept (no phone). In Litochoro, lodgings include the IYHA Hostel (tel: 0352 81 311), Hotel Enipeas (tel: 0352 81 328), Hotel Aphrodite (tel: 0352 81 415) or the more upscale Myrto (tel: 0352 81 398). For others check with the local police (tel: 0352 81 100) or EOS.

A good map and guide are necessary and can be obtained either in Litochoro or before arriving. The climb up during the warm months takes two solid days but more time should be accorded to what is arguably Greece's foremost mountain range. The following paragraphs only give background and are in no way intended to be a guide to trails. Obviously those on a tight time schedule could be tempted to save time by using an overnight train and heading out early in the morning. These people are to be discouraged. It should be remembered that Litochoro is at sea level and the summit is at 2,917m. Attempting this in one day is foolish.

From Litochoro, an 18km marked trail, the E4, along the banks of the Ennipeas River leads to Pronia. There is a road but the views and atmosphere along the trail merit using it instead. The Dimitris Boundolas EOS refuge (open April–November) is halfway between Litochoro and Pronia. The Nazis destroyed the 16th-century Monastery of Agios Dionisos which is about one km from Pronia. From Pronia two main routes lead up: the Gortsia route, considered the prettiest, and the more heavily travelled Pronia route. The Gortsia route leads in about seven hours to the 90-bed SEO refuge of Yiosos Apostolidis, renowned for its unrivalled views of the "Throne of Zeus" as the Stefani Peak (2,909m) is called. Nearby EOS has a small 18-bed Christos Kakkalos refuge, but it is open only in July and August. The Pronia route climbs along the E4 to the EOS Spilios Agapitos refuge and from there to the summit. Returning from the summit, it is possible to take several alternate routes. But, remember to be well equipped, take your time, enjoy the often spectacular views and do not to be taken aback if, and when, the weather suddenly changes – as it frequently does, even in the July–August summer months.

From the Litochoro rail station trains proceed down the main line to the beach village of **Platamon** which is considered the last important stop in Macedonia. Rail photographers should enjoy the view of the main line, and trains passing on the embankment above the beach, just below the crusader castle on the heights. This is one of the finest rail photo opportunities in Greece.

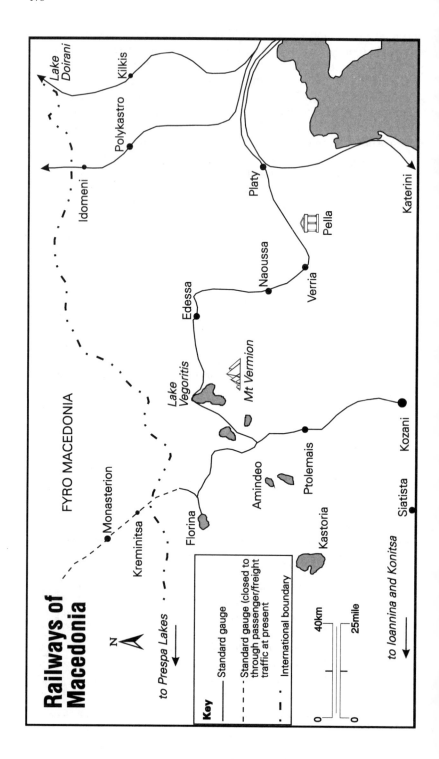

Chapter Thirteen

Thessaloniki–Kozani

Thessaloniki–Platy–Verria–Naoussa–Edessa–Amindeo–Florina/Kozani

INTRODUCTION

This is a 222km standard gauge railway penetrating west from Thessaloniki up Mount Vermion into the very foothills of mountainous Epirus. It was built by a German company during the last years of the Ottoman Empire, though the 60km Amindeo–Kozani segment was added in 1956. It is a railway line that serves mountainous areas more akin to the Balkans than the usual images of sun-drenched Greece. Winter snows, large alpine lakes and cities with fast running waters coursing through their centres remind one more of Central Europe and create a unique and interesting land for discerning visitors wanting to leave the beaten path behind.

There are eight daily trains departing from Thessaloniki towards the west. All trains leave the north/south main line at Platy and go through the Amindeo junction. From there, they serve either Kozani or Florina. Through trains towards one destination will normally have a connecting train at Amindeo for the other branch. For example, Express 723 departing Thessaloniki 08.20 for Kozani will arrive Amindeo at 11.36. A connecting train for Florina (773) departs Amindeo at 11.50.

Two IC trains serve this line. IC 81/80 serves Thessaloniki and Kozani while another IC with an inexplicably long series of numbers (60/65 northbound and 60/62 southbound) connects Athens and Kozani. IC 60/65 from Athens to Kozani leaves the north/south main line at Platy, 39km south of Thessaloniki. This train can be joined from Thessaloniki by boarding express 507 and changing in Platy (it is a long 90-minute wait at Platy).

Trains on this line follow the north/south main line (described in the preceding chapter) to Platy, then leave it on a wide curve to the southwest (right) through the wide, exposed and very flat plain of Pedias Kampanias, along the Aliakmon River that fostered the early Macedonians. This was a lagoon in ancient times and was drained only in 1925 by Venizelos. The outline of the city of Yiannitsa can be made out on the right and that of Verria in the Mount Pieria foothills of Mount Vermion directly ahead.

PLATY TO VERRIA

The rail line runs by the town of Alexandria before passing under the Thessaloniki–Florina road, then proceeds through Xehasmeni (right), and crosses the 152m bridge over the Aliakmon River (which is now on the right) before entering the station of Kouloura. Mesi, a request stop amongst rich plantations of peach and plum trees, is next. The village of Vergina is 10km off to the left.

Vergina, a 1923 refugee village built over an ancient city populated from the Iron Age until Classical times, is better known as the site of the **Royal Tombs of Macedonian King Philip II**. These tombs were only discovered in November 1977 by Professor Manolis Andronikos under a great tumulus mound that had provoked interest for centuries. Finds from the site are on display at the Thessaloniki Archaeological Museum and are considered the richest discovered since Mycenae. They establish that Vergina is the site of **Aigai**, the first capital of Macedon. The administrative capital was moved to Pella, but Aigia continued to be the sanctuary and royal burial site. Andronikos discovered two large definitely Macedonian chamber tombs. The first, looted in antiquity, contained a mural of the rape of Persephone by Pluto: the only complete example of an ancient painting yet found. The second much grander vaulted tomb had been disguised with a pile of rubble from later tomb pillages. This tomb, graced with doric columns and adorned with an exceptional painted frieze of a lion hunt, was intact. Andronikos was astonished to find a marble sarcophagus containing a gold casket of bones bearing the exploding star symbol of the Macedonian royal line on its lid. It also contained five small ivory heads with representations of Philip and Alexander. A facial scar over an eye confirmed that these were indeed the remains of Philip. Though excavations are ongoing, visitors can enter the domed and air-conditioned tomb site (open Tues–Sun 08.30–15.00; admission 1,200, 900, 600Dr; tel: 0331 92 347) and the nearby museum (same days and hours; admission 500, 400, 300Dr; tel: 0331/92 394).

Near these tombs are three other Macedonian tombs; and further along on a low hill marked by a large oak tree are the remains of the 3rd-century BC **Palace of Palititsa**. This was probably the summer palace of the last great Macedonian King Antigonus Gonatus. Here can be seen a fine mosaic. The site is still being excavated and some areas may be off-limits to visitors. But the location itself, with fine views over the valley as well as the existing exhibits, makes the site worth the excursion. Vergina is only beginning to develop as a tourist destination. Rooms can be rented from Mrs Sophia Hatziagapidou (tel: 0331 92 510) in a purpose-built pension near the site.

The rail line then crosses the 98m bridge over the Tripotamos tributary of the Aliakmon and enters Verria.

Verria

Verria (population 38,800), the New Testament Beroia, is the first important stop after Thessaloniki. The railway station is about 3km from the centre of the old city.

History

Verria was the first town from Thessaloniki on the ancient road to Thessaly, protecting the entrance into the valley and acting as a market centre for the region. As such, it was prized by the Macedonians. It was turned over to the Romans the day after the Battle of Pydna, and was used by them as a regional headquarters. The Byzantines developed the city as a centre of textile manufacture, taking advantage of the large number of watermills; in time the city acquired a name for its dyers and bleachers of cloth. Byzantines taken prisoner by the Turks after a difficult siege were sold to Venice (1381-88) and are thought to have expanded Venetian textile skills. Despite many setbacks, Verria's location and industrious citizens prospered and the city once again developed a well-deserved reputation for their skills.

What to see

Though containing few significant ruins of its own, attractive Verria does have a small archaeological museum (Anexios Avenue 47; open Tues–Sun 08.30–15.00; admission 500, 400, 300Dr; tel: 0331 24 972) containing mostly Roman and Byzantine artefacts.

Located about the Roman walls are the several dozen late Byzantine and Ottoman churches (note the 14th-century wall painting of "The Descent into Hades" by Georgios Kalliergis in the Church of the Resurrection of the Lord). There is also the old Turkish quarter with its intact bazaar, hammam baths (not open) and mosques, which will give discerning visitors an idea of life in a prosperous late medieval Ottoman town. Christian churches built in that era were later disguised as barns and houses, but have subsequently been restored. There are fine views from the terraces overlooking the Tripotamos River down through its luscious green valley. The modern city is marked by the usual apartment blocks and much recent commercial development with a wide variety of distractions possible.

Where to stay

Accommodation in Verria includes the Hotel Veroi (Platia Orologiou; tel: 0331 22 866), the Polytimi (Megalou Alexandrou 35; tel: 0331 64 902), and the slightly more upscale Makedonia (Kondogiorgaki 15; tel: 0331 66 902).

VERRIA TO NAOUSSA

The rail line beyond Verria continues north, initially through industrial suburbs, towards Naoussa. It parallels the bulk of Mount Vermion (2,027m) visible on the left. Mount Vermion, the watershed for Thessaloniki, is the most densely forested mountain in Greece, with beech, chestnut, hazel, oak, pine, and evergreen trees sheltering deer and wild boar. It contains ski resorts, and at the village of Seli (1,700m) an 18-bed hostel.

The wine-growing village of Stenamachos (left) signals that entry to the rail station for Naoussa (3km on the left – shuttle bus service meets all trains) is near. Stenamachos was settled by Greek refugee families from near Plovdiv (Philippopolis) in south/central Bulgaria, where most were viticulturists at the well respected wine towns of Asenovgrad.

Naoussa

Naoussa (population 20,100) is a surprisingly large town on the slopes of Mount Vermion, renowned for its hearty red wine. Researchers from the Institute of Enology at France's University of Bordeaux believe that the grape variety grown here since time immemorial, the Xynomavro, could be the distant and rustic ancestor to the celebrated Cabernet Sauvignon variety. This is a wine area where seasonal weather conditions, unlike those in much of Greece, can be difficult during harvest time. It is modern Greece's oldest quality wine-growing area. Many wineries have begun developing tasting and visiting facilities for wine aficionados. They include the Stenamachos winery of the fabled Boutaris family (tastings and slide show, open daily during the summer, no appointment necessary, tel: 0332 42 687); the Chrisohoou family (by appointment: tel: 0332 22 286, fax: 22 112); the Markovitis brothers (tel: 0332 42 402, fax: 41 611) and the Melitzanis brothers (wine shop on Dimarchias Street, Naoussa), to name but a few of the finer properties.

The well-watered town tucked into the folds of the mountain between two tributaries of the Arapitsa River is a delight. It is a modern town, having been destroyed in 1821 and severely damaged in 1944–1948, but its narrow streets remain on the old plan, as do the walkways along the riverside glen that courses down through the centre. The cooling waters used to act as a natural humidifier and refrigerant for wine cellars that honeycombed the ground beneath the town. During its winter carnival (dates are variable) masked dancers holding scimitars symbolise the oppression of the Janissaries.

Excellent nature walks are possible 2km behind Naoussa in the cooling shade of the Mount Vermion area. The Hotel Vermion (tel: 0332 29 311) has quiet rooms, disturbed only by the nearby stream. The Seli Refuge and winter resort can be accessed from here. In the town, the Hellas (tel: 0332 22 006) is the only hotel.

NAOUSSA TO EDESSA

The rail line continues to the northwest through the foothills, but it begins its ascent of Mount Vermion after the stop at Lefkadia. Several kilometres beyond Naoussa at Isvoria near Kopanos (left) is thought to be the site of ancient Mieza and the Nymphaion Sanctuary where Alexander, in the company of Aristotle, learned to "live well".

Excavations at **Lefkadia** have unearthed 4th-century BC Hellenistic ruins with a series of several small tombs containing painted reliefs and mosaics, and the Great Tomb. The Great Tomb (right) before the railway station is built with Doric columns on the ground floor and Ionic above. Here is a frieze depicting a battle between Macedonians and Persians. The Tomb of the Flowers has fine floral and figural paintings; and the Lyson Kallikles Tomb, the Tomb of Palmettes and Kinch's Tomb are all of some interest with their exotic paintings and designs.

Continuing along the rail line are the request stops of Episkopi and Petria, with the railway climbing now to Skydra where it rejoins the Roman Via Egnatia. **Skydra** (population 4,300) is a mountain resort of sorts and the site of a long abandoned and forgotten 48km long, 60cm gauge rail line towards Ardea and Sosandra and beyond to Apsalo. The simple Hotel Adonis (0381 89 231) provides adequate accommodation.

From Skydra the rail line turns to the left, always climbing through mountain country. The 15km beyond, passing through the village halt of Garefi to Edessa, offer fine views of the valley and villages (right) towards the north. Trains, beyond Garefi, thunder through a series of five galleries, the third of which is 641m long. To the right Mount Kaimaktsalan (2,524m) is visible. The rail line has left the plain and become a mountain railway now. A large stand of tall trees signals arrival at the attractive Edessa station.

Edessa

Edessa (population 17,000), with its many streams, cataracts and waterfalls, is called the "garden of Macedonia", and considered by Greeks to be the loveliest city in Greece. It stands on a high bluff at the transition from the plains to the mountains of Macedonia. The town was known in ancient times from an inscription at Delphi and was prized by the Romans for its strategic location on the Via Egnatia. Prior to the discoveries at Vergina it was thought to be the Macedonian capital, Aigai.

The old walls exist and provide an excellent vantage point over the vast green plain of Macedonia. Ancient cemeteries attest to the city's importance during the Roman era. Many of the local finds are in the local Archaeological Museum housed in the 19th-century Yeni Jamii Mosque. Beyond the mosque is an old Roman or Byzantine bridge.

Archaeology is not the main reason to come to Edessa. The waters are. The city is located on the main trajectory of a number of well-channelled streams bridged by simple stone bridges to create a series of canal-lined parks and pedestrian walkways that lead to a 24m waterfall signposted as "Katarractes". A walkway leads to a ledge under the falls, from where visitors can admire the lush country below. Views from the edge of the falls are excellent, with the waters of the Thermaic Gulf being visible behind vineyards and orchards. The effect is soothing and the town has an extremely relaxed atmosphere.

Where to stay
Edessa has quite a few hotels: the simple Alfa (0381 22 221) and Pella (0381 23 541) or the posher Katarraktes (0381 22 300). But be forewarned: the town has a tendency to fill with busloads of Greeks come to admire the waterfalls, and rooms might be full.

EDESSA TO AMINDEO

Beyond the enormous fig tree at the west end of the Edessa station trackage begins a series of sharp curves over three bridges (194, 195 and 130m) and through seven tunnels into a rocky landscape leading to Lake Vegoritida. At Agras, the line passes the first of many hydrolectric power plants in the area. To the right is a memorial to the Macedonian leader Tellos Agapinos, who was hanged from a chestnut tree here while on a truce mission to the Bulgarians in 1907.

Lake Vegoritida comes into view on the left. This calm alpine lake (at 558m) is 19km long from east to west and a maximum of 8km wide. In places it is 49m deep. In antiquity it was much smaller, with the level so low that a village on the isle off Arnissa was exposed. A 1993 earthquake in the area has changed the equation and the level of the lake is falling once again. Mount Kaimaktsalan, whose summit marks the Greek FYRO Macedonia border, is always in view on the right. This mountain was the site of one of the longest and bloodiest battles of World War I, with fighting raging from 1916 to 1918.

The rail line follows the lake for 36km, virtually circumnavigating it. Two villages are found on its shores and they both have OSE rail service. First is the little one-street fishing village of Arnissa, containing the trout hatchery that helped stock the lake in 1958. It is the site of an extensive Tuesday market and walking tours around the high villages of Kaimaktsalan begin from here. Lodging is available at the Megali Ellas (0381 31 232). The next station is Agios Penelimonas, but the station is known as Vegoritis. This red-tile-roofed town has a small beach and a basic campground. Extensive vineyards now come into view.

The railway swings to the left after the end of the lake, with the smaller Petro lake to the right. After a last view of Arnissa behind the train (left), the rail line swings into the Amindeo Junction. It is also known by its former name of Sorovits, for the battle fought here on 22–24 October 1912. It was renamed in honour of the father of Philip of Macedon. The railway was once again destroyed by retreating British irregulars in the spring of 1941.

The Amindeo region has developed into an important region for the production of red wine, with over 550ha planted in the same Xynomavro variety as Naoussa. The local Wine Co-operative and the Boutari Family produce the biggest quantities.

Here at Amindeo the rail line splits, with one branch going on to Florina and the other to Kozani.

AMINDEO TO FLORINA BY RAIL

This 37km standard gauge branch line was one of the first rail lines built by the *Chemin de Fer Oriental* in the late 19th century. Its purpose was to exploit the back country and link the present-day town of Bitola in FYRO Macedonia with Thessaloniki. It was the first line built in the former Ottoman province of Macedonia. The segment from Mesonissi to Florina was completed in 1931. Regular passenger trains through to Bitola, the old Monastir in Yugoslavia, stopped running when the country broke up in 1991. This segment is not exploited at all today. Because the station is on the Mesonissi–Kreminitsa side, OSE trains pull forward to the station then back one kilometre to the switch points for Florina.

The rail line passes through a rather hilly countryside reminiscent of Switzerland, dominated by wheat fields and high mountain pastures where cattle graze. The line climbs to the station of Klidi, which at 769m is the highest point on the OSE standard gauge railway. The pass at Klidi was held for three days in early spring 1941 while the railway installations were blown at Amindeo. After the unusual backup move at Mesonissi, the rail line crosses a girder bridge and proceeds across the high plain of Florina into the Florina station. It is from here that OSE authorities want to push a 110km rail line into Albania.

Florina

Florina (population 12,800) is the rarest of Greek towns. Winters here mean metres of snow and months of below-freezing weather. During the hot summers it is a busy market town, though tourism has dropped off considerably since the break-up of Yugoslavia. Florina is the gateway to the Prespa Lakes and to the old city of Kastoria.

Old Florina, a Turkish border town, occupied both sides of the Sakoulevas river. Some of its picturesque old houses have been restored and one is now the Gallery of Modern Art (Leoforos Eleftheriou 103; open Tues–Sun 18.00–21.00) with a collection of paintings by Greek and European artists. A smaller gallery (Mon, Wed, Sat 18.00–21.30, Sun 10.00–13.30; admission free) in a building formerly used by railway authorities houses a collection of paintings by local artists. The two-floor Archaeological Museum (open Tues–Sun 08.30–15.00; admission 500, 400, 300Dr), also near the railway station, houses finds from the late Macedonian and Roman eras.

Where to stay

Hotels are not in short supply and include: the Hellinis (Pavlou Mela 61; 0385 22 671, fax: 22 815) near the railway station;Antigone (Arianos 1, 0385 23 180);the Lyngos (Tagmatarchou Naoum 1, 0385 28 322, fax: 29 643);and the upscale King Alexander (Leoforos Nikis, 0385 23 501, fax: 23 084) overlooking the town.

Further afield

The objective for many visitors to Florina is to travel on to the high mountain Prespa Lakes.

Prespa Lakes This isolated alpine lake area (850m), surrounded by high mountains creating the borders of Greece, Albania and FYRO Macedonia, is one of those eerily evocative places that stays long in mind. Settled in prehistoric and classical times by outsiders, the area was used by the Byzantines as a place of exile for unruly noblemen, who repented by building a surprisingly large number of churches and other ecclesiastical monuments. Bulgarian Tsars briefly ruled here in the 10th century, before the area sank back into near oblivion under the Ottomans. It was a major battleground during almost all the conflicts of the 20th century, especially the Greek Civil War (1947–49).

There are two lakes: small (Micri) Prespa (43km²) to the south is more shallow and reedy than large (Megali) Prespa (1,000km²), the largest lake in the Balkans, which is the border between the three often antagonistic nations. Given these differences, the military presence is surprisingly low key, unlike further east along the Turkish frontier. This could be due to the fact that only three high passes lead into the area: The Pisoderi Pass (1498m) from Florina, one from Bitola in FYRO Macedonia and the Kristallopigi Pass along the Albanian frontier. Travellers can only use the Pisoderi pass, but permits from the Greek military are no longer necessary.

The region was declared a national park in 1971 to protect the unique birdlife, foxes, bears and wolves which roam the wild areas around the lakes. Birds include large numbers of egrets, cormorants, crested grebes and pelicans, paddling about the reedy banks of Micri Prespa. Over 1,248 types of rare mountain plants have been identified in the Prespa National Park.

The first village into the area (turn off to the left on the road to Agios Germanos) is Mikrolimni on Micri Prespa. Here there are rooms to let (0385 61 221) and good sunset and bird-watching views. A trail leads off beyond the village but it is the main refugee trail from Albania. With the

Folegandros in the Cycladic Islands

ARCHES OLD AND NEW

Left: *Old Mystras*
Right: *Folegandros*

Semeli Winery in the northeast Attica hills near Athens

Above: *Venetian fort at Methoni*

Below: *The seaside village of Koroni*

disintegrating situation there, refugees are becoming more numerous and more and more desperate. Camping is possible here, but, though tolerated, is not recommended during these troubled times.

The excellent Prespa Park Information Centre (mid-March to mid-Sept; open 09.30–13.30 & 16.30–19.30, mid-Sept to mid-March 10.00–14.00) is in the rather large village of Agios Germanos. Though Agios Germanos is on the limit of the lakes, it does have the Centre which can possibly arrange guided tours into the park and it has a variety of Byzantine churches and accommodation. The 18th-century Agios Athanasios church has a selection of saints carved from wood, but the 11th-century Agios Germanos (behind the modern church) has a large quantity of early frescos. The village has several places to stay including old red-tiled *Archontica* (mansions) from the 17th century (0385 51 320) or Les Pelicans (0385 51 442).

A turn off to the left before Agios Germanos leads across the narrow peninsula between Micri and Megali Prespa to the village of Psarades on Megali Prespa. This tiny village has rooms to rent through the Christianopoulos family (0385 51 327) among others. Offshore, on the island of Agios Achillios, are Byzantine churches and monuments: the remains of the 1000AD three-aisle basilica above the hill provides good views, and the Agios Georgios church of the village cemetery has good 15th-century frescos while the early 16th-century Monastery of Porhyra Panagia has fine frescos as well.

Though it is possible to continue on by road to Kastoria, there are few bus connections from Florina and the road is rough in certain places. It is best to access Kastoria through Kozani.

AMINDEO TO KOZANI BY RAIL

This 60km segment of standard gauge was the last major railway built to serve Greek destinations. It was surveyed in the late 1920s to continue through Kozani to Siatista then south to Grevena before coming to a junction with the Thessaly Railways at Kalambaka. The world economic crisis of the 1930s followed by World War II delayed construction until the early 1950s. American economic planners with the Marshall Plan convinced Greek railwaymen to abandon construction after Kozani. Now, with the widening of the track from Paleofarsalo to Kalambaka the extension of this line to complete the circuit at Kozani seems possible; especially if a rail line is built to Igoumenitsa from Kalambaka. Both these two lines would allow goods to be unloaded at the port of Igoumenitsa then be shipped by rail to Central Europe and Turkey via Thessaloniki and to the Near East via Volos. Both these new rail lines seem likely to be built in the first part of the 21st century.

The rail line heads south through a high, wide, fertile plain, with massive high-tension power lines disfiguring the skyline. They come from the huge

Ptolemais hydroelectric power plant built in 1959, which provides over 50% of Greece's total electricity needs. If threats by the Greek Power Company (DEH) to cut FYRO Macedonia from the grid come true, this power plant could possibly provide all the power necessary for the rail mainline electrification scheme. Another hydroelectric dam is planned near the Aliakmon River source that feeds into Lake Vegoritis.

Ptolemais or Ptolemaida (population 25,000) is a growing town whose economy is based on the lignite mines that produce low-grade coal, sulphuric acid and nitrate fertilisers. Behind Ptolemais is the village of Emborio. From here semi-hidden and now little-used mountain trails lead to Siatista and beyond to Kastoria. They were long used by fur traders during the Middle Ages, but last used in any great way by Greek troops fleeing Albania to avoid capture by the Germans in 1941. These trails are easily found, beginning in the shady glen behind the gazebo on the edge of the extensive chestnut forest, which spreads up the mountain slopes behind the town centre. Two hotels are in Ptolemais' colourful market area: the Costis (0463 26 661) and the Pantelidis (0463 53 300, fax: 29 725).

The rail line proceeds south through the crossroads of Azoto (no stop) where the DEH power plant is, then to Komanos village (massive power plant impossible to miss on left). In Komanos there is a strange well from which issues black water. From here, with Mount Vermion visible far on the left, the line wends its way through the villages of Pontokomi, Mavrodendri and Drepano where it attains a high point of 701m before terminating at the relatively new station for the intriguing city of Kozani.

Kozani

This largish city (population 32,400), rarely visited by foreigners, is the communications and transport centre for western Macedonia and Epirus. It is also an agricultural market and important military centre, but has interesting old wooden mansions, winding pedestrian streets terminating in picturesque squares and several museums to detain visitors for a day or so. The region was unfortunately the site of a severe earthquake in the spring of 1995 and some families are still housed in temporary structures near the rail station.

Kozani is not an old town. It was created by voluntary population transfers from the Epirus region in the 14th and 15th centuries supplemented by influxes of people from the Agrafa villages in the 17th century. Artisans specialising in tanning, weaving, bronze work and furs congregated in the city during the 18th century, when Kozani was much favoured by the sultan's mother. Traders fanned out through Central Europe and endowed the city with cobbled streets, fountains, churches and the large two-floored timber-framed houses called *archontiko,* which were begun in the 18th century and recently restored. Greek schools and the first public library in western Macedonia, endowed by Archbishop Meletios (1734–1753), fostered

Hellenism, but the city was not liberated from the Ottomans until 1912. Shortly thereafter Greek cavalry regiments fought the Bulgarians in the Prespa Lakes area and around Siatista from their bases in Kozani.

The park in front of the picturesque Metamorfosis tou Sotiros monument, on the hill northwest of the town, provides commanding views of Kozani and the plain of the Aliakmon River to the village of Servia.

The five-room **Archaeological Museum**, though damaged in the recent earthquake and temporarily closed (Dimokratias St 6; tel: 0461 26 210), has a small but valuable collection of finds from the prehistoric to the Hellenistic era. The Historical and Folklore Museum (P. Charisi Street; open daily 17.00–21.00; admission free) also has a wide range of eclectic exhibits including botanical and geological specimens, tools and machines from local goldsmiths workshops, and even an entire room from the 18th-century Yannis Trantas Archontico.

Where to stay

Accommodation is plentiful in Kozani and includes the Aliakmon (0461 36 015, fax: 26 186), the Katerina (0461 34 856) and the more classic Ptolemais (0461 26 217) and Tselicas (0461 35 997, fax: 37 997). The West Macedonian Regional Tourist Centre (tel: 0461 36 961, fax: 32 633) will gladly provide further information.

Further afield

A road south leads over the Aliakmon River hydroelectric lake via a 2km bridge (the longest in Greece until the Rio-Andiro bridge is finished). The village of Velvendio at the foot of Mount Pieria has Byzantine churches and a lovely waterfall tumbling in front of a hidden cave called the *skepasmeno*. This road leads to Servia (population 3,100), a town deriving its name from a colony of Serbs who were resettled there in the 7th century as a buffer against invaders. The Byzantine fortress on the heights reminds one that the narrow Pass of Sarandoporos was the main north/south route between Thessaly and Macedonia before the modern era.

The road west from Kozani provides access to Epirus, as well as serving the two intriguing and autonomous towns of **Siatista** and **Kastoria**. This road heads directly west from Kozani and parallels the unfinished "ghost railway" 26km to the crossroads of Bara. From there, with the ruined stone rail station, that never saw a train call, on the left, the road forks to the right up to Siatista (930m) nestled on a ridge along a long, narrow valley.

Siatista (population 6,500) is a prosperous fur trading town, probably settled in the 15th or early 16th century by immigrants from Epirus. It is, surprisingly enough, unvisited by travellers today. Very well known during the 17th century throughout Central Europe, its native sons prospered as far afield as Vienna, and with others from neighbouring Kastoria were responsible for organising foreign political and financial support for intrigues against Ottoman rule in the 18th century. The town's location, hidden from the main roads of even the 17th century, was an advantage. Occupying Turks didn't know of it for many decades after they seized control of western Macedonia. Invading Italians in 1941 were routed by the simple ruse of Siatistan horsemen creating an incredible racket with cans tied to their horses' tails. The Italians, unable to see their enemy, thought they were being attacked by an armoured division.

Siatista is composed of two platias: the lower Gerania and the upper Chora linked by a single long street where can be found Siatista's only hotel, the Archonticon (0465 21 298, fax: 22 835). Siatista is surrounded by stark absolutely barren mountains, which used to be widely planted with vineyards. These vineyards were destroyed by the Philoxera in the late 1920s; but the fine, sweet wine of Siatista is still locally produced in small quantities.

Several 18th-century two-storey archontika mansions with their overhanging second floors and typical wattle-and-daub finish over stone foundations have been restored and are open to the public: Poulko (1752–59) in Gerania, and Anousis (1746?), Nerantzopoulis (1754–1755) and Keratzis (1748?) in Chora. The Keratzis mansion is particularly interesting for its colourful wall painting of a harbour scene with peacocks incongruously nesting on clouds. Two 17th-century churches, Agios Dimitrios and Agia Paraskevi, and a surprisingly well endowed public library left by a 19th century scholar, round out the sights.

Siatista is also becoming well known nationally for its continuous 48-hour-long midsummer Assumption of the Virgin Panagyria Festival (14–15 August). Local townspeople wearing multicoloured costumes parade on bedecked horses: they even dance on their patient steeds while accompanying musicians strike up an oddly stirring flute and drum music, unlike anything known elsewhere in Greece.

Beyond Siatista another fork in the road leads south to the agricultural centre of Grevena or 49km north through heavily wooded upland country to Kastoria. The road straight ahead leads through spectacular mountains to the Zagoria Villages, then to Konitsa before entering Ioannina. This will be covered in the *Suggested Itineraries* section (*Part Six*).

Kastoria (population 15,750) on the promontory of a peninsula jutting on to Kastoria's lake, is considered by many to be one of the most attractive towns in mainland Greece. Once again, the fur trade created wealth. As in Siatista, furriers here made their wealth by buying in scraps of mink pelts from here and there and then fashioning them into stylish winter wear. The fur trade is over 500 years old, but the city dates to antiquity. Known to the Greeks and Romans, its walls (only traces of which remain) were built by Justinian. The name was changed from Justinianopolis to Kastron, probably for the beavers who lived in the lake. It was briefly controlled by the Bulgars (980-1018) until wrested back by the Byzantine Basil II. It prospered under Serbian control for almost 50 years in the 14th century before passing into Turkish hands in 1385. It was freed in 1912 and served as the Greco-American forward base for the bloody 1949 assault on the nearby Mount Grammos which ended the military phase of the Greek Civil War.

Most of the remains date from the Byzantine era with over 50 churches – all, with one exception, of the basilica type with barrel vaulted naves. A new Byzantine Museum (Platia Dexaminis; open Tues–Sun 08.30–15.00; admission free) contains a large collection of intricately painted medieval Byzantine icons from the local churches. A visit here is recommended before moving on to the churches. Of the churches, the following merit a visit: the 9–10th-century Agios Stephanos, the 10th-century Church of the Anargyroi and Church of the Taxiarches, the 11th-century Church of Agios Nikolaos Kasnitzes, the 11th-century domed Church of the Panagia and Agios Ioannis the Theologian among the many. The last three are known for their wall painting and show the stylistic progression from the 11th to the 16th century.

Archontika in Kastoria are more plentiful and in better condition than those of Siatista. One 535-year-old house, belonging to the Neranzis Aivazis family, has been converted into the **Kastorian Folklore Museum** (Capitan Lazou 10; open daily 08.30–18.00; admission 400Dr). The large, two-storey house surrounding a small courtyard was inhabited until the early 1970s and is in excellent condition. Its naïve painting of medieval Constantinople without a minaret in sight must be seen. Once the Aivazis mansion has been seen, the others, mostly in the old Christian neighbourhood of Kariadi around Platia Immanouil, will make more sense in the context of Kastoria being a leading city in the 18th-century economic rebirth of Greece.

As well as the church and mansion gazing, Kastoria offers its lake for walking, but perhaps not for swimming – at least not near the city. Halfway along the nine-kilometre trek around the peninsula is the Monastery of Mavriotissa where it is possible to camp. Forbidding Mount Grammos (2,520m), the fourth highest peak in Greece, rises up in the background. It and its neighbour Mount Vitsi (2,360m) form the border with Albania. Left-wing rebels holed up on Grammos in August of 1949 were the object of the first real use ever of napalm. Trekkers there will easily recognise, almost fifty years later, where it was dropped. Many interesting trails up through the valley of the Sarandopotamos River to the summit of Grammos are possible from Kastoria (as well as from Konitsa in Epirus), with one trail to the tiny source of the Aliakmon River. Hikers should stay on marked trails because local shepherds still come across live munitions left over from the campaign to dislodge the rebels.

Accommodation in Kastoria should not prove difficult to obtain: the Hotel Palladion (Mitropoleos 40; 0467 22 493), Acropolis (Grammou 14;

0467 22 537), Anessis (Grammou 10; 0467 83 908), Europa (0467 23 826, fax: 25 154), Kastoria (Leoforou Nikis 122; 0467 29 453), Keletron (11 Novembrio 52; 0467 22 676) and the very upscale Tsamis Hotel (on the lake, 3km from the centre; 0467 85 344, fax: 85 777) overlooking the city. For other accommodation check with the Hoteliers' Association of Kastoria (0467 85 334, fax: 85 777).

The road straight through from Kozani to Konitsa and Ioannina, besides being one of the most scenic in Greece, leads to many trailheads near Konitsa and the Adriatic seacoast at the port of Igoumentisa.

Chapter Fourteen

International Services from Thessaloniki

Thessaloniki has the distinction of being the only major Greek city linked to the rest of Europe with a through railway passenger service. It even looks the part, with its massive railway station, especially since the 79km line to the international frontier at Gevgeli was electrified in 1995. International through passenger trains from Thessaloniki serve Western and Central Europe via Yugoslavia, Eastern Europe via Bulgaria and Turkey through Pythion.

Essentially there are four international routes served from Thessaloniki, through Idomeni, Promachon, Pythion and Svelingrad. Daily IC services through Promachon serve the Bulgarian capital of Sofia. Pythion and Svelingrad are north of Alexandroupolis. The service from Pythion used to serve Istanbul, but the state of this train is in flux. Current schedules show it passing through Pythion on a convenient morning schedule, but this can be and sometimes is disrupted by tensions between Greece and Turkey. It is best to check with railway authorities in Thessaloniki, not in Athens. Athenians tend to ignore what happens outside their walls. The through service from Messonission near Florina to Kreminitsa was terminated with the break-up of Yugoslavia.

The international service east through Promachon and Pythion is dealt with in *Chapter Fifteen*. The rest of this short chapter will deal with rail passenger service north from Thessaloniki to the Greek frontier station of Idomeni. There is just one internal Greek stop on this line, at Polykastro, before the Greek frontier at Idomeni.

This 76km line was part of a grand Turkish railway scheme of 1869, and it was completed in the seventies. It first carried the Orient Express in 1888. There was a possibility at the time that Thessaloniki might become an important port on a direct route from Europe to the far east via the Suez Canal, but this never came to pass. Today, it is the only Greek railway, other than the metropolitan Athens rail line, to be electrified. The electric system (overhead catenary) was turned on during the summer of 1995, but a lack of electric motive power has meant that diesels still·use the line. Six

Railways of Macedonia and Thrace

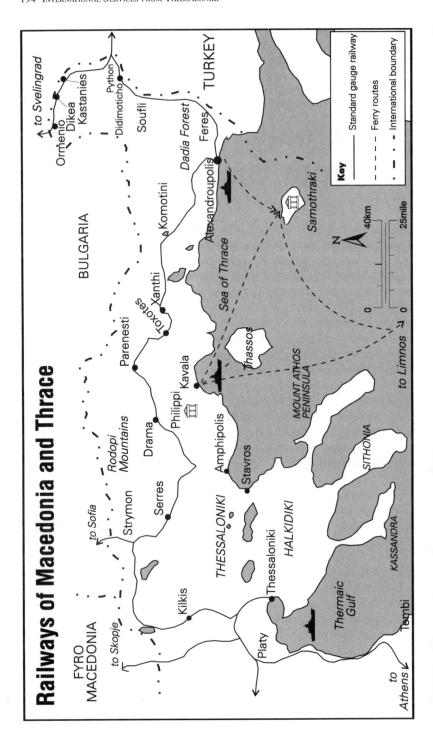

electric locomotives of the Eurosprinter type were ordered in early 1996 and should begin arriving in mid-1997. Whether they will be immediately used is another question because of the never-ending dispute with Greece's northern neighbour FYRO Macedonia over the use of the name Macedonia.

As seen in the preceding chapter, international trains through Idomeni use the same rail corridor out of the Thessaloniki station as all trains, then, after the Alexandroupolis line falls away to the right along the Gallikos River, the international line crosses the Gallikos River over a long 20-span bridge and continues along the marshy plain on a gently rising gradient. On reaching the Axios River near the Gefyra station, the international line turns northward and trains follow this river for the next 200km to the city of Skopje in FYRO Macedonia.

The Axios River is largely controlled by irrigation and flood control works. At Kastanas (no stop) the railway runs between the national road and the old road through the villages. Across the wide plain (left) the slopes of Mount Vermion can easily be made out. The American-built drainage works that reduced the former Lake Amatavon are to the right of Kastanas. Between the villages of Aspros and Limnotopos (no stops), the rail line runs along the alluvial flats reclaimed from the drained Lake Amatavon, then after crossing the Axios on a large bridge, winds with the river to the stop at Polykastro. Polykastro (population 4,700) is where the old and now abandoned Turkish Thessaloniki bypass line, 20km long, connected to the Alexandroupolis line near Kilkis. Polykastro, on the southwest end of Lake Ardzan, is near the Iron Age site of Tsaotsitza. This site has yielded interesting bronze jewellery and evidence of prehistoric housing, as well as vestiges of contact with the Mycenaean peoples from the south.

Six kilometres west of Polycastro is the large viticultural village of Goumenissa, one of the northernmost Greek wine-producing villages, together with Naoussa and Amindeo. Goumenissa, founded in the 15th century, was an important silk and wine centre. Today, silk production has disappeared but the town's wine fortunes are making a comeback. One of the progressive young producers here is Christos Aidarins (0343 41 684) who can be found in his family's store in the centre of the village. In addition to producing wine from grapes, locals produce one of Greece's best distilled spirits, called *raki* (grappa in Italy), from the residue of grape pressings.

From Polycastro the rail line follows the 10km long Tsingan gorge at the foot of Mount Paikon to the border station at Idomeni. This gorge was the main north/south invasion route for all the Slav and Germanic tribes heading to the warmer climates of the Aegean.

Chapter Fifteen

Thessaloniki–Ormenio (Bulgaria)

Thessaloniki–Serres–Drama–Xanthi–Komotini–Alexandroupolis–Pythion (Istanbul)–Ormenio (Bulgaria)

INTRODUCTION

This is the main line of the former Ottoman Empire's *Chemin de Fer Oriental* built in the latter days of the 19th century. As such, this 615km standard gauge single track railway is the longest main line in Greece. It offers spectacular natural scenic wonders like the 100km passage through the Nestos River Gorge, the boundary between Macedonia and Thrace and it offers glimpses into the lives of people and cultures on the fringe of modern Greece. This area, at the northern and eastern limit of modern Greece, is as far from the sunny Aegean Isles in style and temperament as is possible.

This line is slated for significant infrastructure improvements with the right-of-way being strengthened to allow for higher speeds, improved signalisation, and the creation of double track along certain segments. It is highly possible that the line will be electrified, at least as far as the Bulgarian frontier at Promachon.

A multitude of IC, express and local services operate over all or part of this line and there are three through schedules from Piraeus/Athens via Thessaloniki to the eastern frontier: IC 70 Piraeus–Alexandroupolis; expresses 602 (afternoon Athens departure with late evening Thessaloniki departure and morning Dikai arrival in eastern Greece) and 604 (late evening Athens departure, morning Thessaloniki departure, evening Ormenio arrival). From Thessaloniki are: IC 90, with a morning departure, supplementing IC 70; express 614 Thessaloniki–Alexandroupolis; and locals 1630 and 1632 to Serres, and 1634 on to Drama. Drama has an early morning local 1670 to Alexandroupolis and Alexandroupolis has four daily locals (1690, 1692, 1694, 1696) on the 180km transportation corridor north along the eastern Evros River border with Turkey. A new experimental daily service was introduced in July 1996 between Drama and Xanthi through the Nestos River Gorge. It is scheduled to receive steam traction for the 1997 season.

First-class passengers travelling overnight from Thessaloniki (train 602) should be wary of their accommodation. The normal OSE procedure is to place the first-class carriage at the end of the train at Athens so it will be directly behind the engine when the train leaves the dead-end Thessaloniki station. The idea is to be able to provide adequate heat during the winter. The reality is that the intense heat provided is uncontrollable, which forces passengers to open windows so vast quantities of diesel smoke pour into the compartments. It is a loud, smelly, extremely uncomfortable all-night ride. The preferable alternative is to book passage aboard the comfortable second-class coupé/couchette carriage normally coupled to the train at Thessaloniki which is at the end of the train.

Rail travel east from Thessaloniki begins with a westbound exit from the terminal then a sharp curve to the north followed by a 77km run straight north along the Gallikos River before the line begins curving east around the southern edge of Lake Doirani. This was a railway designed to facilitate communications and military transport within the Ottoman Empire. Originally, Thessaloniki was served by a branch line with the main line connecting directly through Kilkis to Yugoslavia.

After the Strymon junction with the Bulgaria-bound branch, the line heads largely southeast to avoid the bulky masses of the Rhodopi Mountains making up the Greco-Bulgarian frontier. It then continues northeast through Drama and the dramatic Nestos River gorge before entering Thrace at Xanthi. From here, with the rolling plain of the Rhodopi foothills on the left and occasional glimpses of the Sea of Thrace to the right, the line continues 47km east to Komotini before curving 68km south to the port of Alexandroupolis. Some observers claim that the Thracian segment of this line was purposely built at least 16km from the coast to minimise possible damage from naval bombardment by big guns mounted on battleships at sea. Though this could be the case, many other observers believe that the rail line was situated there because the ground close to the coast is not stable. The deltas of the three big river systems – Strymon, Nestos and Evros – are large and marshy. This also explains why this coast was not settled until about the 7th century BC.

From Alexandroupolis the rail line follows the Turkish frontier north 175km to its terminus at Ormenio. Along this rail segment Istanbul-bound trains use the branch through Pythion with another entry to Edirne in Turkey (the former Adrinopole) possible at Kastanies, and connections to Bulgaria possible through Ormenio (for Svelingrad and the main Sofia–Istanbul rail line.)

Although interesting views are possible from both sides of the train, passengers towards Alexandroupolis would do well to sit on the right side.

The rail line through the Nestos River Gorge hugs the left bank of the river, and faraway villages with mosques and their tiny spire-like minarets are visible across the Evros river in Turkey from the right. The Rhodopi Mountains and the whitewashed Muslim villages of Thrace are visible from the left side of the train.

THESSALONIKI TO SERRES

Leaving the Thessaloniki station, trains follow the main trunk rail line 8km northwest then leave the main line to Central Europe to head north through the villages of Lahanokipi and Latomio. The Gallikos River is on the left side. Just before the Philadelphia station the train crosses the Gallikos. East of here (right side) near the village of Xirokhori was found a skull (of Ouropithekos Makedonikos) carbon-dated to be 9 to 12 million years old.

The **Kilkis** station was the site of the now abandoned Ottoman rail cut-off that allowed trains to avoid Thessaloniki in case that city fell into enemy hands. Southwest of the rail station (left) is the Sarigol Military Cemetery. Here 659 British soldiers are buried who fell in 1917–18 as part of the Allied attack on Bulgarian positions around Doiran. Kilkis (population 12,000) is a modern, concrete town situated on the edge of a large empty highland plain. It is the major city of its Nome. Nearby is a 14th-century Byzantine fort called Yinaikocastro, because it was so strong that women could defend it. It symbolises the area's role as a battlefield since the time invaders first began to covet lands around the Aegean. It was in this area that the most significant fighting of the Balkan Wars (1912–1918) took place: the June 1913 Battle of Kilkis that checked the Bulgarian advance on Thessaloniki, and the May 1918 Battle of Skra Ravine that resulted in victory for the Greek and Allied armies over the Germans and Bulgarians. A monument and small museum on a hill south of the city records these events.

A small archaeological museum (open Tues–Sun: 08.30–15.00; free; tel: 0341 22 477) contains Greek and Roman finds from various local digs. EOT (0341 97 097) has an office here. Travellers bound for Lake Doiran would do well to at least check to see what the local border situation between Greece and Bulgaria is like. Accommodation is limited to the adequate Hotel Evridiki (tel: 0341 22 304, fax: 23 586).

The railway remounts the Doiranis River towards Lake Doirani past rolling meadows with the border Kerkini mountains rising steeply in front. Passengers observing the pastoral scene from the windows are reminded of the Scottish Highlands. There are large herds of cattle passively grazing – most unusual for Greece. Before arrival at the **Doirani** station a large 12m-high obelisk, guarded by two carved crouching lions, comes into view. This is the British Salonika Force Campaign Memorial. The names of 2,160 fallen without a known grave during the World War I campaign are inscribed on panels attached to the obelisk. The Doiran Military Cemetery nearby contains 1,300 graves (875 of them British).

The Doirani rail station serves a large 11m-deep alpine lake that is divided down the middle between Greece and the FYRO Macedonia. This lake is popular with local fisherman, but the town of Doirani is in the Yugoslavian part of the lake. Other FYRO Macedonian villages are visible off on the left.

The line skirts the calm lake to the southeast then bears northeast across the foothills of the Kerkini. The highest peak with snow on the crest well into June is Demir Kapon (2,032m). It forms the inhospitable border with Bulgaria and the FYRO Macedonia. The halt for Mouries serves the village (left) higher up on the slopes of Demi Kapon. The views from beyond the Kastanonoussa rail station in the area of the narrow Dova Tepea Pass (278m) are extensive and once again more reminiscent of the rolling plains further north in the Balkans than of most notions of Greece.

The Rodopolis station in the centre of the village signifies entrance into a border region with wide alpine meadows. The small town is the centre for services to this area populated by Bulgarians and Macedonian Greeks.

From Rodopolis the railway curves to the east through the village station of Livadia and through marshy land irrigated by the Koumoulis River. Beyond the village of Mandraki, the line enters the valley drained by the Strymon River. The Strymon is dammed further south and man-made Lake Kerkinis is visible to the right. The rail line continues through the villages of Akritochori and Vironia. Between here and the right bank of the Strymon (left) were the silver mines of the Macedonian kings. Beyond the leafy green village of Neo Petritsi (left) the rail line crosses the Strymon on a long bridge near the end of the Rupel Pass, then curves southeast leaving the rail line to Sofia behind (left).

This is a wide lonely plain that abuts the Bulgarian border mountains. The 1965 line to Sofia leaves the main line here and heads straight towards the formidable mountains. The OSE main line passes through Strymon and Sidirokastron.

Sidirokastron (population 6,300) means iron castle and is somewhat better remembered by its Turkish name of Demir Hisar. It is well-sited at the base of a hill with a 14th-century Byzantine citadel. This is an area little used to foreign travellers, although in antiquity and the middle ages it was on the trade routes. Visitors will be met by well-meaning inquisitive locals and those travellers with an ear for languages will easily notice that Greek is not the only language spoken here. Bulgarian and Turkish are the most common languages with Russian occasionally being heard. Two hotels are available for those wanting to stay: the Olympic (0323 23 811, fax: 23 891) and the Pighi (0323 22 422, fax: 22 370).

From Sidirokastron the rail line continues on its southeasterly and steadily downward course through large cotton fields near the villages of Kamaroton,

Gefyroudi and Skotoussa. Beyond Skotoussa is the broad valley of the Strymon River. The villages of Kala Dendra (Good Trees) and Mitroussi lead to the ancient city of Serres. At this point the rail line is at about 28m in altitude.

Serres

Serres (population 51,000) is a modern town with a long, disputed history. At present it is an important and comfortable commercial centre. It was known from 4th-century BC literary sources and 3rd-century BC inscriptions. It was a powerful and independent city in late antiquity and is described as the seat of a bishop in the 5th century AD. It was reinforced by the Byzantines, sought out by the Franks of the errant fourth Crusade, the Bulgars, the Serbs and the Turks. It was reduced to rubble by the time of the Ottoman conquest (1383), but managed to grow into a sizeable city on both the north/south and east/west trade routes during the 17th and 18th centuries. It remained Turkish until 1913, when it was seized by the Bulgarians and burned to the ground. Another disastrous fire struck in 1949.

Since then, the Greek Archaeological Service has restored the 1124 Cathedral of St Theodore and the church of St Nicolaos on the ancient acropolis. Some of the Byzantine gates and walls have been uncovered and parts of the aqueduct are still in place. Several mosques can be seen and the huge brick central Turkish market on the attractive garden-laden Platia Eleftherias has been restored to become the Archaeological Museum (open Tues–Sun: 08.30–15.00; free; tel: 0321 22 257). The Sarakatsanoi people are honoured with a folk museum (62 Ionos Dragoumi). The city merits a visit and should not disappoint the independent traveller. Accommodation is available at the Elpida Hotel (0322 59 311, fax: 36 301), the Park (0322 22 133, fax: 23 533) or the more upscale Gerakina Hotel (0322 23 045, fax: 24 626).

SERRES TO DRAMA

Beyond Serres the rail line penetrates into an area known as **East Macedonia**. This is a hilly area through which passes the Strymon River and its tributaries, as they run towards the sea. The eastern boundary is the Nestos River which is also the traditional boundary with Thrace. Traces of intensive settlements from Neolithic times have been found in several places. It was considered the promised land for Athenians during the Classical period. It passed into Macedonian hands (357BC) after the great powers of Athens and Sparta wore themselves out during the Peloponnesian Wars. The Athenian colony (437BC) of Amphipolis and Philippi (founded in 356BC by Philip II) then came into their own. Amphipolis evolved into one of the most vital ports of the region. Philippi was considered the easternmost great city of the Roman empire. Under Roman rule both cities continued to exert a strong influence over the barbarian mountain tribes in the hinterlands. The usual culprits in the Medieval era succeeded in destroying them both, and the area became a backwater during modern times.

The rail line continues through the villages of Neos Skopos (right), Toumba (right) where a Neolithic settlement has been unearthed, Gazoros (left) with its long Ziliaxoras bridge and Nea Zixni, where the 25km branch line to the port of Amphipolis functioned until 1970. This city, whose origins are described above, commanded "nine ways" or transport routes both by sea and by land. Today a colossal stone Lion of Amphipolis is mounted on a pedestal dredged in 1936–37 from the adjacent Strymon River. Extensive ruins on the hills behind the lion statue and across the river near the derelict railway station attest to its size and importance. Finds from the site are on display at the Kavala Archaeological Museum (see below).

The rail line continues to wind through the local hills of Dafnoudi (left) and Vertiskos and Kerdilia (right). Beyond the villages of Dimitra (left) and Lefkothea (left) the line ducks under a series of three covered galleries as it penetrates through the Petras Defile before passing over the Angiti River. The Nome of Serres is left behind and the rail line is now in the Nome of Drama. Looming Mount Falakro makes its presence known (left). From here, the village of Photolivos, the line enters the great plain of Drama.

Drama

Drama (population 41,000) is a bustling commercial town geared to the tobacco trade, with many green platias and attractive old neighbourhoods shaded by tall trees. It is probable that Drama occupies the site of a settlement of Thracians who wiped out the first Athenian attempt at colonising the area (465BC). The second attempt resulted in Amphipolis. The Byzantines were somewhat involved in Drama and evidence of their ninth century walls have been found. Drama gained in importance with the abrupt decline of Philippi.

Its business orientation will soon be felt by the traveller, but it is a gateway for treks to nearby Mount Falakro (2,232m), as well as to Kavala on the coast. Falakro means bald in Greek but the impressive limestone hulk is anything but that. Buses from Drama lead to the trailhead at the village of Volakos on Falakro's northwest flank; other buses lead to another trailhead at Pirgi on Falakro's southwest slope.

Oenophiles should call on the Lazaridi brothers who have made impressive strides in creating world-class wines from grapes grown in the Drama plain. Both their estates use cutting-edge technology to produce dry white, rosé and red wines from a variety of grapes. They are responsible for the revival of quality wine production in Drama. Visits can be arranged by calling Chateau Lazaridi (tel: 0521 36 616, fax: 31 453; address: PO Box 101, 66100 Drama) or Ktima Kosta Lazaridi (PO Box 157, 66100 Adriani-Drama; tel: 0521 82 348, fax: 82 320).

Where to stay

Accommodation in Drama is available at the Apollo (0521 25 551) or the Marianna (0521 31 520, fax: 31 756). The Hoteliers' Association of Drama (tel/fax: 0521 22 568) can also help with lodgings.

To Philippi and Kavala by road

Most travellers will want to proceed to Kavala (38km), with or without a stop at the ruins of Philippi (open Tues–Sun: 08.30–15.00; admission 500Dr). This city, using Kavala/Neapolis as its port, rose to prominence when the Roman Via Egnatia passed through. It guarded a narrow gap between hill and marsh through which the road had to pass. The vaunted Battle of Philippi (42BC) between the forces of Antony and Octavian on one side and those of Brutus and Cassius on the other helped decide the fate of the Empire. St Paul began his European mission from here (49AD) with the conversion of the Philippians. His converts created one of the earliest Christian communities in Europe. Most ruins on the site are from this community. A tidy museum (open Tues–Sun: 08.30–15.00; admission 500Dr) has finds from the earlier era, but most of the better discoveries are in Kavala. The presence of the Via Egnatia meant that many travellers passed through Philippi. The Arab geographer Idrisi visited the city in the 12th century. He described the lively commercial activity and makes specific mention of viticulture. Inevitably, the Turks came, in 1387 and the city was abandoned when the malarial marshes overcame the plain.

Approaching Kavala by road, down through the residential area lined with apartment blocks, does not do the attractive city justice. It is one of the prettiest seafacing cities in all of Greece. Those continuing on to (or returning from) the island of Thassos will be rewarded with stunning views.

Kavala

Kavala (population 61,000), butting up against the lower slopes of Mount Simbolon, is the second largest city in Macedonia and the principal port for northern Greece. It also has the dubious distinction of being the largest Greek city without any railway service.

Kavala, known as **Neapolis**, was the port of Philippi. As such it was the traditional port for travellers from the Holy Lands bound for Europe. The origins of Neapolis are unclear, but it is believed to have been settled from Thassos (7th century BC) and Paros in an attempt to quell attacks from the hostile Thracian tribes on the mainland. Kavala was an ally of Athens and continued to prosper under the Macedonians, as it was the principal port for the shipment of precious ore, principally gold and silver, from the near hinterlands. In the early Christian era the name changed to Christoupolis. The aforementioned Arab geographer Idrisi admired the city, calling it a strongly fortified place with a busy commercial harbour.

The Normans in 1185, Catalans and Serbs in the early 1300s and the

Ottoman Turks in 1385 laid waste to the city, which became a barracks with the first recorded use of the name Kavala being in the 15th century. A settlement of Jews (1526) from Hungary sparked an economic resurgence that led the city to expand beyond its limited walls on the high, rocky promontory called the Panagia District. Noted sultan Suleyman the Magnificent (1521–1566) had new walls built around the expanded city and the port. The imposing aqueduct (still a major city landmark) was constructed during the same era. By the late 17th century, Kavala was an imposing city with a series of domed mosques, two-storey stone houses and a booming port.

From the middle of the 18th century, Kavala entered into intensive commercial trade with Marseilles, and the city took on the air of a prosperous international transit centre. In the early 19th century, the father of Mehmet Ali – who would found a ruling dynasty in Egypt – built a large mansion on the Panagia heights over the site of the Temple of Parthenos and the impressive 18-domed Imaret complex, housing an Islamic theological academy (Mendreses) and poorhouse, was built on the western walls. After Greek Independence in the south, Macedonians began to assert themselves, taking over control of the harbour and building churches. The city was finally liberated from the Turks in 1913.

Much of Kavala's rich past is on display in the fine **Archaeological Museum** (17, Erythrou Stavrou St; open: Tues–Sun 08.30–15.00; admission 600, 400, 300Dr; tel: 051 222 335, fax: 224 717). The Municipal Museum of Kavala (Fillipou S; open Mon–Fri: 08.00–14.00, Sat: 09.00–13.00; admission free; tel: 051 222 706) houses the collection of the former Folk and Modern Art Museum plus works of the Thassos born sculptor Polyganos Vagis (1894–1965).

Travellers to Kavala will find a bustling, vibrant city turned towards the harbour. All services are grouped around the large central Platia Eleftherias and the enchanting Panagia District on the promontory to the left of the harbour. Here are the Byzantine Castle (open: Tues–Sun 08.30–17.00 with later hours during the midsummer music and dance festivals, admission free; tel: 051 838 602), Mehmet Ali's house (open Tues–Sun: 10.00–14.00; admission free) situated behind a large statue of Ali on horseback and the intriguing Imaret which has recently been transformed into a large and lovely café/bar with some of the most enchanting sea views in Greece.

Accommodation is available in the Panagia District at Giorgios Alvanos rooms (Anthemiou 35 in Panagia; tel: 051 228 412). These rooms in a joyously restored 300-year-old house are the most highly recommended; in the centre the Parthenon (Spetson 14; tel: 051 223 205), the Nefeli (Erythrou Stavrou 50; tel: 051 227 440) and the upscale Galaxy (Eleftheriou Venizelou 27; tel: 051 224812) are recommended. Camping places abound east of the city along the long beaches, with the Irini (051 229 776) and the Alexandros (051 316 347) sites being the closest to town.

Moving on from Kavala, travellers have a choice of ships to Thassos, Limnos, Rafina and Samothraki, with some continuing on to Alexandroupolis, or of buses to Thessaloniki or on to Xanthi in Thrace. Rail travellers and those interested in seeing the Nestos River gorge area would do well to return to Drama and continue east by rail.

DRAMA TO XANTHI

The 105km railway line from Drama to Xanthi has the most dramatic scenery on this route and possibly in Greece. The highest point is reached at Platania, when the highly scenic and tortuous railway should keep all riders glued to the right-hand windows as it runs along the banks of the Nestos River from Paranesti all the way to Xanthi (right).

The Nestos River, also known as the Mesta, has its sources high in the Bulgaria section of the forested Rhodope Mountains. Under the 1913 Treaty of Bucharest, it formed the boundary of an expanded Bulgaria that reached to Alexandroupolis and beyond. Today it forms the boundary between the modern Greek provinces of Macedonia and Thrace.

The river winds its way through 234km of wild, primitive gorges mostly above Paranesti. Its banks are home to over 250 bird species, of which close to half, such as the Dalmatian pelican, imperial eagle and peregrine falcon, are either rare or endangered. On the upper Bulgarian side segments run through the Rila and Pirim national parks; and the Nestos delta is one of eleven Greek wetlands declared protected under the international Ramsar convention.

Greece and Bulgaria are embroiled in long-standing disputes over its waters and environmentalists are concerned both by Bulgarian plans to divert water and by the desire of the Greek Public Power Corporation (DEH) to build four hydroelectric plants along its banks. The future of this wild river is not assured and travellers are advised to see and experience it now.

The rail line starts climbing the mountains almost immediately after departure from Drama. By the first halt, Nikiphoros, it is already in the mountains. After Nikiphoros it crosses a trestle bridge and the village of Platanovryssi comes into view on the right with Mount Lekani (1,298m) visible on the left and its deep gorge on the right. The Platania station in the centre of the village on the watershed limit between the Angitis and Nestos Rivers indicates the highest point (322m) on the entire Thessaloniki–Pithion rail line.

After Platania, the rail line descends through the Korpilon narrows by means of galleries and tunnels, then across a 150m iron bridge with the Nestos a surging torrent here most of the year. The rail line penetrates the Nestos gorge with a brief halt at Paranesti. Beyond Paranesti, the rail line continues through the gorge with Mount Koula (1,827m) visible on the left and Mount Lekani still visible on the right. The next station, Sterna, signals the province of Thrace – leaving Macedonia behind. Paschalia station is the first Thracian rail station. The rail line continues to pass under galleries and tunnels through the tiny villages of Neochori, Stavroupolis (extremely impressive canyon scenery from here to the west), Komnina and Livera. The Nestos is never far away and at times its spray from the tumbling rocks mists train windows. The premier local crop, tobacco, can be seen growing near the village of Livera. The rail line and the Nestos part company at Toxotes with the river wending its way south (right) into a broadening valley while the rail line bears slightly to the north (left) into the Xanthi plain. The main Thessaloniki–Alexandroupolis highway which passed the Nestos Gorge by another route further south rejoins the railway here.

Thrace

Western Thrace, as the Greek province is called to distinguish it from the large eastern plain in Turkey, only joined Greece in 1920. It has a population of about 360,000.

In antiquity Thrace was considered the fourth "continent" (after Europe, Asia, and Africa (Libya)) as it differed so greatly from the rest of Greece. Geographically the region seems Balkan with rivers that flow year round and a coastline with few safe anchorages. The area is marked by the Rhodope Mountains which rise to 2,278m and, though mostly in Bulgaria, form the boundary with the Balkan nations to the north. The mountains are indented by five major river systems creating broad fertile valleys. Until late in the 20th century, population centres were located mostly in the foothills to avoid the pestilential marshy lowlands near the coast, and the constant flow of marauders and invaders sweeping east and west.

Railway building commenced late in the 19th century at the urging of Ottoman military leaders who understood the strategic value of rapid troop movements along the iron rails. The particular geography of the region dictated that the railway should be away from the coast but, given the location of the cities in the hills, the railway could not penetrate directly to their centres. Alexandroupolis was served by a bypass, so that in case of attack the main line would not be threatened. Both the major cities Xanthi and Komotini are served by railway stations that are relatively far from the city centre.

Rail speeds are not high. IC trains operate to Alexandroupolis and major track work is under way. A branch line from Xanthi to the developing oil port of Kavala is being surveyed. OSE has begun negotiations with Romania and Ukraine to provide fresh agricultural produce on a fast, regular schedule. This will add to the impetus to improve rail transport facilities on the single track railway.

Toxotes is an old established Turkish Muslim town with mosques and minarets clearly visible from the train (left).The newer drab concrete towns (usually on the plain/right) characterised by long apartment blocks were built to house Greek refugees after the 1922 Near East debacle.

The Greeks, with a large army relatively unscathed by World War I, encouraged by the Allied Powers to occupy Turkey, took the initiative, and saw an opportunity to implement the traditional Greek dream known as the "Great Idea" of the recovery of lost Greek territories with a large-scale invasion of the ancient Greek settlements on the Aegean coast of modern Turkey. When they overextended themselves and the Allies ceased their support, the seminal Turkish leader Attaturk seized the moment and literally drove the Greeks into the sea. The ancient Greek city of Smyrna – now Ismir – was burned to the ground, and with it all realistic hope of Greek territorial expansion at the expense of the disintegrating Ottoman Empire.

The subsequent Treaty of Lausanne (1923) called for a massive exchange of population with over 400,000 Turks forced out of Greece and over a million Anatolian Greeks resettled in Greece. The large Muslim population of Thrace was not affected by this exchange, but Greek authorities desiring to restore the population balance created a great many refugee settlements which unfortunately still exist. When the Berlin Wall fell in 1989, a great many Greeks from the Black Sea communities near present day Trabizond, who went to Russia in 1924, returned to Greece. They were also resettled, much to their chagrin, in jobless Thrace.

The Thracian "problem" for Greece is multifaceted. Ancient inhabitants of Thrace were Indo-European but not considered as Hellenes. They spoke a language which is still undeciphered and Bronze Age improvements seem to not have reached them. Greek colonisation began in the 7th century BC, but was limited to coastal settlements.

The people and wildlife (lions and bears) in the hinterlands were considered too dangerous. The Macedonians and then the Romans subdued the area, but the long era of the Middle Ages brought about a mixing of peoples with Slavs, mostly Bulgars, and Turks settling into the area. Thrace is still the only Greek province where Greek and Turk coexist as they did during the days of the Ottoman Empire. Approximately one-third of the population is considered Muslim with Turks, Pomaks and Gypsies making up the mix. A Muslim deputy or two usually serve in the Greek Parliament and they are actively solicited when coalitions are needed which is often. Over 336 mosques can be found in Thrace.

The Greek government points to the success of its "minority policy" though there is a nucleus of Islamic discontent. The left-leaning PASOK Party partially diffused this in the 1980s by finally allowing Muslims to own, trade and sell private property. Muslim schools exist and flourish, and teachers and theological support staff must be educated at the appropriate schools in Thessaloniki.

Despite this activity, Thracian political leaders decry a perceived lack of support and interest from the central government in Athens. Since the post World War II era, public figures sense neglect, with investment centred in the Peloponnese and Thessaly. Any funds destined for northern Greece usually find their way to Thessaloniki. The Mayor of Alexandroupolis, Ilias Evangelidis, stated at a press conference in March 1996 in Athens: "The geostrategic position of Thrace is coming back to the fore. It is the centre of a broad region and the hub of Greece's links with the Balkan and Black Sea communities." A well publicised tour of Thrace by the Prime Minister and several high government officials then followed.

The discerning traveller to Thrace will find an exotic region where the entire fabric of Balkan and Mediterranean culture is still tightly interwoven. A range of languages can be heard with the Turkish "yok" for no and the Russian "da" for yes possible in the same neighbourhood. Cities are clean with attractive squares, extensive walkways and old neighbourhoods where half-timbered houses still possess the second-floor enclosed balcony often seen in Muslim countries. The muezzin's appeal to prayer coexists with the incense that issues from domed Orthodox churches.

Continuing east from Toxotes, the rail line curves slightly towards the north. Deep forests are visible on the slopes of the Rhodope and a succession of small Greek and Muslim villages are visible left and right. The rail line traverses extensive fields cultivated with tobacco. This is the preferred crop of Muslim farmers who drink no alcohol.

Xanthi

This attractive town (population 37,500) on the lower slopes of Mount Koula at the opening of the narrow valley of the Esketze River – the ancient Kosintos – offers a sample of what Thracian life is all about.

The railway station, currently undergoing extensive renovations to create a park and full service café/shop, is about 2.5km from the city centre. The coming of the railway in the late 19th century increased Xanthi's importance. Originally a summer resort for the Turks, it supplanted nearby Yenisea as the regional centre.

Xanthi is the centre of tobacco cultivation and possesses a new university. A Byzantine citadel above the town protected the nearby pass from Bulgar invasions and now provides excellent views of the plain down to the coast. It has a large café-lined central Platia with an imposing cathedral located just off it. The main attraction is a quaint old 19th-century **Turkish quarter** on the hill with winding cobbled streets and traditional houses. Two old mansions in the old town belonging to the tobacco magnates the Coumtzogli brothers have been renovated and converted into a **folk arts museum** (Antika St 7; open daily: 10.00–13.00 and 18.00–20.00, winter 17.00–19.00; admission 200Dr). It is also the site of an extensive vibrant Saturday morning market frequented by the Muslim villagers from the surrounding regions.

Summer evenings in the centre hark back to Xanthi's past as a resort with cafés and pedestrian streets full of revellers. Xanthi would make an attractive base from which to explore the surrounding area.

Where to stay

Accommodation includes the Lux Hotel (Georgiou Stavriou 18, near the central Platia; tel: 0541 22 341), the Dimokritos (28 Octovriou St 41; tel: 0541 25 111), the Sissy (Lefkippou 14; tel: 0541 22 996) and the more expensive Hotel Nestos (tel: 0541 27 531).

Further afield

South of Xanthi in tobacco country is the previously mentioned Yenisea. Now a nondescript farming town, its former glory is expressed by the large but sadly derelict 400-year-old mosque behind the centre. This low white-washed mosque is one of the oldest in Thrace. Another closed mosque with its tall minaret is behind the service station. After Yenisea comes marshy lowland near the coast. Xanthi is close (38km) to several beach resorts around Porto Lagos, notably Fanari. An in-season campground is available at Fanari (0535 31 270). Further along the coast near the present-day village of Avdira is the site of ancient **Abdera** (open daily 09.00–15.00; free).

Abdera was traditionally said to have been founded by Hercules. In reality, it was probably founded by Greek refugees fleeing a Persian occupation of their land near the present-day city of Ismir. Democritus, Protagoras (the first Sophist) and Anaxarchos (counsellor to Alexander the Great) were all born here. The city was important in early Christian times but vanished, probably because of the marshy lowlands nearby. Excavations continue on the site and a museum is being prepared in the village, but most finds are in Kavala and Komotini.

The surrounding marshland along the Vistonian Gulf is an important and perhaps too easily accessible bird sanctuary. The economy is based on fishing with live eels being exported to Central Europe. The abundant aquatic life probably explains the large variety of water-birds.

Behind Xanthi, towards Bulgaria, attractive mountain scenery vies with several interesting and ethnically mixed towns such as Sminthi and Miki, for visitor interest. The large market village of Ehinos serves the surrounding Pomak community. These are Bogomil-Christian Slavs who were forcibly converted to Islam in the 16th century. Their women still wear long black full-length veils.

XANTHI TO KOMOTINI

Beyond Xanthi the rail line continues directly east through tobacco and cotton fields. The main Thessaloniki–Alexandroupolis highway following the course of the Via Egnatia is on the left, and wide-angle views down to the sea are possible on the right. Soon though, the plain flattens out and the rail line passes through the dusty little farm villages of Polysitou, Kopteron where the Nome of Komotini begins, Iasmos and Polyanthos (where there is a Byzantine castle).

East of Kopteron, before Iasmos (left), are the fine remains of an old Roman town – Amastasioupolis or Peritheorion – near Amaxades. It was a fortified station on the Via Egnatia located on the edge of Lake Vistonia; and its extensive fortifications continue on both sides of the lake.

The large village of **Iasmos** (population 2,900) on the banks of the River Kompsatos was of some importance in bygone days and has remains of a Byzantine church and an attractive medieval bridge with two arches, a central pier and the original surface intact.

After Sostis (note the 75m-long rail bridge over the Akmar River) and just before entering the area of the Komotini rail station (town on the left) is the large silver-capped minaret of **Miskos** (left). Near Miskos are the remains of the Norman capital of Mosynopolis. Originally called Porsula, Diocletian gave it city rank and renamed it Maximianopolis. Good sections of the city walls can be seen on the site, with architectural fragments and inscriptions in the Komotini Museum.

Komotini

Komotini (population 41,000), the capital of its Nome, is palpably more Turkish than Xanthi, with the population split between Greeks and Turks. There are more than a dozen functioning mosques in the city and some are being extensively renovated. The city is on the plain and has somewhat of a military garrison town air about it due to the presence of the Bulgarian frontier 22km distant.

The OSE rail station is about 1.5km from the town centre. It too is being restored and renovated.

The flourishing market city is largely laid out in a grid plan except for the extensive Turkish quarter behind the Platia Ifastou. This bazaar has many antique shops on narrow streets where hawkers crowd the sidewalks with their various wares and little cafés where Turkish is the *lingua franca*. Market day is Tuesday. Travellers planning on continuing their voyages to Turkey would do well to stay several days in Komotini. The Muslim presence here is so strong that young Greek men assigned here for their obligatory 24-month military service often have serious difficulty adjusting.

A branch of the University of Thrace is located here as well as a Muslim secondary school. The city provides a guide to the area (tel: 0531 22 644) and an excellent **Archaeological Museum** (A Symeonidi St 4; open daily: 08.00–17.00; admission free; tel: 0531 22 411) has well displayed artefacts from the relatively little-known Thracian sites of Abdera and Maronia. Behind the museum are traces of the Byzantine walls (which can also be seen on entering the town). Around the corner from the museum on the pedestrian street leading into the centre is the community centre (Leski) for the recently returned Pontic Greeks from Tashkent and Alma Ata. These people are a font of knowledge about travel possibilities in the areas along the Central Asian Silk route.

The Greek presence began to be felt in the mid-19th century, with wealthy Greeks funding schools and academies. One such school has become Komotini's **Folk Museum** (Agios Georgiou 13; open Mon–Sat: 10.00–13.00; free).

Where to stay

Accommodation is not a problem, with a large variety available: the older Hellas (Dimokritou 31; tel: 0531 22 055), the Dimokritos (tel: 0531 22 579, fax: 23 396), the Astoria (Platia Irinis, tel: 0531 35 054, fax 23 396) or the upscale Anatolia (Anchialo St 53; tel: 0531 36 242, fax: 23 170). Otherwise, several small hotels in the bazaar area near the main mosque behind the clock tower and the taverna of Moumin Mehmet Mouhsin offer possibilities, but don't expect many creature comforts or English-speakers in this area.

Further afield

North of Komotini in the large Nympaia forest are walking trails, cafés and, on the heights, the Byzantine fortress. Views to the sea, and on clear days to the islands beyond, are possible from here.

KOMOTINI TO ALEXANDROUPOLIS

The 67km rail line beyond Komotini to the east begins with a curve to the south through prominent hills. It passes a handful of small villages on its route towards Alexandroupolis. This area is decidedly less populated but with a more Muslim orientation than even Komotini. The Krovilli station is the closest rail access to the ancient site of Maronia (8km distant).

The modern village of **Maronia** with its pleasant square and cafés is the site (2km distant towards the sea) of an important classical city of the 4th to 3rd centuries BC. This coastal city was allegedly founded by Maron, son of Dionysos. The open site, in olive groves at the base of Mount Ismaros, contains traces of the old 2m high, 2–3m thick walls and large square towers. The 10.5km circuit of the walls attests to Maronia's power and importance in ancient Thrace. Besides the battlements and a large double monumental gateway near the harbour, there are Hellenistic mosaics, and remains of the theatre and sanctuary. A café and restaurant are on the heights on the seaward edge of the site (look for traces of the walls in the ancient harbour). This is probably the most noteworthy and evocative archaeological site in Thrace, if not the easiest to grasp. An evening spent here, after viewing the exquisite sunset over the Thracian Sea, would not be wasted. The only hotel in the area is the King Maron Beach Hotel (tel: 0533 61 345, fax: 61 347).

At Mesti begins the Evros Nome which is part of the sensitive Greek/Turkish border region. The rail line crosses the east/west highway here. It then climbs severely on a sharp grade to Sikorachi through a series of barren hills. This area is a favourite local hunting area for wild boar. The Kirki station is the alighting point for miners heading to the tin and silver mines north of the village (left). The railway follows the valley of the Iren stream through the village of Potamos (where the large plain begins) down into the outskirts of Alexandroupolis.

Potamos is where the now abandoned Alexandroupolis bypass line left the port branch to connect with the main rail line near Feres. The Alexandroupolis area was the focal point for two competing railways in the late 19th century, and at one time the area around the little city had five different rail stations.

Trains curve around outer residential districts then stop at a station labelled Alexandroupolis in the midst of rail marshalling yards with an industrial harbour at a distance (left). This is not the city-centre station and passengers should not leave the train here. The centre station is about five minutes further on. Through trains bound for the northeast head directly into the two-track "stub-end" terminal then exchange engines to continue the trip.

Alexandroupolis

This straightforward port and resort town (population 39,250), known to the Turks and Bulgars as Dedeagac, is not often a direct destination in itself. It is the jumping-off point for ornithological visits to the protected Evros River Delta (if the military allow), expeditions to the 5km deep Cave of Polyphemus (the one-eyed Cyclops who attacked Odysseus and his men on their return from Troy) on the outskirts of the village of Makris to the west, and it is also the port for ferries to Samothraki and other islands including Thassos. The massive lighthouse on the foreshore at the passenger ferry quay entrance acts as a symbol for the city.

This city is basically a transit point with an interesting (though rarely open) Ecclesiastic Art Museum in the grounds of the St Nicholas Cathedral. Orthodox icons and ecclesiastic ornaments saved from Asia Minor are the major cultural attractions.

Contrary to popular belief, Alexandroupolis did not come upon its name from "the Great" but from the Greek king Alexander who visited the town just after its independence from Turkey in 1920. It is probably on the site of a Roman town – Salis – parts of whose cemeteries have been found under the modern town. The Turkish name (Dedeagac – tree of the holy man) derives from a colony of mystic dervishes implanted during the 15th century. It was just a fishing village until the railway from Edirne arrived in 1872, then it began to boom. (This should makes it the first major town in modern Greece to be linked by railway to the outside world. But it did not become Greek until 1920, so it doesn't count...sort of.)

Alexandroupolis is set for another boom shortly. A new multi-lane motorway is planned from Igoumenitsa to Istanbul and a major crude-oil pipeline from the Russian port of Burgas will soon be coming to the city. These two large-scale projects could also alter the ecological balance of the protected Evros River Delta.

The 11km wide Evros River Delta near Loutra Trianoupolis, 20km southeast of Alexandroupolis, is considered one of Europe's most important wetlands; close to 250 species of birds have been recorded with some 15 pairs of royal eagles and more than 200,000 migratory birds spending part of the winter here. Visits here are possible, but it is an extremely sensitive military area. Local ecologist Stella Kladara (Mosconision 1; tel: 0551 22 124) can offer advice on going to the Evros, as can members of Greenpeace or the World Wildlife Fund in Athens. Both groups are extremely concerned by the potential effects of damage to the projected oil pipeline. The area itself is full of fishing shacks, sandbars and sandy high-spots that remind one more of Louisiana than Greece. A large saltwater lake, Limni Drakonda, is at the mouth of the delta. The area definitely merits a visit.

Ferries from Alexandroupolis regularly serve the islands of Samothraki and Thassos and the mainland port of Kavala. Schedules permit a daylight passage to both these islands with an early evening arrival in Kavala. Check with the port police (tel: 0551 26 468) for schedules. Any number of travel agencies in the city – behind the lighthouse – will provide fare information,

It is also a rail junction. IC trains from/to Thessaloniki/Athens originate here, as do a number of daily north/south services to the Greek cities along the Evros River border with Turkey.

Where to stay

There is a lively downtown area with a plethora of cafés, restaurants and accommodation: near the train station is the Metropolis Hotel (Athanasiou Diakou 11; tel: 0551 22 443) and the Hotel Acteon (Karaoli Dimitriou; tel: 0551 28 078); on Dimocratiou and behind the port are: the Ira (Dimocratiou 179; tel: 0551 23 941), the Lido (Paleologou 15; tel: 0551 28 808), and the Okeanis (Paleologou 20; tel: 0551 28 830). Camping is available in Nea Hili, 3km west towards Makris, and Camping Alexandroupolis (tel: 0551 28 735). The helpful Municipal Tourist office (City Hall on Democratiou St; tel: 0551 24 998) dispenses maps and can offer information on other lodgings as well as help with ferries schedules to Samothraki.

International connections

OSE offers several possibilities for rail travel from Alexandroupolis via Istanbul to **Turkey** and **Bulgaria**: through Pythion by local train 1690 (05.20 departure, 07.10 arrival at Pythion) then Turkish State Railways (local train 82801 departs at 07.58) for Istanbul (when dealing with Greeks, use the city's old name, Constantinople); or through Ormenio for Svelingrad then on to Istanbul. The first option should be possible by using through express 602, with direct through coaches from Thessaloniki for Istanbul (departure

Alexandroupolis 05.34, arrival Pythion 07.50 then on to Istanbul). But given the extremely tense nature of recent international events in the area, the through service may or may not be operating. Check with railway authorities before travel. They are all still extremely sensitive about this.

The second option, of travel through Bulgaria, could be complex, as Bulgaria requires a visa for most visitors. Once again confirmation of possibilities and visa requirements is advised to avoid unnecessary inconvenience. A third option, simpler and more intriguing, entails leaving the train at the little OSE station of Kastanies (a request stop) then walking across the nearby Turkish border for a quick (7km) ride to the interesting old city of Edirne (Adrianople to the Greeks) then a Turkish train to Istanbul. At the time of writing, the Kastanies border crossing was only open 09.00–13.00 daily. This entails taking a train from Alexandroupolis that arrives in Kastanies in time (05.20 on the local that originates in Alexandroupolis or the slightly later 05.38 Evros Express 602 – but this train comes from Athens and could be late. The 09.35 local originating in Alexandroupolis is an option, but this arrives at 12.28 which is cutting things a bit short. There are no tourist services at Kastanies.

ALEXANDROUPOLIS TO DIDIMOTICHO

The 172km railway line north of Alexandroupolis is one of the earliest rail lines built in the Balkans. It pushed south from Edirne in 1871 and reached Alexandroupolis in 1872. It has much to offer the discerning rail traveller, though few make the effort to explore the region. Tourism facilities are not abundant but travellers should have no trouble finding accommodation and meeting people who appreciate adventurous foreigners.

After leaving the Alexandroupolis port area behind, the rail line heads towards the east: 11km past the airport and the village of Loutra Trianoupolis (no stop) along the Thracian Sea coast before turning sharply north. The marshy lowlands of the Evros Delta lie on the right. The historically significant **Skai River** is crossed. On the east bank of this river was the ancient village of Doriskos. This was a Persian fortress and staging area established by Darius I in 512BC. Xerxes massed over 200,000 men here in 480BC for his invasion of Athens.

The rail line almost immediately comes into sight of the Evros River. The river area is followed virtually the entire way, as the rail line proceeds north.

The headwaters of the Evros rise near Sofia in Bulgaria. The river then proceeds more than 500km before spilling into the Aegean near Alexandroupolis. Only two bridges cross it below Edirne: at Pithion and at Ipsala. It is navigable by small boats to Edirne and since 1923 it has been the border between Greece and Turkey. Both sides maintain large military presences discretely placed on either bank of the river. Despite the tanks, minefields and constant patrols, the area is a favourite for smuggling contraband and illegal immigrants to Europe.

Feres (population 4,900), 29km north of Alexandroupolis, is the first stop. This town (on the right) is the last stop before the highway bridge over the Evros into Turkey. It has an imposing 12th-century Byzantine church with many frescos (somewhat defaced) from the same era. The church, built by Isaac Comnenus, was the central hall, or katholikon, of the no-longer-existing Monastery of Theotokos Cosmosoteira. The Anthi Hotel (tel: 0555 24 201) in the centre is adequate for those wishing to experience tense frontier life on the Evros.

Beyond Feres, the rail line passes pine forests and lowlands through the village stops of Poros (right), Vrissoula (left) and Peplos (left). **Peplos** is where the long highway bridge crosses the Evros into Turkey on a route taken by the Via Egnatia to Ipsala. At times it is possible to walk into Turkey from here. If not, it might be possible to hitch a ride across. If the military do not allow this, then the alternative is to return to Alexandroupolis or proceed further north and try again. **Ipsala** is on the site of the ancient Thracian capital of Kypsela which was in steep decline by the 4th century BC. The Frank, Boniface de Montferrat, was ambushed and killed here by Bulgars in 1207.

Tycheron (left), Phylacton, Lagna and Lykophos are the next three stations as the line heads north, never far out of sight of the Evros. Lykophos (59km from Alexandroupolis)is the stop for the 35,000 hectare **Dadia Forest Reserve**. Of the 38 species of raptor known in Europe, 36 can be found here. This protected forest of oak and pines, where rare and endangered black vultures roost and wildlife migratory routes pass, is one of the oldest uncut areas in Europe. The black vulture, with a wing span of three metres, is joined by the also black griffon, and the single bearded vulture – all rare. As few as 20 black vultures survived here in the 1980s, but the Dadia reserve now boasts up to 100. Altogether, more than 200 species of birds have been recorded in Dadia and 40 kinds of reptiles and amphibians, the perfect food for eagles and hawks. The information centre (tel: 0554 32 397) is about five kilometres through rolling hills from Lykophos. There is inexpensive visitors' accommodation (tel: 0554 32 263) in the forest.

After the village of Kornofolia, comes the intriguing little town of **Soufli** (population 5,000). Soufli has been an important centre of sericulture since the Byzantines controlled that trade early in their existence. The mulberry trees preferred by the silkworms are largely gone, but silk is still made in Soufli. It retains a number of Turkish-style wattle-and-daub houses, one of which has been converted into a Silk Museum (hours and days vary), explaining silk manufacture and displaying the machines used. Two hotels are available in Soufli: the Egnatia (Vassileos Georgiou 225; tel: 0554 22 001) and the Orpheus (Vassileos Georgiou and Tsimiski; tel: 0554 22 305).

The stop of Mandra permits access to a series of small villages up a wooded valley near the Bulgarian frontier at Mikro Derio. The rail line curves sharply to the right to follow the river valley. The hills visible in the distance off to the right are in Turkey. The line passes through the hamlets of Lavara, Amorion and Psathades. The next important stop is Didimoticho, the biggest town in the area.

The original wooden station building is being renovated as a youth hostel. The new glass-and-steel station is strangely reminiscent of the Xilokastro station in the Peleponnese. The town is to the left one kilometre up the hill from the railway station. Standing on the platform in front of the stationmaster's office, it is possible to make out minarets on hilltop mosques across the Evros river. This is a favourite spot for illegal immigrants to wade across into Greece. Station railwaymen have become adept at picking out offbeat-looking people trying to buy tickets and board trains. Though these people are not harmful, it is always a good idea to take care when wandering around at night in this area.

Didimoticho

This town (population 8,500) acquired its name from the double walls that encircled the town. Historically, the town controlled the outer defences of the Byzantine empire's capital – Constantinople. Remains of the Roman town of **Plotinoupolis** have been found nearby. Those who have visited the Komotini archaeological museum will remember the gold bust found here. Didimoticho was briefly the first European capital of the Ottoman Empire when it fell to the Turks in 1361: Constantinople didn't fall for another 92 years. The large, rectangular and surprisingly plain 14th-century mosque (closed for urgent repairs) is considered to be the oldest (built by Murad I in 1368) and largest in Europe. Beyond the mosque in the town centre, up towards the hill, is a small but delightful triangular square with a frog-shaped fountain. Not surprisingly, the square is named Platia Vatrahos – Frog Square. Above the square on the right is the well-organised **folk museum** (Vatatzi Street; open evenings 17.00–20.00) in an old timber-framed house in the Turkish neighbourhood. Crowning it is the modern Cathedral of Agios Athanassis overlooking the town, the intensely cultivated valley behind it, and the Evros river area in front of the town. Parts of the substantial Byzantine walls are visible here. Up the valley along the Erithropotamos River beyond Kiani is the attractive hilltop farming village of Metaxades, considered one of the prettiest in the area.

Where to stay

Didimoticho is the kind of town worth spending a night in. Accommodation includes the Hotel Anesis (tel: 0553 22 050) in the centre, and the Plotini (tel/fax: 0553 23 400) on the southern outskirts. The youth hostel at the OSE station should open soon as well.

DIDIMOTICHO TO ORMENIO

Continuing beyond Didimoticho, the rail line curves sharply to the east (right), and proceeds through the villages of Praggion and Petrades. The rails run parallel to the international bridge to Turkey at Petrades. The next important stop is **Python**, which has the remains of a 13th-century Byzantine tower fort, and walls that are impressive and worth a slight detour.

Python's claim to fame is the major international rail junction with Turkey. Disappointingly it is basically a dusty little border town with Greek Immigration and Customs being housed in a simple chicken-shack-sized building. The old Turkish rail line used to run west from here through Greece, but a new line was built east of the Evros to avoid traversing Greece.

Coaches to and from Turkey are uncoupled here from their respective trains, then recoupled on the corresponding country's train. Several years ago the international train ran on an all-night schedule that called for an extremely inconvenient middle-of-the-night stop at Python. The long, sloppy and unprofessional customs and immigration controls would last an incredible amount of time, and were seemingly designed to create maximum discomfort and embarrassment. Yard locomotives would then haul the train a few kilometres to the Turkish customs station, and the entire farce would be repeated. When the international train developed an important following among smugglers (dope, guns and illegal immigrants) the schedule was changed and custom controls became more professional. Subsequently this train, on a new daylight schedule, has become the preferred way to travel between Greece and Turkey. Unfortunately it is sometimes held "hostage" to the political differences between the governments of the two countries. Travellers are advised to check schedules and conditions before embarking.

Departing Python, trains in Greece serve a slew of small villages with Orestiada (through the station of Nea Orestias), Kastanies, Dikea and Ormenio being the most important. **Orestiada** (population 12,000) was founded after the 1923 population exchange, and is one of the few successful refugee settlements to work as a town. It has banks and hotels that could be helpful to those coming into Greece from Bulgaria and Turkey. Hotels include the Acropolis (Vasilleos Constantinou 46; tel: 0552 22 277); the Alexandros (tel: 0552 27 000) and the Vienni (Orestou 64; tel: 0552 22 578, fax: 22 558); more upscale is the Electra (A Pantazinou 50; tel: 0552 23 540, fax 23 133).

Kastanies means customs house. The hamlet is in a forested area along the banks of the wooded Ardas River with lovely walks and picnic areas nearby. But it is so close to Turkey (minarets from Edirne can be spotted through the trees) that paranoia among the Greeks is palpable. In the spring of 1996, local Greek housewives organised self-protection units whereby they learned the mysteries of holding, loading and, even, using submachine guns. EOT (tel: 0552 85 205) provides tourism and border-crossing information here.

The Kastanies road border with Turkey is only open in the morning (09.00–13.00). Travellers bound for Edirne should not have much difficulty walking into Edirne. Edirne was refounded in AD125 by Hadrian, reached its peak as the Ottoman capital from 1367–1458, and remained important until the decline of the Ottoman Empire. Among its impressive buildings and monuments is the fine Selimiya Jami Mosque built by the notable architect Sinan.

Beyond Kastanies the rail line comes to the end of the modern Greek world at Dikea where most trains terminate. Several others continue on to the small border village of Ormenio. There OSE trains exchange cars with Bulgarian State Railways trains in an atmosphere which is less tense than in Kastanies 26km further south.

Part Six

SUGGESTED ITINERARIES

TRAIN • BUS • FERRY

Chapter Sixteen

Itinerary One

Athens–Epirus–the Ionian Islands

Travel is from Kalambaka by road west through Metsovo, Ioannina and the exotic Zagoria Villages to Igoumenitsa; then by ferryboat via the Ionian Isles of Corfu, Ithaca, Cephalonia and Zakynthos to Patras.

This route entails visits to two regions often not associated with the typical images of Greece: the Pindos Mountains of Epirus in the northwest of Greece and the Ionian Islands of the Adriatic Sea. Though both regions are within the borders of modern Greece, their history and geography away from the Aegean mean that they have evolved differently. Epirus is marked by the lofty barren peaks of the Pindos Mountains, carved by the canyons of five major rivers. Its relative isolation meant that it turned inward and could allow the development of local customs, with despots like the 18th-century Ali Pasha. The likewise green and lush Ionian Isles are situated on all main sea trade routes between Western Europe and the Greek mainland, and were prized by all who wished to control events along this route.

This itinerary calls for two days in Athens, followed by a half-day train journey to Kalambaka, one night in Kalambaka for the Meteora, then departure for Metsovo and Ioannina. After two nights in Ioannina take the short ride to Igoumenitsa, then a ferry to Corfu, two nights in Corfu, then an inter-island ferry south through the Ionian Islands to Patras. Alternatively, this could be the beginning of a trip to Greece, with a ferry from Italy to Igoumenitsa then following the same itinerary to Ioannina, Metsovo and Kalambaka by road for a return to the railway there. Obviously, with so much to do, flexibility is the key.

BY ROAD TO IGOUMENITSA

The road from Kalambaka to Epirus over the Katara Pass (1,707m) is the main all-weather route from northern Greece into the region. Up to three daily buses pass through during the summer. The route begins at the KTEL terminal near the OSE railway station then climbs gently through the valley of the Pinios River. The embankment of the abandoned railway (left) is followed 31km to Kani Mourgani. Here the railway cutting follows the road towards Grevena on the right while the Epirus road traverses the Pinios by way of a narrow one-lane bridge.

The road winds up, through and around Mounts Orthovouni (1,106m) and Kratsovon (1,565m), before dipping slightly beneath Pevki. From there, 81km from Kalambaka, it mounts above the snowline to the Katara Pass (1,707m). Tall snow-poles placed at regular intervals along the road attest to the difficult nature of this passage in the winter.

This pass is commonly cited as the reason the Vlachs are in Greece. They were allowed by the Romans to graze their animals in this area in exchange for guarding the Pass.

The road starts its zig-zag descent beyond the Katara watershed into Epirus. The first important settlement, only ten kilometres from the Katara, is the large Vlach market centre of Metsovo (population 3,500, elevation 1,100m).

Metsovo

The town is attractively built on terraces descending from the beech-clad slopes of Mount Zygos (1,555m). All five major rivers beginning in the Pindos have their sources near here. The prosperous town is of two-storey stone houses linked by well-maintained and steep cobbled stone paths. Voices heard in the streets are often not Greek, and the image of being elsewhere is reinforced by the traditional dress of the local people congregating in the main square. Residents of Metsovo still practise local crafts like barrel making and hand weaving, and produce their own cheeses and wine in community efforts that are becoming rare in the modern era. Two famous sons of Metsovo, George Averoff (1815–99) and Michael Tositsa (1885-1950), have endowed the town, contributing to the rebuilding and rejuvenation of the many 18th- and 19th-century buildings, as well as fostering local crafts and products.

Metsovo can be conveniently divided into two parts: that which receives sunlight, "Prosilio"; and that which does not, "Anilio". From the heights of Prosilio the construction site of the new tunnel and road that will render the Katara less vital is visible below along the chasm of the Metsovitikos River.

A first stop by visitors should be to the **Museum** (Fri–Wed: 08.30–13.00 & 16.00–18.00; admission 400Dr) in the recently restored Archontiko Tositsa and, if open, the Women's Weaving Co-operative. Both provide glimpses into the former wealth and quality of Metsovo daily life. The fine red wines of Metsovo, made from grapes whose vines are planted in what are some of the highest vineyards (850–900m) in the world, can be tasted in the newly rebuilt cellar (contact the Athens office of Averoff Katogi Oenopiitiki for information on visits: tel: 01 36 42 419, fax: 36 04 511). The **Averoff Gallery** houses a permanent collection of 19th- and 20th-century paintings and sculptures by Greek artists.

Trekking is possible from Metsovo and a winter sports and ski centre (tel: 0656 41 211) is nearby. **Accommodation** is plentiful: the Athinea (tel: 0656 41 332) and the Filokseni (tel: 0656 41 020) are simple and inexpensive, while the Egnatias (tel: 0656 41 263; fax: 41 485) and the Apollon (tel: 0656 41 844; fax: 42 110) are plushier.

The road beyond Metsovo continues its winding descent around Mount Mitsekeli (1,562m) offering good views of Lake Pamvotis and exotic Ioannina: its towering minarets giving it a most un-Greek air.

Ioannina

Ioannina (population 75,000) spreading around the southeast shores of Lake Pamvotis must be one of Greece's most exotic and least visited (by foreigners) big city. It is the capital of Epirus, the gateway to the Vikos-Aoos National Park and, as such, the jumping-off point for visits to the isolated, romantic Zagoria villages hidden high in the mountains.

Ioannina was founded in 1020 and may have taken its name from a monastery of St John the Baptist. Its location in the only large, flat place in Epirus ensured that it gained commercial prosperity during the Ottoman centuries. Ioannina was most conspicuous during the reign of the Turkish-appointed Albanian-born despot Ali Pasha (1741–1822), who succeeded in creating something of an autonomous Epirot state. Locals today downplay the marked penchant for debauchery, murder and savagery of this self-anointed "Lion of Ioanninas". They point instead to his rebellion against the Sultan and other foreign powers like Great Britain and Napoleon's France. Ali Pasha ruled for 33 years in semi-autonomy and is credited with being the first independent ruler of a large Greek-inhabited area since the Turcocratia began.

The city centre area is dominated by the old town within the walls. At the high point, dominated by the minaret of the **Aslam Pasha Jami Mosque**, is the Popular Arts Museum or the **Municipal Museum** (summer Mon–Sat 08.00–20.00, Sun 09.00–20.00, winter daily 08.00–15.00; admission 550Dr) under the dome of the mosque. Ioannina's old-established Jewish population is represented by the surviving synagogue on Ioustinanou Street within the walls, although the community disappeared during World War II. Another large mosque in the Its-Kale inner citadel, the **Fetiye Jami**, counts one of the best preserved minarets (closed) in Greece.

Under the walls outside the main gate is the extensive bazaar area with its large number of Turkish buildings and crafts shops. Metal-smiths (copper, tin and silver) still play an important role in the city's economy, and pastry makers, much prized in old Constantinople, still create their delicacies here.

The fine **Archaeological Museum** (25th March Street 6; open Tues–Sun 08.30–15.00; admission 500, 400, 300Dr; tel: 0651 33 357) behind the imposing clock tower on the city's main square houses important finds from local paleolithic, classical and Roman sites. It is useful for those planning to visit the nearby classical theatre and oracle of Dodoni.

The pleasant lakeside area is lined with cafés and offers towering views of the sheer wall-like Pindos Mountain escarpment, as well as the ferry (every half-hour from 06.30–23.00, 200Dr) dock for the car-free island of Nissi in the centre of Lake Pamvotis.

Five monasteries are located on the little island and include the **Monastery of Pandelimonos**, where Ali Pasha was finally brought down by the Sultan. The cottage where he was killed (the shot came through the ceiling – Ali Pasha was hiding on the second floor) is now a small museum (150Dr) with mementos and period pieces. There are several other monasteries on the other side of the island: the 13th-century Agios Nikolaos Philanthropinon, the 11th-century Stratigopolou Diliou and the 18th-century Eleoussas which houses gory 16th-century Byzantine frescoes and important icons. The frescoes can be visited by asking for the key from the resident family in the forecourt of the Philanthropion. This island also offers the best and quietest accommodation in Ioannina: rooms for rent by Delas Sotinos (tel: 0651 73 494) and Varvara Vasilios (tel: 0651 24 396). The only disadvantage is that island transport begins too late to make the earliest bus connections for the Zagoria Villages.

In Ioannina proper are many hotels, including the Hotel Paris (Tsirigoti Street, near the bus station; tel: 0651 20 541); Hotel Egnatias (Dangli St 2 also near the bus station; tel: 0651 25 667), the Tourist (Koletti 18; tel: 0651 26 443) and the Metropolis (Kristalli 2; tel: 0651 26 207); more expensive is the Palladion (Botsari 1; tel: 0651 25 856). Camping is possible within the city limits on the grounds of the local water-sports club (tel: 0651 29 402). The EOT office (Central Platia; open Sept-June on Mon–Fri 07.30–14.30 plus July–Aug 17.30–20.30 and Sat 09.00–14.00) is one of the best in Greece. The local tourist police (28 Octovriou; tel: 0651 25 673) are also very helpful. Information on trekking through the nearby Vikos gorge and in other Pindos locales can be had through EOS (Despotatou Ipirou 2; evenings 19.00–21.00; tel: 0651 22 138) or through Robinson Travel (Merarhias Gramou 10; tel: 0651 29 402, fax: 27 071) for longer treks.

Ioannina could act as the base for a longer stay and discovery of the intriguing surroundings.

Four kilometres from Ioannina are the relatively recently discovered **Perama Caves** (08.00–17.00; admission 800Dr; tel: 0651 23 440) in the village of the same name. Supposedly found by guerrillas fleeing the Nazis in World War II, they are considered among the deepest and with the most interesting stalagmites and stalactites in Greece. Lodgings are also possible here at the Ziakas pension (tel: 0651 81 611).

Further to the west is the large wine-producing village of **Zitsa**, where some of the best dry and sparkling white wines in Greece are made. The

Zitsa Wine Co-op (tel: 0651 70 961, fax: 77 941) has been responsible for the rejuvenation of this old wine-growing area, where the Dobina variety has been cultivated since the early middle ages.

Dodoni at the base of Mount Tomaras, 21km southwest of Ioannina, is Epirus' major ancient and rarely visited site (Mon–Fri 08.00–19.00, Sat–Sun 08.00–15.00; admission 500Dr). The Oracle of Zeus at Dodoni is Greece's oldest oracle with worship in the area said to have begun around 1900BC. The theatre, built during the time of Pyrrhus (297–272BC), is one of Greece's largest, along with those of Argos and Megalopolis in the Peloponnese. Accommodation is available at the Andromachia pension (tel: 0651 82 296).

The main reason to go to the Ioannina area is to walk through the **Vikos River Gorge** and to visit the many villages around it, called the Zagoria, like the well-cared-for Monodendri and Megalo and Mikro Papingo villages at either end of the Vikos. The Vikos can be walked in one long day, but that presupposes being at the trailhead early in the morning. Accommodation is available in Monodendri, at the Monodendri (tel: 0653 71 300) or the Vikos (tel: 0653 61 232) among others; or in the delightful Papingo villages: Megalo at the Hristodoulou family Inn (tel: 0653 41 138) or the pension of Kalliopi Ranga (tel: 0653 41 081).

This is some of the best trekking in Greece. It offers the gleaming Lake of Drakolimni tucked in a saddle of Mount Gamila (2,497m), and a series of well built, high arched stone bridges built during the 19th century by itinerant craftsmen. There are also several isolated monasteries such as the 13th-century Molivdoskepastou and the 18th-century Stomiou.

The area of the Zagoria is quite near the frontier of Albania and is, in fact, the site of the only land crossing possible at Kakavia (OSE runs a weekly bus from Patras to Tirana through Kakavia). The Vikos is still the main refugee trail for destitute Albanians heading south. Though they are normally not dangerous, they possess virtually nothing and can cause difficulty if not approached with caution.

A more pressing danger comes from the aftermath of a series of earthquakes in the late summer of 1996 that have caused many problems with newer buildings around Konitsa. The houses in the town have been condemned and should not be entered, but those in the outlying villages are still to be inspected by the authorities. Konitsa is the starting-point for many long treks in the area. For those not so inclined, it has a good example of a stone packhorse bridge over the Aoos River east of the city. The bus ride from Konitsa around to the rail head at Kozani is one of the most scenic in Greece. The picturesque village of Pendalofos, on this route, was the headquarters of the British Mission to the Greek Resistance during World War II.

This road will lead close to the Vlach homeland in the isolated village of Samarina in the Mount Smolikas (2,637m) range. No paved roads branch off from this main road, but many well defined paths lead off it into an area that is mostly above an altitude of 1,700m. Samarina is best accessed by public transport from Grevena between Kozani and Kalambaka.

Igoumenitsa

This town (population 7,100), 110km from Ioannina, is the most important Epirot port, and Greece's third passenger port with frequent connections to the Ionian Isles and Italy. A coastal road leads to Parga, Prevesa, Messalongi and Nafpaktos. The Andirio ferry connects this section of Western Greece with the Peloponnese at Patras. Igoumenitsa is a transit point situated on a former marsh and has no inherent interest nor any archaeological sites. If a stay is necessary, try the Lux (Saldari 19; tel: 0665 22 223) and the Stavrodromi (Souliou 14; tel: 0665 22 343). Camping is possible at Kalami Beach (tel: 0665 71 211) 10km south from the centre. EOT (in the harbour; Mon–Fri 07.00–14.00; tel: 0651 22 227) has an office here as well.

Small landing-craft-like car ferries and larger steamships regularly ply the waters between Igoumenitsa and Corfu. The larger international ferries, much like cruise liners, also go to Corfu, but will not carry local passengers. All the major Greek and Italian ferry companies have offices in Igoumenitsa. The tourist police (tel: 0665 22 222) will help with shipping information.

THE IONIAN ISLANDS

This group of islands consists of seven major islands (hence its Greek name "Eptanissia" meaning "seven isles") and their small outlying dependencies. Starting in the north, the major islands are: Corfu, Paxi, Lefkada, Ithaca, Cephalonia, Zakynthos and Kythera. Kythera is administered from Piraeus while the others, more closely grouped, are administered together from Corfu. Visits to one island cannot characterise all of them but they do have similarities. They do not suffer from the hot summer winds that blow from Africa, and they all receive a great deal of winter rain. These islands are all colonies of the important Greek city-states located further south. Their history is inextricably linked with the western powers of Venice, France and Great Britain. They suffered little under Turkish control: in Corfu, the Turks did not stay long enough for their presence to cause long-term effects, while elsewhere they were unable to break through the prevailing Venetian influence. They were all reunited with Greece in 1864. Today they see an inordinate amount of package tourists flying in for two weeks during July and August, but are tranquil the rest of the year.

Corfu

Corfu (port police tel: 0661 32 655) is grouped with the smaller islands of Erikousa, Mathraki and Othoni. This large (second of the Ionian group, population 105,000), extremely green island is considered to be the most beautiful of Greece's many islands. Unfortunately, it is one of the busiest in the high summer tourist season, with almost hourly charter flights shuttling into the tiny airport. Luckily, it is so big that the discerning traveller can get away from the masses with surprising ease. Corfu is green partly because of the consistent winter rains but also for the three million olive trees, give or take a couple of hundred thousand, that perennially put the island near the top of world olive-oil production. Something like 3% of the world's olive oil comes from Corfu. Discerning travellers will discover the island that inspired Edward Lear, Lawrence Durrell and Henry Miller, if they leave the crowded east-coast beaches and venture into the hills to villages like Vatos near the surprisingly large Ropa Valley (quaint rooms with fine views are available from Despina Moulinou in Vatos, tel: 0661 94 309) in the direction of Paliocastritsa, or head up to the north to unspoilt mountain villages like Peroulades in the region of Mount Pantocrator (914m).

Corfu Town (population 75,000) is actually a city, and a quite charming one at that, snuggling around two large forts on their respective hills. The old Byzantine fortress is open for visits (08.00–19.00; free) and hosts a sound-and-light show. The other Venetian fort is an important Greek Navy base and closed to the public. The Splanada, or Liston, promenade with buildings designed by Napoleon and a cricket pitch is one of Greece's most delightful and eclectic Platias. Without many classical ruins, Corfu (colonised from Corinth) has to make do with a modest archaeological museum (A Vraila St 1; open Tues–Sun 08.30–15.00; admission 800, 600, 400Dr; tel: 0661 30 680); a small Byzantine Museum (tel: 0661 38 313; open Tues–Sun 08.30–15.00; admission 500, 400, 300Dr) in the 16th-century Antivouniiotissa church; and surprisingly a museum of Asiatic Art, once housed in the now restored British governor's mansion (Palace of St Michael and St George) but now seeking a new home. A must on any visit to Corfu Town is a respectful visit to the ornately decorated St Spiridon Church named in honour of the Saint who lies inside and is credited with miraculously saving the islanders many times. He is paraded around the city four times per year (Orthodox Palm Sunday, the following Saturday, 11 August and the first Sunday in November). Other than these and other sights, aimless strolls through the atmospheric old Venetian neighbourhoods of Campiello between the Splanada and the old port and the town's Jewish quarter (between the old KTEL bus terminal and the main G. Theotoki Street) will give a good idea of what the real Corfu is like.

A variety of **accommodation** is available from basic hotels in the old city like the Hotel Konstantinoupolis (tel: 0661 39 326), the Hotel Cyprus (Agios Paterou 13; tel: 0661 40 675); or in the new international port area: the Hotel Europa (tel: 0661 39 304). Smarter options abound with the suburb of Kanoni overlooking Corfu's world known Pontikonissa (Mouse Island) a good place: the Hilton International (tel: 0661 36 540, fax 36 551) and the seasonal Ariti (tel: 0661 33 885, fax 33 889). An IYH youth hostel (tel:

0661 91 292) is in Kontokoli 4.5km from town, as is a campsite (tel: 0661 91 202). Finding adequate accommodation should not be a problem: in most cases it will find you first. EOT (tel: 0661 37 520) and the more helpful tourist police (tel: 0661 30 265) will provide the usual brochures and island maps.

The little and little-known islands of Erikousa, Mathraki and Othoni offer the best bets for solitude. They see only a limited number of visitors, but are well enough equipped to satisfy the needs of those who want to get away: Erikousa has a hotel (tel: 0663 71 555) and rooms; Mathraki is known as a nesting place for the large loggerhead turtles who migrate mostly to Zakynthos; and the larger forbidding-looking Othoni has an attractive traditional village among the tall cypress trees (rooms, tel: 0663 71 640).

Paxi

Paxi (port police, tel: 0662 31 259), with its smaller neighbour of Antipaxi, is low-lying, low-key and the smallest of the big Ionian islands. It manages to maintain its poise, even during the annual tourist migrations. Olive oil, some say Greece's best, is Paxi's main attraction. The attractive port village of **Gaios** will be the first place most visitors go, but rooms are scarce. Try the Paxos Beach Hotel (tel: 0622 31 21, fax: 31 166), the tourist police (tel: 0622 31 222) or the private agencies in the town. The island's only sandy beach is a 45-minute walk south on the islet of Mogonissi (with a causeway to Paxi), but better sand beaches can be found on Antipaxi. The sheer chalk cliffs at Erimitis near the hamlet of Magazia are an extremely romantic place to catch the sunset.

Small caiques connect Paxi with Antipaxi and Parga on the mainland. Check with the port police for details. Parga is the connecting-point for buses to the island of Lefkada. Ferries also serve Ithaca, Cephalonia and Patras from Paxi.

Lefkada

Lefkada (port police, tel: 0645 22 322), which neighbours Meganissi and nine other outer islands, is the fourth largest Ionian island, and is joined to the mainland by a 25m-long bridge over a canal dug by the Corinthians (8th century BC) that cut the natural isthmus. The series of Venetian Castles on the way over the causeway attest to its importance when they called it Santa Maura. It is mountainous (several peaks over 1,000m) and fertile. The surprisingly large inland plain is a fine destination for those interested in tiny, quaint villages like Spanochori or the embroidery village of Karia. The southern village resort of Vasiliki beyond Poros is considered an exceptional windsurfing spot. Caiques sail from here to Cephalonia. The road around the precipitous cliffs off the west coast eventually leads to Cape Lefkas at Land's End at the island's southernmost point. This is the legendary spot where Sappho leaped to escape her unrequited love. Today, hang gliders hold a festival in July.

Camping seems to be the way to go on this mostly adventure travel island: there is Episkopos Beach Camping (tel: 0645 23 043) on the east coast halfway to Nydri from Lefkada Town which also has ferry service to the other islands. This village was thought to be Odysseus' palace until further research placed it at Ithaca. Beyond Nydri, organised camping is possible near Vliho at the Desimi Beach Camping (tel: 0645 95 225) or on Rouda Bay near Poros (tel: 0645 95 452). Hotels in Lefkada Town include the Hotel Byzantio (tel: 0645 22 629), the Hotel Patras (tel: 0645 22 359) or the upscale Hotel Lefkas (tel: 0645 23 916). The tourist police (tel: 0645 22 346) can help finding other accommodation in the many rooms on the island.

Meganissi linked to Nydri seems somehow to have escaped the tourism era, and remains a charming place. It does have one hotel (tel: 0645 51 240) and genuinely friendly village folk willing to practise the traditional greetings to outsiders, known as *philoxenia*, that seems to be lost on the major tourist trails.

Ithaca

Ithaca (port police, tel: 0674 32 909), the second smallest of the Ionian chain, has gained a reputation as being relatively unspoilt, despite its world-wide fame as the home of wandering Odysseus and his faithful wife Penelope. Odysseus, or Ulysses, was King of Ithaca and an important figure during the siege of Troy (the horse was his idea). According to Homer's Odyssey, our hero incurred Poseidon's wrath and it took him ten years to make it home where his wife waited patiently despite the advances of many suitors. Ithaca doesn't have great sandy beaches or architectural ruins as such but it is an extremely pleasant walking island. On the southern part of the island near the port, it is possible to walk to the Cave of the Nymphs where the sleeping Odysseus was placed on land; or further away to visit the Fountain of Arethusa, where on his return to Ithaca Odysseus dressed as a beggar to meet his swineherd Eumaeus.

The northern part of the island is connected to the south by a narrow, precipitous isthmus. Here are quiet little villages and small pebbly beaches. Fair-sized Stravos, at the base of Mount Nisiti (806m), is a base for walks either down to Frikes (half-an-hour) which has a small pebbly beach and the Nostos hotel (tel: 0674 31 644), or 1km up to the Venetian fort in ruins at Pelikata. Better yet is the 4km track up to the church at Exoyi, for spectacular views over the island from the bell tower.

Enough rooms are available on the island, but two mid-priced hotels in Ithaca town, or Vathi, are recommended: the Hotel Odysseus (tel: 0674 32 381) and the Mentor (tel: 0674 32 433). The tourist police (tel: 0674 32 205) can also help. Ferries sail from Ithaca to Vasiliki on Lefkada, Astakos on the mainland, Patras and Sami, Agia Evfymia and Fiskardo on Cephalonia.

Cephalonia

Cephalonia (port police: Sami, tel: 0674 22 031; Argostoli, tel: 0671 22 224; Poros, tel: 0674 72 460) is the largest and possibly most rugged of the Ionian Isles. It is an important nesting ground for the endangered Loggerhead Turtle, has notable wine and is currently experiencing a package tourist boom, despite having no major archaeological sites and some rather desultory towns (the result of mass destruction during the 1953 earthquake); with the exception of the picturesque fishing port of Fiskardo on the island's north coast. It is so big that beach and village holidays are possible without really sensing the package crowds.

Wine aficionados should make an effort to taste the fine dry white wines based on the Robola variety unique to Cephalonia and long considered one of Greece's best. Good Robola is produced by the Calligas Cousins (telephone in Athens 01 29 92 231, fax: 01 29 92 301) for visits to the Cephalonia winery in the village of Calligata. Another well known producer is Nicholas S. Cosmetatos (tel: 0671 41 618) in the village of Minies near Argostoli.

Other than wine, visitors should consider exploring the high country around 1,632m Mount Enos, recently declared a national park to protect the indigenous fir trees named after the island; and the breeding grounds of the turtles around Potomakia Beach near Skala. Campers are asked to not use the beach during breeding season, as the turtles are endangered and they do not like sharing the beach with humans. Another site to visit is the village of Markopoulos for the unusual spectacle associated with the 15th of August Assumption of the Virgin festival. Small harmless snakes, bearing a natural cross-type marking on their foreheads, occasionally make forays among the worshippers. These reptiles are respected as having curative powers. But they do not emerge every year.

Argostoli will be the base for many visitors, as it is the largest town. Here are the Archaeological Museum (tel: 0671 28 300) and the Historical and Cultural Museum (tel: 0671 28 221). Accommodation includes: Argostoli Camping (tel: 0671 23 487) about 2km from the town; the Hotel Pathenon (tel: 0671 22 246), the Hotel Tourist (tel: 0671 22 510) and the Hotel Agios Yerassimos (tel: 0671 28 697). Ferries from Argostoli call at Kylini south of Patras. Sami is the main port with ships to Patras, Corfu and Italy. It has a variety of accommodation including the Caravomilos Beach Camping (tel: 0674 22 480) and quite a few hotels including: the Hotel Kyma (tel: 0674 22 064), the Melissani (tel: 0674 22 464) and the slightly better Ionion (tel: 0674 22 035). Fiskardo pays for its quaintness and is the centre of island tourism with yachties and package tourists sharing the narrow streets. Accommodation includes the Hotel Panorama (tel: 0674 51 340) or rooms from Anna Barzouka (tel: 0674 51 572). This little port has ferries to Ithaca, but is busy and those wishing to stay should call well in advance.

Zakynthos

Zakynthos or Zante (port police, tel: 0695 22 417), which neighbours the smaller Strophades, was long considered the most beautiful of the Ionian Isles, but has suffered from extensive tourism around its shores. Inland, it still preserves its natural beauty – there are quite attractive villages like Maherado, Kiliomeno, or Agios Nikolaos, and Maries on the mountain road, surrounded by fine pastoral landscapes. Good white and red wine is produced here, from the Robola. One of the best producers is also one of Greece's oldest: the Comouto Family (tel: 0695 92 285, fax: 92 284). They have been making wine at their Ktima Agria estate since 1638.

Loggerhead turtles use the fine sand beaches around the Bay of Laganas, as do hordes of sun worshippers. It may be a good idea to avoid the beaches at Laganas, Kalamaki and especially Geraki during the turtles' nesting period. The romantic golden sand beach with the rusting hulk of a wrecked ship represented on the postcards is on the northern tip of the island near the village of Volimes. Near here is the Anafonitria Monastery, reputedly the refuge of Saint Dionissios.

Accommodation in Zakynthos town includes: Zante Camping (tel: 0695 24 754) at Tsilivi, five km away, the Hotel Ionian (tel: 0695 22 5111), the Hotel Oasis (tel: 0695 22 287), the Hotel Apollon (tel: 0695 22 838) and the Palatino (tel/fax: 0695 45 400). The tourist police (tel: 0695 27 367) can help with other accommodation.

Strophades is a large, remote, uninhabited and rarely visited island south of Zakynthos. It has a Byzantine monastery fortress with only a handful of monks. It is mostly used by hunters shooting doves.

Chapter Seventeen

Itinerary Two

Athens–Thessaloniki–Alexandroupolis–Samothraki–Thassos–Kavala–Thessaloniki–Athens (directly by rail or through the Sporades and Volos)

This route goes from Athens to Alexandroupolis by rail, then by ferry to the islands of Samothraki and Thassos with a visit to Kavala, then by train from Xanthi back to Thessaloniki and either to Athens by rail or to the Sporades and Volos by ferry for a return by rail from Volos to Athens.

The itinerary calls for two days in Athens followed by a half-day train ride to Thessaloniki; two nights there then a half-day train trip to Alexandroupolis, followed by a ferry to Samothraki and Thassos with a night in each island then another ferry to Kavala (one night there); then a return to Thessaloniki for either the half-day rail descent to Athens, or a several-day descent by ferry through the Sporades to Volos, then by rail to Athens.

SAMOTHRAKI

(Port police, tel: 0551 41 305.) This small (176km²) verdant and isolated island 32km off the coast of Alexandroupolis has long been considered one of Greece's most beautiful islands. It is topped by the striking granite peak of 1,611m Mount Fegari (moon mountain) and it contains an important archaeological site: the **Sanctuary of the Great Gods** (open Tues–Sun 08.30–15.00; site and museum have individual admission of 500, 300Dr; tel: 0551 41 474). This island, without an airport and without much tourism-based infrastructure, is far off the main tourist trail: there are no package tourists here. The main attractions are the surprisingly wide range of natural attributes (greenery, waterfalls, mountains and plains) and the Sanctuary.

Arrival is at the sole island port of **Kamariotissa**. This sleepy port situated at the base of unwooded hills could be a base for explorations into the interior, but it is best used as a jumping-off point for the more attractive villages of Chora in the interior, or Paleopolis and Loutra (Therma) around the north coast. A daily excursion boat circumnavigates Samothraki from Kamariotissa in three to four hours and will give a good idea as to why many believe that, after Santorini, Samothraki has the most dramatic profile of any island. Accommodation in Kamariotissa includes the Kima Pension (tel: 0551 41 268), Niki Beach Hotel (tel: 0551 41 561) and Aeolis Hotel (tel: 0551 41 596).

The old, picturesque, hillside village of **Chora** offers striking panoramas and is totally untouristy. It is possible to walk from here to the Sanctuary at Paleopolis (two hours), to the summit of Mount Fengari (five hours) or to a variety of small villages in the region.

Paleopolis on the coast is where the Sanctuary of the Great Gods is located. This Sanctuary was considered as sacred and important to the ancients as the Mysteries of Elefsina. It was a site of worship from about 1000BC, when the island was first settled by Thracians, to the 4th century AD when paganism was abolished. The evocative site is where the famous Winged Venus of Nike Athena was discovered in 1863. The original is at the Louvre in Paris, but a reproduction is here at the museum. A visit to the museum will help put the site in context. On the site are a variety of distinct edifices including the hall of initiation, the Anaktoron, followed by the Arsinoeion: the largest circular ancient building known in Greece. Then the Temenos and the Hieron buildings are where, respectively, the feasting and a higher level of initiation took place. Beyond is the outline of a theatre, and on a ridge, the Nike fountain where the statue was found. Above is a monumental gateway to the great gods dedicated by Ptolemy II. Accommodation at Paleopolis is available at the Kastro Hotel (tel: 0551 41 001).

Continuing around the rough coast from Paleopolis, the next populated area is little Loutra, or Therma. Loutra is the best place to stay in Samothraki, with a variety of accommodation including two campsites: the Loutra (tel: 0551 41 784) and the Multilary (tel: 0551 41 494) . There are also two hotels, the Karivos (tel: 0551 41 577) and the Mariva (tel: 0551 41 759), among the other pensions and rooms for rent.

The main reason for coming here is to amble up to the summit of **Mount Fengari**. Along the way you can see the extensive variety of fauna, like frogs, toads, turtles and lumbering tortoises, as well as pass through deep, dark, boulder-strewn glades, gurgling springs and thick brush, to the 1,611 metre summit. From here, it is possible, as Poseidon allegedly did, to see over to the Galipoli Peninsula and the plain of Troy in the east, the Rhodopi Mountains to the north and the Mount Athos peninsula in the west. Besides the climb to Mount Fengari, Loutra has thermal baths and a 12m waterfall near Fonias, a one-hour walk from the town centre.

Regular ferries sail from Kamariotissa to the islands of Limnos (during the summer) and Thassos as well as returning to Alexandroupolis.

THASSOS

(Ferry information, tel: 0593 22 500.) This large (398km²), almost circular "island in the mist", as the Delphic oracle called it, is just ten kilometres off the coast from the mouth of the Nestos River. It is luxuriantly green, blessed with abundant precious metals (mined since antiquity), significant oil reserves (exploited since the 1970s) and long silvery beaches bordering its deep blue seas. Package tourism has discovered Thassos, but the high-rise hotel strips are mostly restricted to the southwest coast. Ships call at the port of Limen, better known as Thassos, in the north. A coastal road encircles the island.

The main attractions include the town of Thassos built over the ancient town (founded in the 8th century BC) and its beaches. But discriminating visitors should try to explore some of the delightful and surprisingly intact hill villages, like Potamia, from where the trail leads for the ascent of Mount Psarion (1,142m), Thassos' highest mountain.

Thassos town offers the greatest concentration of ancient sites on the island. These include the ancient agora, acropolis and theatre. The theatre is still used for classical drama, staged as part of the Kavala Festival of Drama. The **Archaeological Museum** (Great Alexander Street 18; tel: 0593 22 180) is currently closed for renovation but when it reopens will merit a concerted visit for its informative displays. The ancient 5th-century walls complete with monumental gates are largely intact, and make for a fine two-hour stroll. For those interested, attractive and well-marked, though shadeless, trails lead in five hours to the hill village of Panagia. From here another trail leads to Potamia for the climb to Mount Psarion. Both of these charming villages provide great views down across Potamia Bay.

Accommodation in Thassos Town is plentiful even during the busy summer months of July and August. It includes the budget favourites: Acropol (tel: 0593 22 488), Athanasia (tel: 0593 22 545) and Victoria (tel: 0593 22 556). Other well respected properties include the Timeleon (tel: 0593 22 177, fax: 23 277) and the seasonal Amfipolis (tel: 0593 23 101, fax: 22 110). Note that Thassos' resort status means that many hotels are not open during the winter. Off-season visitors are invited to contact the Hoteliers Association of Thassos (tel: 0593 22 177, fax: 23 277) for further information.

Important beaches east of Thassos Town include the Golden where the Chryssi Ammoudia Campsite is (tel: 0593 61 207) and Paradise Beaches. Both these beaches are near the villages of Panagia and Potamia. These can be used as bases, if avoiding beach crowds is a priority. In Panagia, near the always flowing fountain, are the Hotel Helvetia (tel: 0593 61 231), the Hotel Chrysafis (tel: 0593 61 451) and the Thassos (tel: 0593 61 612) among others.

Inland villages include Theologos, the medieval and Turkish-era capital,

10km from Potos on the south coast; Kastro Limenaria and, above Prinos, the nunnery of Agios Pandelimonos. Agios Pandelimonos is accessible via a one-hour walk, mostly uphill from Prinos. From there unpaved roads lead on to Sotiros or Maries.

THE SPORADES

These consist of **Skiathos** (port police, tel: 0427 22017), **Skopelos** (port police, tel: 0424 22 189), **Alonissos** (port police, tel: 0424 65 595), **Skyros** (port police, tel: 0222 91 475). This eleven-island archipelagos is scattered (thus the Greek *sporades*) off the Thessalian shore from Volos. These small, hilly and extremely attractive islands much resemble the nearby Pelion Peninsula from which they were detached many millennia ago. Only four of the eleven are populated and the first two, Skiathos and Skopelos, are well on the package-tour charter-flight circuit. As such, they are overcrowded during July and August. Those who wish to discover their quaint villages and hidden monasteries are recommended to visit in the spring or early summer. In general and like many small islands, most people live in one big town with the back country acting as a large garden. They all have excellent beaches and the full range of tourist-related services.

Skiathos

Skiathos is the third largest island (78km^2), the most densely populated (6,000), and the most popular because it is the most accessible by air. It contains a quaint 19th-century, red-tile-roofed town, built around an attractive bay closed off by the forested Bourtzi islet. Beyond the town are the popular southern beaches, protected from the hot summer Meltemi winds blowing from the north; the more isolated northern beaches; and the relatively unpopulated interior.

The town contains the home, now a museum, of the late-19th-century writer Alexandros Papadiamantis (1851–1911). The simple house can be visited daily from 09.30–13.00 & 17.00–19.00. His works, in translation, describe the condition of Greeks during the last days of the Turkish hegemony. They are available in island book shops or in Athens at the Compendium Bookshop (Nikis 28, Syntagma Square).

Lodgings in Skiathos are in a large variety of pensions and rented rooms, or in its hotels which include: the Australia Hotel (tel: 0427 49 312), the Hotel Karafelas (tel: 0427 21 235), the Morfo (tel: 0427 21 737) and the Alkyon (tel: 0427 22 981). During the July–August crush or the winter off-season, the tourist police (tel: 0427 23 172) will help secure other accommodation.

The main south-coast beach is the long crescent-shaped sandy Koukounaries. This is reputed to be Greece's best beach. Here are any number of hotels and a good campground (0427 49 290). The rough northern coast is accessible by caique and rough roads. On one wide beach-front glade at Megali Aselino is Skiathos' other recommended official campground (tel: 0427 49 312).

A long walk straight across the island will lead through the 18th-century Moni Evangelismos monastery to the medieval island capital of Kastro. Moni Evangelismo (daily 08.00–12.00 & 16.00–20.00) is well sited over a 450m chasm and surrounded by fragrant pines and cypress trees. Islanders claim that the blue and white Greek flag was raised here for the first time in 1807. The hero of the War of Independence Kolokotronis declared his willingness to fight from here. Along the way are two abandoned monasteries: the 15th-century Panagia tis Kerias and the 17th-century Haralambos. Beyond Haralambos a path leads the 3km to the abandoned Kastro town.

Kastro (1538–1829) is built on a rocky headland overlooking the sea. It was formerly connected to the island by a drawbridge, but is now linked by steps. At one time containing over 300 houses and 20 churches, it is a ghostly unoccupied ruin today with only two churches in a reasonable state of repair. When piracy was eliminated after Independence, islanders moved down to the ancient site at Skiathos town.

Skopelos

Skopelos is the second largest (122km^2) and most obviously agricultural of the Sporades. It has not escaped the holiday-island image of its neighbour Skiathos. Skopelos has one paved road running from the main port at Skopelos Town through the minor storm port at Agnontas up to the picturesque hilltop village of Glossa (which also has a small sea port at Loutraki). Ferries usually call at both Loutraki and Skopelos town.

Skopelos Town is rather attractive, rising up in terraces behind the port. It has over 120 churches for the devout, and those interested in Orthodox architecture and iconography. A beautiful walk/scramble over trails and donkey paths leads in an hour to two nunneries: Evengelistria and Prodromos (both open from 08.00–13.00 & 17.00–19.00). A small folk art museum on Hatzistamati Street is open in the evenings (19.00–22.00).

Most ferries call at Skopelos town which has the majority of tourist services. Accommodation includes: the Hotel Rania (tel: 0424 22 486), the Eleni (tel: 0424 22 393), the Pension Ulla (tel: 0424 22 637), the upscale Delfini (tel: 0424 23 015) and the fine Arhondiko Inn (tel: 0424 22 765). Once again, during the busy summer months or slow winter period, the police (tel: 0424 22 235) will come to the aid of those unable to find lodgings.

Whitewashed Glossa at the other end of Skopelos seems to have kept its traditional integrity while providing for tourists. A sizeable and attractive town, Glossa has a range of accommodation, including the Hotel Atlantis (tel: 0424 33 223) and many pensions, of which the Pension Valentina (tel: 0424 33 694) is recommended. Beyond Glossa, a path leads in 90 minutes to the semi-secluded beach of Perivoliou.

Other good island beaches include Stafilos, the nearest to Skopelos Town, and its neighbour Velanio; also Milia and Elios.

Alonissos

Alonissos is the smallest (62km²) and most remote of the inhabited islands, and often the least appealing at first glance. The vineyard blight Phyloxera wiped out the economy in 1950, and in 1965 a severe earthquake led to a decision by the ruling Athenian Junta to abandon the old settlements. Many people subsequently left and are only now returning.

The waters around the island have been declared a marine park, partially as an effort to protect the endangered monk seal. This is the European animal most in danger of extinction. Around 800 of these sea mammals exist in the world, with the largest concentration being in the sea caves of the islet of Piperi off the coast of Alonissos. The Hellenic Society for the Protection of the Monk Seal (HSPMS) is based in the tiny fishing hamlet of Steni Vala. They have been successful in reintroducing several orphaned monk seals back into the wild, and they ask tourists and travellers to respect the monk seal's natural habitat and refrain from snorkelling and especially spear-fishing in the area. The Ikaros Camping (tel: 0424 65 258) is located in Steni Vala. HSPMS welcomes inquiries from those interested in preserving the monk seal. Breeding grounds on Piperi have made the isle off-limits to all except those with special permits. Check with HSPMS (Solomou Street 53, 10432 Athens; tel: 01 52 22 888, fax: 52 22 450) for details.

Accommodation in Alonissos is available at the Camping Rocks (tel: 0424 65 410); the Alkyon Guest House (tel: 0424 65 450); the Ladromia Hotel (tel: 0424 65 521) and the posh Galaxy Hotel (tel: 0424 65 251).

Skyros

Skyros is the largest (205km²) and most unusual of the inhabited Sporades, with its southerly location and customs. At times, it seems like a barren Cycladic isle and at other times it resembles the Caribbean with its unusual pre-Lenten Carnival. It is home to a race of small wild ponies distinct to the island and has a long tradition of wood carving. The goat dance by masked revellers in the streets of Skyros town associated with Skyros' pre-Lenten celebrations is featured in a book by Joy Koulentitianous, *The Goat Dance of Skyros*. It also has the grave of the poet Rupert Brooke and the site of the New Ages Skyros Centre of Holistic Healing (in London: tel: 0171 267 4424, fax: 284 3063; 92 Prince of Wales Road, London NW5 3NE, UK). Several museums recall that the island had mythological associations: the Archaeology Museum (open Tues–Sun 08.30–15.00; admission 500, 400, 300Dr; tel: 022 91 327) has a good selection from Mycenaean and Roman times. The Municipal Traditional Skyrion House (open Mon–Sat 11.00–12.00 & 18.00–20.00; admission 300Dr) and the private ethnographic Faltaitz Museum (Mon–Sat 10.00–13.00 & 17.30–21.30; free) are the other cultural activities possible on the island.

Skyros' main town, called Chora, high on a bluff and crowned by a 13th-century Venetian fortress, is a compact car-free zone and has a definite Cycladic-style feel about it. Within the fortress is a decaying convent (St George the Arab) built in 962, and once famous for its miracles. Accommodation in Chora includes: Skyros Camping (tel: 0222 92 458), the Hotel Eleni (tel: 0222 91 738), the Nefeli (tel: 0222 91 964) and the fine Lykomedes House (tel: 0222 91 697).

Two relatively modern resort towns have developed in the bay below Skyros town: Mazagia at the bay's southern and Molos at its northern end have long sandy beaches and the full range of tourist amenities. Other good beaches are at Atsitsa and Kyra Panagia on the island's northwest coast. Another road leads south around Ahili Bay, then traverses the island, skirting Mount Kokilas (782m) south towards the Treis Bokes Bay site of Rupert Brooke's tomb in an olive grove.

Skyros has ferry service through Linaria, 10km from Skyros Town, to Volos and Kymi on Evia. It is theoretically possible to take a train from Athens to Chalkis, then catch a bus to Kymi and sail from there to Linaria. This trip should take about five hours.

Chapter Eighteen

Itinerary Three

Athens–Peloponnese–Crete–the Aegean Isles–Athens

This route goes from Athens or Patras to Kalamata by rail, then either by ship to Crete, or first to Gythion then to Crete, and from Crete to Santorini and by ferry directly to Piraeus or to other islands before returning to Piraeus and Athens. Between the Peloponnese and Crete are the untouristy islands of Kythera and Antikythera. Both of these islands represent interesting stopovers or destinations in themselves.

The itinerary calls for a train to Kalamata from either Athens (after two nights) or Patras (after one night), then one night in Kalamata (or more time along the west coast or in the Mani), then a ferry to Kissamos in Crete with two nights in Chania, then directly to Iraklion for one or two nights before taking the ferry to Santorini for one or two nights, then directly to Piraeus or the other Aegean islands. Note that this itinerary requires the most planning or the most flexibility as ferry connections from the Southern Peloponnese to Crete and from Iraklion to Santorini sail less frequently than those from Piraeus directly to the Aegean and Crete.

KYTHERA AND ANTIKYTHERA

Port police are at Agia Pelagia (tel: 0735 33 280) and at Kapsali (tel: 0735 31 222). A large (30km long by 18km wide) and relatively unspoilt island at the base of the Peloponnese, **Kythera**'s claim to fame in antiquity is that it is where Aphrodite was born. It played a strategic role for the Venetians who knew it as Cerigo. The completion of the Corinth Canal led to a steep decline in shipping around the Peloponnese and contributed to the isolation of this island: many natives have emigrated to Australia. Today it is a rather sleepy island without many tourists.

Sights include the ruined medieval capital of Paleohora east of Potamos, and traditional villages like Karavas in the north near Potamos and Milapotamos in the south. Paleohora is an exceptional Byzantine site that reminds one of Mystra. Built in the 14th century, it became the hidden refuge of Byzantine nobility after the fall of Monemvasia and Mystra to the Turks. It was discovered in 1537 by the Turkish Admiral Barbarossa, despite its seemingly impregnable site, sacked, and all its inhabitants sold into slavery. The town was never repopulated, nor has it been seriously excavated. Karavas and Milapotamos are oasis towns nestled in leafy, deeply wooded valleys with swiftly running water coursing through the villages. These are the exceptions to a largely rocky island.

Ferries call at either Agia Pelagia in the north or Kapsali in the south. Both have the gamut of visitor services but not in any great number. In Agia Pelagia are the Faros Taverna (tel: 0735 33 282) and the Hotel Kythera (tel: 0735 33 3221) as well as a number of rooms for rent. Up the winding road that clings precipitously to the sheer cliff is the village of Potamos with rooms available in the Porfyra Pension (tel: 0735 33 329). Kapsali offers Kythera's sole official camping (tel: 0735 31 580) and luxury rooms at the Raikos Hotel (tel: 0735 31 629). Above Kapsali in the island's present capital called Chora, an attractive village, are lodgings at the recently renovated 19th-century mansion Hotel Margarita (tel: 0735 31 694) and the simpler though no less desirable Pension Keti (tel: 0735 31 318).

Antikythera (population 75) is the definitive isolated island. It seems to have one of everything, doctor, shop and telephone, but it does have two boats per week in the summer. Shipwrecks in the treacherous straits between it and Kythera seem to be its forte. One in the 1st century BC was salvaged; its bronze and marble sculptures are now in the National Archaeological Museum in Athens.

CRETE

Port police stations are at Kissamos (tel: 0822 22 655), Chania (tel: 0821 89 240), Rethmynon (tel: 0831 29 950), Iraklion (tel: 081 282 002), and Agios Nikolaos (tel: 0841 22 312). The largest (8,259km²) island in Greece and the fourth largest in the Mediterranean, Crete is big and populous (540,000) enough to stand on its own as a free country, which it briefly did in the later years of the 19th century. Its history is long and convoluted, but essentially linked with that of the powerful Bronze Age Minoan Civilisation. These mysterious and still mostly unknown people built majestic unwalled cities throughout Crete and on other nearby islands. Crete is further south than northern Tunisia, and boasts an excellent climate which results in high-quality agricultural produce and fine sandy beaches. This, and its location on all important shipping routes between Europe, Africa and the Near East, means that it has been coveted by all, including Venetians, Crusaders and Turks. They have left an important architectural legacy.

The fact that Crete looks toward Greece and Europe is well represented by the five ports on its north coast. High roadless mountains dominate the west coast and much of the centre of the island. The high fertile plain of Lasithi east of its capital, Iraklion, gives way to a tropical feel on the eastern coast near Vai and Ierapetra on the southeastern coast: Europe's southernmost town.

The main attractions on a very long list include King Minos' extensive palace at Knossos (among the half-dozen other Minoan sites on the island) near Iraklion (which has a fine Archaeological Museum), and the imposing Samaria Gorge in the high country behind the charming city of Chania.

Arriving at the port of Kissamos, you should make a quick trip to nearby Chania. Note the large statue in Kissamos' centre. It is of Crete's "Great Man", Eleftherios Venizelos, arguably modern Greece's most charismatic and influential public figure. A fine road follows the coast from here all the way to the eastern extremity of the island. At times it hugs the coast so closely that spray from the beach enters the bus (best views from the left side).

Chania

Chania (tourist police, tel: 0821 24 477) is Crete's traditional capital. It has been, since 1971, its second city (70,000); the administrative capital then moved to Iraklion. It is Crete's most attractive city though, with a centre that retains a great deal of its Venetian/Turkish charm. The skyline is dominated by the often snow-capped peaks of the nearby White Mountains. It is gateway to the Nome of Chania and the much-touted Samaria Gorge on the south coast. It is a good base to organise treks to the back country, or you can simply relax and enjoy the cosmopolitan atmosphere (especially around the old port dominated by the now closed Mosque of the Janissaries). An archaeological museum (Halidon St 24; open Mon 12.30–18.00, Tues–Fri 08.00–18.00, Sat–Sun 08.30–15.00; admission 500, 400, 300Dr; tel: 0821 90 334) in the 16th-century former church of San Francisco and the spacious late-19th-century Central Market should retain the visitor's interest; while treks to the 16km Samaria Gorge (May–Oct; 1,000Dr), Europe's longest, can be organised. This can be done individually (check with the tourist police for details) or through an agency. Chania's chapter of EOS (Tsanakaki 90; tel: 0821 24 647) or an agency like Trekking Plan (Dimitriou 15; tel: 0821 44 946) can help with this or longer treks to the White Mountains.

Lodgings include Hania Campground (tel: 0821 51 090), the IYHA Hostel (tel: 0821 53 565), Piraeus Hotel (Zambeliou 14; tel: 0821 54 154), the Thereza (Angelou 8; tel: 0821 40 118), and the more upscale Hotel Samaria (1866 Square; tel: 0821 71 271, fax: 71 270) near the KTEL bus station.

Chania has hourly buses to the east and many to the south. Try the lovely village of Paleohora for a laid-back resort. A nightly ferry sails year-round to Piraeus from Chania's port at Souda Bay. This is also the largest NATO naval base in the eastern Mediterranean. In case of difficulties on NATO's eastern flank, the area fills with American and European sailors.

Rethymnon

Rethymnon (tourist police, tel: 0831 28 156). This is a small (population 25,000), charming port city at the base of an over-large 16th-century Venetian fort. The old quarter is more compact than Chania and offers more Venetian/Ottoman charm in a smaller area. It is a good base to explore the back country. From here, it's possible to leave the north coast and take an alternative route through the more barren south coast and then circle back to Iraklion. On the south coast are Agia Galini which boasts 340 days of sunshine and the cave-ridden port of Matala, one of the few places in the world that actively relishes its hippie past. Twenty-three kilometres from Rethymnon is the 16th-century Orthodox Monastery of Moni Arkadiou. It gained renown during the 1866 insurrection when the several hundred Cretans taking refuge there from the besieging Turks chose to blow themselves up with their attackers rather than surrender. Trekking in the charming back-country region of the Amari Valley can be organised through the local offices of EOS (tel: 083 22 710) or Trekking Plan (Portaliou 18; tel: 0831 20 123).

Places to stay include: two nearby campsites: Camping Arkadia (tel: 0831 28 825) and Camping Elisabeth (tel: 0831 28 694), the IYHA Hostel (Tombasi St 41; tel: 0831 22 848), Achillion Hotel (Arcadiou 151; tel: 0831 22 581), The Byzantine (Vosporou 26; tel: 0831 55 609) and the smarter Hotel Fortezza (tel: 0831 21 551, fax: 20 073).

Buses leave from the KTEL terminal above the port for all points and ferries leave three times weekly for Piraeus.

Iraklion

Iraklion (tourist police, tel: 081 283 190). The capital and largest city (125,000), Iraklion is big, bustling and difficult to like. But, it has one of the best Archaeological Museums (Xanthoudidou St 1; open Mon 12.30–17.00, Tues–Sun 08.00–17.00; admission 1,500, 1,100, 800Dr; tel: 081 224 630) and one of the most fascinating archaeological sites, the Knossos Palace (open daily 08.00–17.00; admission 1,500, 1,100, 800Dr; tel: 081 231 940), in all of Greece. The 16-room museum and the grand 22,000m^2 palace help place the enlightened, though still mysterious, Minoan (3000–1100BC) culture in its proper context. The city has long since expanded outside the massive Venetian fortress (1462–1562), but the seven bastions and four towering gates are still much in evidence. Iraklion's land-side walls are complete and have a recently installed promenade along the top of the ramparts that leads to the simple and poignant tomb of Greece's best modern writer Nikos Kazantzakis (1883–1957). The excellent Historical Museum (open Mon–Fri 09.30–16.30, Sat 09.30–14.30, admission 600Dr) near the port should help put Crete's long and convoluted contemporary history in perspective.

Beyond the Knossos site are two large, green agricultural valleys, Peza and Archanes, whose speciality is lovely white and red wine made from grape varieties cultivated there since antiquity. Visits to the Miliarakis Brothers' Minos Cretan Wines winery in Peza can be arranged by telephoning 081 741 213, or at the Archanes estate of the Boutari Family.

Once again, hiking and trekking can be arranged from Iraklion, through the local EOS (Dikeosinis 53; tel: 081 227 609) which owns a refuge on Mount Ida (2,456 m). Other tours to the villages where Kazantzakis grew up and to the fine Minoan palaces other than Knossos (Phaestus, Gortyn and Agia Triada) can be arranged by the Iraklion branch of Creta Travel (Epimendou 20-22; tel: 081 223 749).

Iraklion has a plethora of places to stay from the gritty to the glamorous. A selection includes the IYHA Hostels (two locations, at Vironas 5; tel: 081 286 281 and at Handakos 24; tel: 081 280 858), The Hotel Rea (Kalimeraki 4; tel: 081 223 638), Lena Hotel (Lahana 10; tel: 081 223 280), the Hotel Metropol (Odos Karterou; tel: 081 242 330) and the fine Astoria Hotel (Platia Eleftherias 11; tel: 081 229 002, fax: 229 078).

The two KTEL bus stations by the port and the third KTEL terminal outside the land walls provide regular bus service to all parts of the island. The international port has several daily ships to Piraeus and regular departures to the islands and Thessaloniki. When times are good there are even ships to Italy. An international airport east of the city has multi-daily flights to Athens and charters to every destination.

The road east from Iraklion leads past Chersonissos and Malia, two erstwhile fishing ports which are now grim package-tourist ghettos. There is little of value in these places: just a plethora of hotels, restaurants, cafés and bars catering mostly to northerners seeking several weeks in the sun. Malia does have an important Minoan palace site (open Tues–Sun 08.30–15.00; admission 800, 600, 400Dr) east of the centre. Beyond this bus stop, the road begins to climb over the headlands to the Nome of Lasithi, and its principal port of Agios Nikolaos. The small traditional market town of Neapolis with its large central church is a gateway to the inland Lasithi plateau. Every square inch of this large plain seems to be cultivated, but the dozens of windmills that are always identified with it are now seldom used.

Agios Nikolaos

Agios Nikolaos (tourist police, tel: 0841 22 321), an attractive port around the picturesque Bay of Mirabello, is inundated with tourists in the busy summer months: the population doubles. At the town's centre is the small Voulismeni Lake, 64m deep. According to mythology, Athena and Artemis enjoyed swimming here. A fine Archaeological Museum (K. Paleologou St 74; open Tues–Sun 08.30–15.00; admission 500, 400, 300Dr; tel: 084124 943) displays finds from eastern Crete. There is also an interesting museum of local folklore (Paleologou St; Sun–Fri 10.00–13.30 & 18.30–21.30;

admission 250Dr).

Accommodation tends to be difficult to find in the summer. The tourist police and the laudable Municipal Tourist Office (Paleologou St tel: 0841 22 357, fax: 26 398) will help find something. But try Gournia Moon Camping (tel: 0842 93 243) east of town near the Minoan Gournia site, the IYHA Hostel (tel: 0841 22 823), the Pension Vasilia Inn (Ariadnis 6; tel: 0841 23 572), the Linda Hotel (tel: 0841 22 130) and the plush Coral Hotel (tel: 0841 28 363) both on the western end of the city near the waterfront.

As expected, KTEL buses serve the island, but services to the east and south are less frequent than those to the west. Ferries call here to and from Piraeus and serve the islands of Milos (where the Venus in Paris's Louvre Museum was found) in the Cyclades, and Rhodes, through intriguing Karpathos in the southern Aegean.

Eastern Crete is a large quiet area with its share of fine beaches and intriguing sites. The cities of Sitea and Ierapetra on the south coast seem less European than somewhat Near-Eastern whereas the resort of Vai with its soaring palm trees and extensive sand dunes looks positively Polynesian.

Santorini

Santorini and Thirassia (port police, tel: 0286 22 239). This is the Aegean Island destination par excellence. It seems to have everything (except sand on its many beaches). There are fine Minoan ruins on the southern end near Acrotiri (open Tues–Sun 08.30–15.00; admission 1,000Dr) and quaint geometric blue-and-white villages everywhere. Pyrgos is a personal favourite. The main town of Fira is very lively, while Oia at the other end of the island is serene and content, with some of the best sunset views in Greece.

But the main attraction of this island is the spectacular entrance by sea into the port. Santorini, or Thera, is an island over a still seething and very active volcano. The last important eruption blew the island's top and destroyed Minoan Civilisation in Crete, more than 70 nautical miles away. But that was about 3,000 years ago. Today, entrance into the Caldera, as it is called, reveals dramatic multi-hued cliffs rising hundreds of metres from sea level. The cliffs are topped with tiny cubist villages.

Surprisingly, for an island with little natural water and volcanic ash for soil, its agricultural produce is remarkably good. Santorini is known for tiny and sweet cherry tomatoes, succulent fava beans and excellent white wine produced in both a dry and a sweet style from the unique Assyrtico variety. Lately, this wine has experienced great international success and local vintners have built state-of-the-art wineries and created smart tasting rooms. The best of these big wineries are Santos Wines (highly recommended), at Pyrgos overlooking the Caldera, and Boutari at Megalochori; of the individual producers try George Sigalas on the beach in Oia and Canava Roussos in Fira. All of these wineries are open for tastings and visits, but harvest time in mid-August can be hectic for the small producers.

Lodgings run the gamut as can be expected. A selection includes Camping Santorini (tel: 0286 22 9440), but there are several others. A youth hostel, the Kontonari, (tel: 0286 22 722) is in Fira near the cable car; also in Fira is the Hotel Takati (tel: 0286 22 389); the Locos Hotel (tel: 0286 22 480) and the fine Kallisti Thira (tel: 0286 22 317). In Oia are the Hotel Fregata (tel: 0286 71 221) and the Hotel Anemones (tel: 0286 71 220). In the wine country around Megalochori is the Hotel Zorbas (tel: 0286 31 433). The beach resort of Kamari has two campsites: Kamari Camping (tel: 0286 31 453) and Galanakis Camping (tel: 0286 81 343).

Thirassia, the small island across the Caldera, is more traditional than its bigger neighbour and is a good place to see the volcano smoke and smoulder.

THE OTHER CYCLADIC ISLANDS

Beyond Santorini are so many islands that it is difficult to do them all justice. The name Cyclades comes from the fact that all the islands form somewhat of a circle around the sacred island of Delos. They have been settled since prehistoric days and have been at the centre of all trading and warring activities ever since. In the days before steam ships, many islands played an important role as stopping harbours. The digging of the Corinth Canal began the decline of these islands, and then wholesale emigration before and after World War II depopulated many of them. Only with an upsurge in tourism during the late 1970s have some islands begun to see their former residents return, if only for the summer.

Quiet little **Anafi**, raging **Ios** (visible from Oia in the north of Santorini) and magical **Folegandros** are all near Santorini. Ios is for the college-age non-stop-party crowd.

The little island of **Folegandros** (population 620) is typical of the pre-20th century era when rampaging sea pirates forced villagers to hide themselves and their settlements out of sight. From the ferry, it is impossible to tell where the village, Chora, is. The tarred road leading out of sight up over the hill gives away the location of the delightful little village (270 inhabitants). Here there are almost as many donkeys as people (probably more so in the winter). The main activities seem to be relaxing under the almond trees and smelling the jasmine. In Chora, a walk up to the Church of the Panayia, built over the ancient town's walls, will reward the intrepid with magnificent views over the islands of Sifnos, Thira and Crete. The minuscule walled Castro (1212) provided what further protection islanders needed from potential invaders.

A word of warning is necessary. Rooms here are extremely scarce in July and August. Without a reservation during those months, the only place to sleep is at the campground (tel: 0286 42 203) near the port of Karavostassi.

Up in the town, Chora, try the Hotel Danassis in the Castro fort (tel/fax: 0286 41 230), the Hotel Odysseus (tel: 0286 41 237), or the Hotel Fani-Vevie (tel: 0286 41 237). The island stretches 15km to the north where there is a small though sprawling settlement called Ano Meria. Trails lead from the escarpment down to a number of secluded beaches. Near Folegandros is the equally small island of Sikinos which hasn't yet the cachet of Folegandros, but most probably soon will.

Ferry schedules to Folegandros alter regularly, and changes to other ferries are often necessary at Ios or Paros for other islands. Contact the port police (tel: 0286 41 249) for current schedules.

Syros

Syros (population 30,000) with its large capital of Ermoupolis (20,000) is a bit off the foreigner's path but it also deserves a special mention. The island (22.5km by 9km) is the capital of the Nome of the Cyclades and with the large Neorion Shipyards seems to be prospering without mass tourism. The city is crowned with two conical hills, each the province of its respective religious community: closer to Ermoupolis (lower and on the right) is the Orthodox hill of Vrodado; while Ano Syros (on the left from the port) has one of the oldest Catholic communities in the Aegean with its Baroque Cathedral of Saint George and a Capuchin Monastery of St Jean (1535). Great views across to the islands of Andros and Naxos are possible from the ramparts of Saint George.

The fact of the matter is that Syros was mainly Catholic from the time the Franks took it in 1207 and succeeded in converting the population. As a result the mostly Catholic Western Powers protected the island. Because it wasn't involved in the War of Independence, Syros was spared the usual atrocities, and received a large number of Orthodox refugees from the other islands. This, of course, altered the religious equation without creating major problems, though both communities did guard their integrity on their own hills. The island is the seat of an Orthodox Archbishop and a Catholic Bishop. Ermoupolis prospered after Independence and became the major Greek port and city before the Corinth Canal; but afterwards it was quickly supplanted by Piraeus and Athens.

The bustling city is based around the large Platia Miaouli which acts as its transport and entertainment centre. The large distinguished neo-classical town hall is another creation of the Bavarian architect Ziller. Arcade-covered streets line the Platia on two sides, and near its left-hand corner is a fine outdoor summer cinema. The Apollo Theatre, opened in 1864 and reopened for the 1996 season, is said to be modelled on Milan's La Scala, though in miniature. It is on the right behind the town hall, on the Platia Vardaki. The city has a charm, with many narrow commercial streets and unhurried calm neighbourhoods featuring a great number of neo-classical buildings, that many of Greece's other large cities lack. The Vaporia neighbourhood between the seashore and Evangelistra Street is one such neighbourhood and certainly merits a visit.

The island itself has good beaches, notably the large beach at Galissas on the west coast and smaller ones south around the coast at Finikas and Posidonia. These and other beaches beyond Galissas can be reached by walking around the splendid headland from Galissas. Syros has two campsites. Both are at Galissas: the Hearts Camping (tel: 0281 42 052) and Camping Yianna (tel: 0281 42 418).

Excellent wine is produced on the island by the noted ship owner Yannis Vatis in his striking estate at Agia Paraskevi, overlooking Ermoupolis. His wines, under the Vatis and Chateau Vatis labels, can be purchased in Ermoupolis, but the estate is not open for visits.

Accommodation in town is plentiful: the Europa Hotel (tel: 0281 28 771), the Hotel Hermes (tel: 0281 23 011) and several converted mansions including: Homer (Omirou Street 43; tel: 0281 84 910), the Palladion (Stamatiou Proiou 60; tel: 0281 86 400, fax 86 436) and the Villa Maria (tel: 0281 81 561, fax: 86 536) are only a few of the possibilities. The Syros Hoteliers Association has set up a kiosk on the harbour to help with accommodation: they can be telephoned on 0281 61 761.

Ferries sail from Ermoupolis to all the big and small islands of the Cyclades and there is a tri-weekly sailing to Thessaloniki. Through the adjacent island of Naxos there are sailings to Ikaria, Samos and the Dodecanese near the coast of Asia Minor. The port police (tel: 0281 22 690) will gladly offer information on sailings.

Epilogue

The Future of Rail Travel in Greece

A bright future for rail travel in Greece seems assured.

Massive investment in infrastructure and rolling stock is creating a modern railway well capable of serving the needs of passengers and shippers. There is a noticeable change in the attitudes of Greeks towards the railways. Television advertisements feature attractive actors riding fast trains; and Athenian art galleries hold major exhibitions of oil painting on various aspects of railway life. Greek railway modellers present their meticulously crafted miniatures in well received shows, the likes of which have never before been seen in Greece. Volunteer railway activists are maturing and taking important decision-making roles in OSE and other public agencies. Even OSE has embarked on a programme to promote interest in the railway's heritage, by rebuilding and operating steam locomotives over various rail lines throughout the country.

More importantly, public transport policy is forcing travellers to choose between the illusion of independence granted by the private automobile and the attractive alternative of train travel. Tolls on motorways between Patras and Thessaloniki are rising steeply and regularly. The price of imported fossil fuels is increasing continuously. Public authorities are cracking down severely on irresponsible motorists behind the wheels of unsafe cars. Cities are restricting the use of automobiles in their centres. But there is more than simply restricting auto use. Other methods of transport are being made available. New heavy rail transit systems will soon be available in the two major cities and the present intercity rail network is being constantly improved with plans for expansion moving forward. Valid plans exist to complete the Kalambaka–Kozani rail link and to extend the line from Kalambaka through Ioannina to the Ionian port of Igoumenitsa; the port of Kavala could obtain a rail line and Albania could be linked into the Greek railways through Florina.

By the way, the tiny steam locomotive on display in the dock area of Iraklion, Crete, came from the Peloponnese but was put on display to commemorate the temporary 6km-long rail line used during the construction of the modern port of Iraklion.

Appendix One
The Hellenic Association of Railway Friends

Spyros Fasoulas, President

A short history

Soon after its creation in 1979, the Hellenic Railway Museum, situated not far from the Athens railway stations, became a centre of attraction for many train enthusiasts who used to meet there regularly and exchange views about their favourite subject. This led gradually to the idea of creating a "friends-of-the-trains" society. It was a dream which came true in 1983, when a group of twenty initial members officially founded the Hellenic Association of Railway Friends (HARF).

This Association is today an influential group of 350 people of all ages and walks of life who unite their efforts and expertise in order to serve a common cause: the development of the railway in Greece.

The necessity of promoting the Greek railway network is, indeed, a real and challenging one. Its construction got under way in 1869, much later than in other European countries, and even then it was piecemeal: the construction of the most important part of the network started only in 1881 and was not completed until 1909. And we must not forget that railway development in Greece was impeded from the beginning by unfavourable geographic conditions (high mountains, many islands). Moreover, the fact that all big Greek cities of the 19th century were built on the sea coast, which is very extended, reduced the importance of the railway: it had to face the hard competition of sea transport, especially after the opening of the Corinth Canal. Nevertheless, the railway network was continually extended until the outbreak of World War II. During the occupation and resistance which followed, bridges, locomotives and rolling stock were almost totally destroyed. After the war, only part of the system was rebuilt. Priority was given to road building and the development of car transport, so much so that the actual railway network is insufficient, with its three main routes and a few more branch lines. Double tracks cover a rather small part of the network; single tracks cause delays and commuter frustration. Locomotives and other rolling stock are often obsolete, and high-speed trains rare. Further development has been held back by the indifference of successive governments or by the action of deeply entrenched interests. Similarly, the tram was also victim of this situation: up to the end of the 1950s, all tram transport was brought to an end in every big city in Greece (Athens, Thessaloniki, Patras, Piraeus, Kalamata) and all tram tracks removed. In Athens alone 42km of tram rails were removed from 1953 to 1960.

Projects

Such is the reality that the Association of Railway Friends has to face. It is motivated by the firm belief that the train is the best of transport means on land and has, in particular, many advantages over the car. The train is environment-friendly: it fits in any landscape without damaging it, and relieves road congestion as well as destructive pollution and noise caused by cars. Faster than the car, it is also more economical in energy costs. Moreover, it has a much greater carrying capacity and is not affected by adverse weather. And last but not least, the Association takes into account that collective memory has invested the train with high cultural and aesthetic importance.

Considerations of this kind led the Association to form the following general projects:

- to contribute in every possible way to the modernisation and development of the railway, as well as of the metro and noiseless tram

- to organise all sorts of campaigns in order to promote the cause of the railway, the metro and the tram

- to take action for the safeguard and preservation of all sorts of important railway material and equipment

- to keep records and form a solid documentation on technical, cultural and historical railway matters

- to encourage and promote railway modelling

The Association statutes make provision for all these activities, carried out in five specialised Sections: those of Public Relations, Appliances, Museum Pieces and Rail History, Documentation and Rail Promotion, and Organisation. Two publications reinforce the effort of the Association, the half-yearly *Sidirotrochia (Rail)* and a calendar issued every year with rail related illustrations.

Achievements

During the thirteen years of its existence, the Association has made serious and often successful efforts to achieve its aims:

- It has organised a great number of successful conferences, meetings, exhibitions (of rail models, photographs, etc), festivities and excursions in order to bring a large public into contact with the railway and its advantages. Part of this success is to support two very popular "sound and image" spectacles about the train, created by one of its members.

- In 1987, the European Year for the Environment, the Association presented a campaign for the promotion of the railway and tram as the most environment-friendly transport means. This programme was selected and subsidised by the EEC.

- It has tried (and is still trying) through the commission of specialist studies, the media, ministry lobbying, co-operation with Universities, municipalities, local authorities and organisations to halt the development of road transport and promote instead railway travel and freight systems, as well as the introduction into Greek cities of metros and trams. Many of its suggestions have been adopted by the authorities. Lately the Association has been co-operating with the Mayor of Athens and the Technical University of Athens in an effort to reintroduce the tram in the city of Athens. In spite of many adverse reactions to this plan, there is hope that the tram will be reintroduced in the Greek capital in several areas.

- It has played a pivotal role in the reopening of the local lines of Nafplion (Peloponnese), the spa of Loutraki (Corinth Gulf) and Stylis (Maliakos Gulf), with trains running to 80% capacity during the week and over-full at weekends.

- It has played a pivotal role, too, in the recent revamping and reopening of the station of Agios Dionyssios (in the port of Piraeus), now the starting point for the immensely popular "Intercity" express to Thessaloniki. This express links now distant Aegean islands to the mainland and especially to northern Greece.

- It is supporting very actively the plan to reopen the Athens–Lavrion line, and the introduction of a light suburban train, both in East and West Attica (Athens–Mesogeia–the new airport of Spata (under construction)–Lavrion and Stavros–Elefsina–Megara). Besides radically reducing the asphyxiating pollution levels in the greater Athens area, this plan aims to serve the booming villages of Attica as well as to link Attica via Lavrion to the island of Kea and other Aegean islands.

- On the association's initiative and with the assistance of the concerned municipalities, part of the abandoned Athens–Lavrion line has been repaired and is used by our members for short trips.

- It has contributed, by expert studies and the personal work of its members, to the renovation and update of the Markopoulo station (Attica), used extensively as a cultural centre for the whole area of Mesogeia.

- It is struggling very actively, too, for the linking of the Adriatic port at Igoumenitsa to the Aegean Sea by rail. This will allow the creation of a rail link from Italy via Greece to the Middle East. This railway route will be combined with two ferry-boat lines, Brindisi–Igoumenitsa on the west and Volos–Middle East on the east. In the project it presented, the Association is suggesting that the existing Volos–Paleofarsalos–Kalambaka route could be quickly extended via the Katara Pass near Metsovo to the Adriatic port, at relatively low cost.

- It has taken action, in co-operation with the local authorities, for the reopening of the Agrinio–Kryoneri route (Western Greece). The work on the restoration of this line will start soon.

- It has contributed, also, in co-operation with the local friends of the train society, to the reopening of the picturesque 60cm gauge Volos–Milies (Mount Pelion) route served by an old-fashioned little train drawn by a steam engine dating from 1903. The great Italian painter Giorgio De Kiriko, who was born in Volos, was fond of this train and has represented it in many of his paintings as a background motif.

- It actively opposed the closure of several branch lines recommended recently by the British Company Transmark. Fortunately, these closures never took place.

- It is firmly supporting the effort of the Hellenic Railways Organisation (OSE) for a high-tech update (including state-of-the-art communication systems and the laying of double tracks) on two main routes, Athens–Thessaloniki in the mainland and Athens–Patras in the Peloponnese.

- It has taken action against the possible closure of the branch route from Katakolon, the cruise-ship port-of-call for ancient Olympia. Moreover, in a study the association presented to the mayor of Olympia, it recommended that the approach to the classical site be solely by light-weight observation trains as opposed to the already planned motor way access.

- It contributed to the safeguard, restoration and re-operation of the vintage steam engine from 1895 which hauls the rack railway of Kalavryta, Peloponnese.

- By the Association's insistent action, many old locomotives of all origins, old trams, old electric cars and, in general, all sorts of rail museum pieces have been saved. It was also able, by presenting a well-founded expertise study, to safeguard several Simplon Orient Express wagons-lits and wagons-restaurants (which were operating in Greece until recently). These carriages were listed by the Ministry of Culture with a preservation order on them. It is noticeable that this was the first case in Greece of moveable things being listed.

This brief survey cannot include, of course, the totality of the Association's activities which exceed largely the space available in the present publication. Even so, the commitment of its members to the cause of the train as well as their hard work and relentless efforts should be clear enough. The members struggle most of the time to overcome the inevitable technical and financial problems and combat entrenched interests. In this struggle, every small advance is welcomed as a victory.

HARF, Siokou Street 4, 10443 Athens, Greece.

Appendix Two
Further Reading

A Literary Companion to Travel in Greece (1994), edited by Richard Stoneman for the J Paul Getty Museum, 17985 Pacific Coast Highway, Malibu, CA 90265-5799, USA.

Athens and the Peloponnese (1995), Everyman Guide, David Campbell Publishers Ltd, London, UK.

A Traveller's History of Greece (1991) Timothy Boatswain & Colin Nicolson, Efstathiadis Group SA, Athens, Greece.

Blue Guide, Greece (1995), A&C Black (Publishers) Ltd, 35 Bedford Row, London WC14 4JH, UK.

Grèce, Autrement Revue, 4, rue d'Engheim, 75010 Paris, France.

Greece, The Rough Guide (1995), Rough Guides Ltd, 1 Mercer Street, London WC2H 9QJ, UK.

The Greeks: The Land and People since the War (1994), James Pettifer, Penguin Books Ltd, 27 Wright Lane, London W8 5TZ, UK.

Greek Travel Pages, a monthly by International Publications Ltd, 6 Psylla and Filellinon Streets, 10557 Syntagma, Athens, Greece.

Greek Wine Guide (1996), Nico Manessis, Olive Press Publishers, Loutrouvio, Benitses, 49084 Corfu, Greece.

Harling Mission 1942 (the Gorgopotomos Operation) (1993), Themistocles Marinos, Papazisis Publications, 2 Nikitara Street, Athens, Greece.

Insight Guides, Greece (1992), APA Publications, Hong Kong.

Le Livre de l'Olivier (1992), Marie-Claire Amouretti and Georges Comet, Edisud, La Calade, 13090 Aix-en-Provence, France.

Roumeli: Travels in Northern Greece (1966), Patrick Leigh Fermor, Penguin Books Ltd, 27 Wrights Lane, London W8 5TZ, UK.

Salonique (1850-1918) (1992), Editions Autrement, 4 rue d'Engheim, 75010 Paris, France.

Siatista, Macedonia and Our Ancestors (1995), James Siotas, Souliou 6, 15235 Ano Vrilisia, Attica, Greece.

Stathmoi – Greek Railway Stations (1995), Yannis Skoulas, Themelio/Ikona, Solonos 84, 10680 Athens, Greece.

The Peloponnese (1995), E Karpodini-Dimitriadi, Athenian Editions, Vissarionos 1, 10672 Athens, Greece.

The Rise of The Greeks (1987), Michael Grant, Collier Books, Maximilian Publishing Company, New York, USA.

The Unwritten Places (1995), Tim Salmon, Lycabettus Press, P.O.Box 17091, 10024 Athens, Greece.

The Wines of Greece (1990), Miles Lambert-Gocs, Faber and Faber, 3 Queen Square, London WC1N 3AU, UK.

Thomas Cook Guide to Greek Island Hopping (1995), Frewin Poffley, Thomas Cook Publishing, PO Box 227, Thorpe Wood, Peterborough PE3 6PU, UK.

Traditional Inns in Greece (1996), Vertical Advertising Publishing, Katehaki Street 61A, 11525 Athens, Greece.

Trekking in Greece (1993), Marc Dubin, Lonely Planet Publications, PO Box 617, Hawthorne, Vic 3122, Australia.

Vanishing Greece (1992), Clay Perry, Abbeville Press Inc, 488 Madison Avenue, New York, NY 10022.

GRADIENT PROFILES

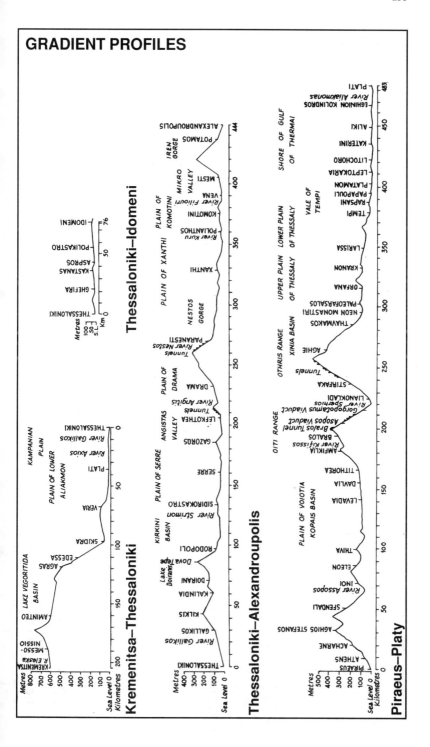

Thessaloniki–Idomeni

Kremenitsa–Thessaloniki

Thessaloniki–Alexandroupolis

Piraeus–Platy

254

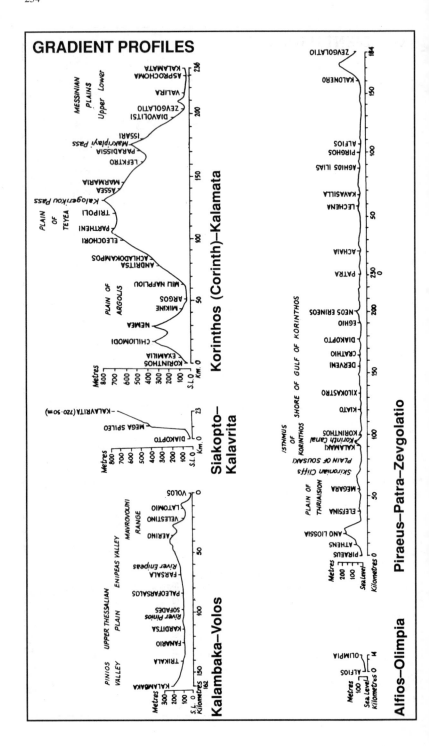

GRADIENT PROFILES

Korinthos (Corinth)–Kalamata

Siakopto–Kalavrita

Kalambaka–Volos

Piraeus–Patra–Zevgolatio

Alfios–Olimpia

FORSYTH TRAVEL LIBRARY

▚▚▚▚▚▚▚▚▚▚▚▚▚▚▚▚▚▚▚▚▚▚▚▚

EUROPEAN RAIL PASSES
ORDER FORM
Prices are U.S. $ Effective until December 31, 1997

AVAILABLE IN NORTH AMERICA ONLY

Visit our comprehensive home page on the world wide web for all the latest prices on all rail passes, hostel memberships, timetables. Even learn how to earn frequent flyer miles when you purchase rail passes.

http://www.forsyth.com

GREECE is one of the 17 European countries included in Eurail Pass. Travel to and from Greece via select ferries between Brindisi, Italy and Patras, Greece on ADN/HML.

EURAIL PASS (17 Countries) - 1st Class

15 Days	❑ $ 522	2 Months	❑ $1,188
21 Days	❑ $ 678	3 Months	❑ $1,468
1 Month	❑ $ 838		

EURAIL FLEXIPASS - 1st Class

10 Days in 2 Months	❑ $ 616
15 Days in 2 Months	❑ $ 812

EURAIL SAVERPASS

Starting in 1997 – valid for 2 to 5 people traveling together from Jan. to Dec.

15 Days	❑ $ 444	2 Months	❑ $1,010
21 Days	❑ $ 576	3 Months	❑ $1,248
1 Month	❑ $ 712		

EURAIL SAVER FLEXIPASS

10 Days in 2 Months	❑ $ 524
15 Days in 2 Months	❑ $ 690

EURAIL YOUTHPASS - * 2nd Class

15 Days	❑ $ 365	2 Months	❑ $ 832
21 Days	❑ $ 475	3 Months	❑ $1,028
1 Month	❑ $ 587		

EURAIL YOUTH FLEXIPASS* - 2nd Class

10 Days in 2 Months	❑ $ 431
15 Days in 2 Months	❑ $ 568

Pass holder must be under age 26 on first day of use.

For Travelers from North America

CALL TOLL FREE 1-800-367-7984 – ASK FOR DEPT. BGT7
(Charge to Visa or MasterCard)

FORSYTH TRAVEL LIBRARY, INC.
1750 E. 131st Street, P.O. Box 480800, Dept. BGT7, Kansas City, MO 64148

Forsyth Travel Library, Inc., is the leading agent in North America for the European and British Railroads and distributor of the famous Thomas Cook European Timetable. We are international rail travel specialists. Members: ASTA, Better Business Bureau of Kansas City, MO and International Map Trades Association. Free catalogs upon request listing all rail passes, timetables, hostelling information and maps. All prices shown are US Dollars.

SHIPPING Allow 14 days for delivery but most orders are shipped much sooner. There is a minimum $9.50 shipping charge generally using UPS/2nd DAY AIR. RUSH service also available using Fed-Ex or Express Mail with next day delivery where such service exists for a minimum charge of $25. Call for details. Sorry, no COD's.

NOTE : All prices for all passes are subject to change, alteration and/or cancellation. Customers should expect prices to change and increase in 1998.

256

FORSYTH TRAVEL LIBRARY

ORDER FORM
European Rail Passes
Prices are U.S. $ Effective until December 31, 1997

EUROPASS – First Class
Unlimited travel in France, Germany, Italy, Spain & Switzerland

	Adult	2 Adults*
Any 5 Days in 2 Months	❏ $316	❏ $253
with 1 associate country	❏ $376	❏ $301
with 2 associate countries	❏ $406	❏ $325
with 3 associate countries	❏ $426	❏ $341
with 4 associate countries	❏ $436	❏ $349
Add extra days (10 max)	❏ $ 42	❏ $33.⁵⁰

*Prices per person based on 2 people traveling together, includes 40% companion discount. Children from 4-11: half adult fare. Under 4: Free

EUROPASS YOUTH – Second Class
Unlimited travel in France, Germany, Italy, Spain & Switzerland

Any 5 Days in 2 Months	❏ $210
with 1 associate country	❏ $255
with 2 associate countries	❏ $280
with 3 associate countries	❏ $295
with 4 associate countries	❏ $303
Add extra days (10 max)	❏ $ 29

Passenger must be under age 26 years of age on the first date of travel to use this pass.

EURAIL & EURO DRIVE PASS

There are excellent Rail/Drive programs that combine a Eurail or Euro Pass with either Avis or Hertz Rental cars in Europe. And, you can reserve your auto rentals even before leaving home! Call us for a complete brochure and prices.

FLASH!
Europass is now the top selling Rail pass for travel in Europe!

ASSOCIATE COUNTRIES

Extend the geographic reach of your EuroPass by adding the following Associates Countries. Name which Associate Countries you want added to your pass when ordering.
Also known as "Additional Zones"

❏ **Greece** (includes Greece & ADN/HML Ferry services between Greece & Italy)
❏ **Austria & Hungary** (Danube Zone)
❏ **Benelux** (Belguim, Netherlands & Luxembourg)
❏ **Portugal**

EASTERN EUROPEAN PASS - 1st Class
Austria, Poland, Czech, Slovakia, Hungary

5 Days in 1 Month	❏ $195
Add'l Rail Day (5 max)	❏ $ 21

GREEK FLEXI RAIL 'N FLY PASS - 1st Class

3 Days in 1 Month	❏ $ 202 Adult
	❏ $186 Child (4-11)

Includes 2 air journeys on select Olympic Airways flights to Greek islands

Add'l one way air journeys	❏ $ 66 Adult
	❏ $ 33 Child (4-11)

Not Shown: Passes for Britain, France, Benelux, Germany, Italy, Scandinavia, Spain & Portugal, Switzerland, Austria, Hungary, Rail & Drive passes. Call for rates and free brochures.

PASS PROTECTION: All Travelers should consider buying Pass Protection Insurance. This protects your pass for loss and theft and only costs $10 per pass at time of purchase. Ask us for details.

Order Toll Free – call 800-367-7984. Ask for Dept BGT7
Charge to Visa or MasterCard

INDEX